DATE DUE

YOU CAN'T
BLOW HOME
AGAIN

YOU CAN'T BLOW HOME AGAIN

HERB PAYSON

HEARST MARINE BOOKS

NEW YORK

Library of Congress Cataloging in Publication Data

Payson, Herb.
    You can't blow home again.

    1. Payson, Herb.   2. Sea Foam (Ketch)   3. Voyages
and travels—1951–   . I. Title.
G477.P395   1983   910.4'5   83-16099
ISBN 0-688-04069-1

Printed in the United States of America

First Edition

1 2 3 4 5 6 7 8 9 10

To mother
who bore and forebore
and to the memory of my father
who encouraged

CONTENTS

YOU CAN'T
BLOW HOME
AGAIN

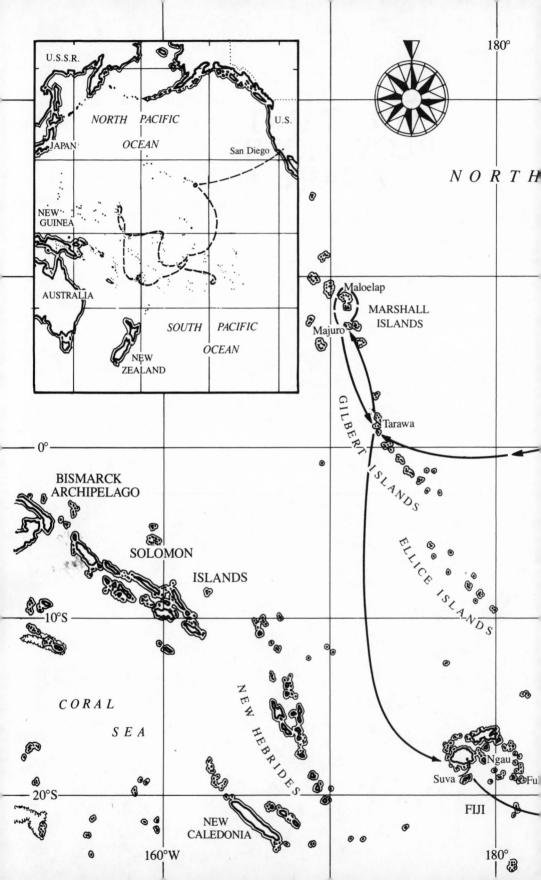

180°

NORTH

U.S.S.R.

NORTH PACIFIC

OCEAN

JAPAN

U.S.

San Diego

NEW
GUINEA

AUSTRALIA

SOUTH   PACIFIC

OCEAN

NEW
ZEALAND

Maloelap

MARSHALL
ISLANDS

Majuro

0°

BISMARCK
ARCHIPELAGO

SOLOMON

ISLANDS

Tarawa

10°S

CORAL

SEA

NEW HEBRIDES

GILBERT ISLANDS

ELLICE ISLANDS

Ngau

Suva   Ful

20°S

NEW
CALEDONIA

FIJI

160°W

180°

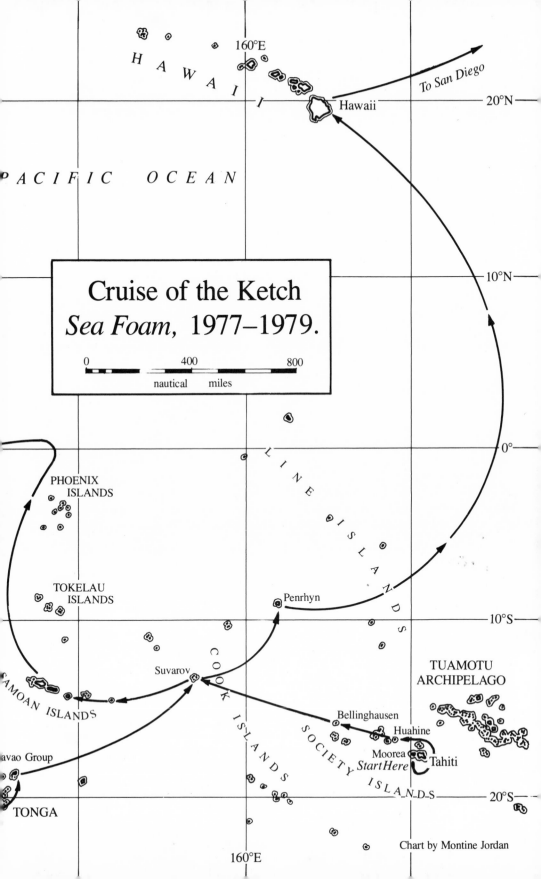

160°E

To San Diego

20°N

H A W A I I

Hawaii

P A C I F I C   O C E A N

10°N

Cruise of the Ketch
Sea Foam, 1977–1979.

0   400   800

nautical   miles

0°

PHOENIX
ISLANDS

L I N E   I S L A N D S

TOKELAU
ISLANDS

Penrhyn

10°S

TUAMOTU
ARCHIPELAGO

C O O K   I S L A N D S

Suvarov

SAMOAN ISLANDS

Bellinghausen

Huahine

avao Group

SOCIETY   ISLANDS

Moorea

StartHere

Tahiti

TONGA

20°S

Chart by Montine Jordan

160°E

INTRODUCTION

This book concludes the story of our cruising adventures begun in a previous book entitled *Blown Away,* adventures in which we sailed 45,000 miles of the Pacific in our 36-foot ketch, *Sea Foam.* The year is 1977. We have survived the delivery of Leaky *Lissa* from Tahiti to Los Angeles, spent four months in California, and have bought several thousand dollars worth of stuff to ship to ourselves in Moorea, French Polynesia, where *Sea Foam* awaits our return.

My wife, Nancy, and I have an extended family of six children. All of them spent time with us cruising on *Sea Foam,* but by 1977 all but one had spun off to take up the threads of their lives. The remaining personnel were Nancy, 15-year-old Craig, and myself.

In going back to *Sea Foam* we crossed a threshold. Our problems remained pretty much the same, but our perceptions of them had deepened. We had grown stronger as seamen and as a team. Our experience of the cruising life now included both the good and the bad, but even after the treats of four months of Stateside living, we were eager to return to our boat. Maybe we'd sail to Singapore, maybe to Bali. Maybe we'd round South Africa, or instead head up to Suez. It didn't matter. What did matter was that we'd be back aboard *Sea Foam,* moving with the wind, rediscovering slow, compelling rhythms, taking the time to see.

It was this change of pace that to me was so special. Normally an *A-to-B-er,* when Nancy and I go on hikes, I trudge, head down, watching where I step. When I get to B, most all I can tell you about the route is the condition of the path. Nancy is always stopping to look around. She insists on interrupting my dogged plodding by making me notice a bird, a flower, or the way the light filters through the trees. I stop, often grumpily, humoring her, impatient to get on with it. And while I might worry about being caught out in the dark, Nancy rejoices in the colors of the setting sun.

The tempo of sailing was slow enough that I became less tunnel-visioned, even though I never completely got over it. In writing our story I will no doubt keep my eye on where we're going and how to get there (which is no guarantee that I won't get lost). Nancy, if I know her, will read over my shoulder and insist that I pause frequently to enjoy where we are.

I / BAD NEWS

It was a rainy morning in Orange County, California, a soggy, raw morning, which is the way I remember most of the times that I've gotten bad news. Nancy and I were in the spare bedroom of Nancy's granny's house, which was really Harold's house, but it's all part of Nancy's family so the details aren't important. What's important is that we were living on *land* at the time. Nancy was painstakingly scrawling recipes on three-by-five cards for her someday cruising cookbook. I was sitting at my typewriter, wrestling sentences from it at an increasingly slower rate. For the tenth time in 30 minutes I got up and started pacing.

"You're pacing," said Nancy, absently chewing on an eraser.

"He's late again," I said. I was referring to the mailman, whose expected arrival has elicited most of the peak anticipations of my middle age. As a freelance writer, not only my mood for the rest of the day, but also our economic future for weeks and maybe months depended on what he might bring.

"Relax. Pacing won't bring him here one minute sooner."

"You can't be sure of that," I said, following my custom of taking exception to everything when I'm fretting. Nancy, writing again, refused to pick up the gauntlet. Once, during a similar wait, I wrote in my journal, "Never ask what your mail can bring to you, but only what you will *send* in the mail," the idea being that it's better to focus on sending out material than to dwell on acceptance or rejection. My own advice was absolutely impossible for me to live up to. So I paced.

"I think I hear him," said Nancy, 83 of my steps later. Disregarding the rain, I made the round trip to the box in my shirt sleeves.

"Nothing," I said, dripping, my hands full of envelopes. "Not a damn thing. No word from *Pacific Yachting,* no check from *Boating,* and nothing from *SAIL* about my book."

"Terrific," said Nancy. "That means all of your irons are still in the fire." She took the mail and riffled through it. "Look! Here's a letter from Tahiti. It's from Ed. Shall I read it?"

"I suppose so," I said.

"Dear Herb and Nancy," she read, "I'm sorry, but I've got bad news for you. Your boat is in terrible shape. I took a day off from work and sailed over from Papeete to Moorea like you asked me to. We were going to bring *Sea Foam* back to the boatyard, but no way. She's a mess. I mean it. Full of mildew and that smell of tropical rot. Rats have gotten in and done a lot of damage, and there's rat shit all over. If you don't get back here quick and do something you're going to lose her. She'll be so far gone you'll never bring her back. She may be already.

"The three of us tried to clean her up a little, but there wasn't much we could do in half a day. Believe me, I hate to write you this and spoil your visit home, but it's better to know the truth than to lose your boat. Regards, Ed."

"Is that all?" I asked.

"That's all." She got up, her blue eyes troubled and not shining with her usual joie de vivre. For myself, I must confess to a morbid satisfaction that this news should match the weather and my disappointment.

"I thought Mark was supposed to look after her," said Nancy.

"He was. But we're five months later than we thought we'd be."

"We'd better get our asses back there."

"What on?" I asked.

Because what we'd done was to deliver Mark's boat, *Lissa,* from Tahiti to Los Angeles, for which we were paid by the mile. Then we'd cleaned her all up and sold her, earning as a bonus a certain percentage of everything she'd brought over a certain amount. However, we'd had an inflated idea of what she'd sell for, and our bonus had been minimal. Furthermore, selling her had taken a long time, and our personal expenses had continued. What could, if all had gone well, have been a mildly profitable venture had turned out to be a break-even situation.

"I guess we'll just have to borrow enough to get us going and keep us eating for six months or so. By then you'll have sold some more articles and we'll be getting the advance on your book," said Nancy.

"Who says the book will be accepted? And who's going to lend us any money?" I demanded, leaving the room.

The thing that depressed me even more than our lack of cash was the fact that I hadn't seen the situation coming. We had been merrily buying gear for *Sea Foam*: an almost-new Avon dinghy; a preowned ham radio; a small, portable Honda generator (new); a used Canon Ftb with two lenses; three new boat batteries; paid half down on three new sails; bought new tools; a bolt of acrylan for a new awning; and nearly $1,000 worth of paint, varnish, line, caulking, rigging spares and engine dittos, all with no real regard for what we were spending. Somewhere I had in the back of my mind that we'd wait around in southern California till one of my pending deals came through, or until Nancy had gotten a job, or an advance on her cookbook. Nothing definite, but if you chum, and lay out enough baited hooks, and if there are fish around, usually you'll catch something. And that much we'd done.

But now Time, which cruising had taught us to treat like a rubber band, had become rigid and finite. Get back to Tahiti now, or you'll lose your boat; your beautiful, classic, 36-foot ketch that's carried you and your family from San Diego down to Panama, across to the Galápagos, the Marquesas, Tuamotus, Societies, Tonga, Fiji, New Zealand, and then back to Tahiti via the Austral Islands; your boat, which is 90 percent of all the equity you have in the world. There was nothing vague about Ed's message. Act now! That meant paying full fare for air tickets, instead of waiting around for cheap standby tickets that occasionally were available. And it meant not waiting around to see if my book would be accepted, and how much of an advance against royalties I could expect, if any. In other words, it meant going back to *Sea Foam* with nothing for the future except crossed fingers.

"How can you possibly love me?" I demanded, stomping back to where Nancy was and hugging her. "I'm a lousy lover, a lousy writer, and such a horse's ass."

"You're not a lousy lover," said Nancy, nuzzling. (I keep hoping for more, but Nancy believes in The Truth.) "And you're a fantastic writer. And one of the reasons you're a fantastic writer is that you write about being a horse's ass" (which if you don't examine too closely, represents total support).

We had met in a bar nearly eight years before. She was working as cocktail waitress, I as entertainer. Each of us had three children, and all except Craig, her youngest, were teenagers. Teenagers are nearly people and have put up with parental nonsense long enough to be eager to turn the tables. I firmly believed that my children's escapades were vendettas, designed specifically to prove to the world what an inept parent I was. After the crowd had left and the cleanup work done, Nancy and I would sip nightcaps and exchange horror stories about our children's behavior. As I look back, our kids were no worse than most growing-ups; but their adventures in sex, drugs, and their minor brushes with the law all seemed at the time uniquely catastrophic. When eventually my playing engagement came to an end and I went to work at another nightspot, I found that I missed our concerned sharings, and after work I would drive for miles just to bring Nancy up to date on the next chapter of 'Teenage Revenge'.

In spite of our reluctance toward a second marriage, Nancy and I decided to legitimize our sex life (and risk, in the process, ruining it). We invited a few friends, all our children, and were married in Nancy's family's vacation cabin. The cabin sits among tall pine trees on a hillside next to Big Bear Lake. The winter night was breathtaking. Huge snowflakes drifted down, smothering all sound. The justice of the peace was in his seventies, recently retired because of a heart attack, and we feared he wouldn't make it up the stairs to the cabin. He rested in a chair in front of the fire for a half-hour before he was able to perform the ceremony. But perform it he did, and at the end he made me repeat Nancy's new name, and made both of us repeat the date—January 17, 1970—which, but for him, I would have promptly forgotten.

"How much do I owe you?" I asked him as he was putting on his overcoat. Color had finally returned to his face, and his breathing was less raspy.

"Just pay me what it's worth," he said, and I knew his faculties were fully recovered.

"I won't know for a while," I said. "How about 20 bucks to tide you over?" He smiled, so I guess it was enough. I'm never sure about those things. Now, exactly seven years later, hugging Nancy on a rainy January morning, I realized that if he were to send me a bill with the same condition, I would gladly come up with more money. However, it would have to be an IOU.

Nancy and I hadn't always been undercapitalized. When we were both working, prior to going cruising, we were making a comfortable living, and with the help of MasterCard, Visa, American Express, Overdraft Privileges, BankAmericard, and credit cards from Sears, Penneys, Buffums, Robinsons, Bullocks, May Company, Exxon, Mobil, Amoco, and Texaco, we were able to have all the amenities. But the trouble with our 'thing hunger' was that it was neurotic—i.e., could never be satisfied—and not only were we unslaked and unsated, but we were also constantly nervous about our deficit finances. There are people, I've heard, who can use credit cards as conveniences and not as vehicles for compulsive buying, but I've never met one, and if I did I probably couldn't relate to him. We bought all we could afford, and then a bit more, worried about how to pay for it, and in the interim wondered why what we bought didn't make us happy.

Now we were on a cash basis that in simple terms said that if you can't pay, you don't go, and our boat was 4,000 miles away, dying of neglect. If there is one thing worse than the burden of debt, it's a feeling of helplessness. And this, except for Fortune Land, is what we had.

"We could sell Fortune Land," I suggested. Fortune Land was a small investment I'd made nearly a decade before in the one area of southern California that refused to boom. It had become to us like mama's bank account in the play, *I Remember Mama,* a talisman of last resort. It was an asset with no potential buyers, as liquid as a building lot on the back side of the moon. But it was equity, and as such it had comforted us several times during our cruising when we wondered where our next dollar was coming from. As long as we held it, we were never broke.

"Who would we sell it to?" asked Nancy. "Besides, we aren't that desperate yet. Not this morning, anyway." For Nancy, postponement made her cheerful again, and her cheerfulness turned on the nightlight in my chrysalis of woe.

"There's one thing we can do," I said, "and that's sit down and deal with the numbers. Knowing exactly the amount we need is a giant step toward getting it." I didn't really believe this, but I'd read it somewhere, and it was indeed something we could do.

The task didn't take long. We started with air fare, Los Angeles to Tahiti, for Nancy, Craig, and me. We had a cousin who worked for a shipping company and learned from her how much it would cost to ship all our goodies. We added in the cost of the additional paint and supplies we'd need to refurbish *Sea Foam*'s interior. We figured the cost of a much-needed haulout based on what we'd paid for a haulout in Tahiti three years before. New sails were being shipped to us in Tahiti from Hong Kong, and we threw in the balance due. We estimated the cost of one more month's living in California plus six months' provisions for *Sea Foam*. Add 20 percent for inflation and other imponderables, and subtract the money we still had in the bank. Needed: $3,000.

"You didn't allow anything for fun," said Nancy.

"We can't afford fun," I said. This was the most ridiculous statement of the week, as fun was what we always afforded first, after which we'd look around to see what else we could do. But we were trying to be responsible, so Nancy bought it.

"Three thousand dollars isn't so much," she said brightly.

"Then you find it," I said. And so matters stood for the rest of the day.

I'd like to relate that Nancy and I pulled a coup, scooped a quick profit out of the stock market, ran a string of luck at the crap table, or took some other kind of risk and came out smelling roselike; but it wasn't that way. Months before, when we'd first arrived in California with *Lissa,* one well-to-do friend had asked if we needed any money to tide us over. We'd said no, which was true at the time. Now I remembered the offer and called her.

"How much do you need?" she asked.

I told her.

"Is that all?" was her answer. I was flooded with unexpected emotion, to the extent that I could barely finish the conversation without choking up. If there are any blessings that accompany need, one of them must be discovering one's friends.

But the fact remained: self-reliance would have died but for an emergency transfusion, and cash-and-carry independence now bore a debt. In exchange, our cruising life had acquired a new lease. Nancy, Craig, and I could return to *Sea Foam,* fix her up, and once more sail into the sunset. When the chips were down, that was where our priorities lay.

II / *SEA FOAM* AFTER *LISSA*

The DC-10 slid down out of a slippery sky, landed and taxied quickly to the terminal. More than three hundred people who had spent nine hours without enough knee room stood, stretched, emerged from their air conditioned womb and were assaulted by the hot sponge that is Tahiti's summer.

The night before, a chilly February evening, Nancy and I had arrived at the Los Angeles airport looking casual even for Californians. I was wearing a cotton shirt and shorts, Nancy a cotton dress; both of us were in go-aheads. Now, as we stood waiting in line for French Polynesian customs, it was our turn to be amused while other passengers shucked sweat-stained winter clothing, mopped brows, and swore.

"Is it as hot as I think it is?" asked Nancy, fanning herself with her sandalwood fan. Nancy's thermostat has worn out, and recently in Maine's woods I caught her fanning herself while I was trying unsuccessfully to get warm by chopping more energetically at our Christmas tree.

"It's really hot," I said. "We didn't notice it so much before 'cause we were sailing and the change was gradual."

"Damn, it feels like a steam bath."

"I know," I said, thinking of *Sea Foam*. "It's a perfect climate for fungus, mold, mildew, and rot."

"You sure know how to cheer a girl up."

Having worked hard to finish up our Stateside business quickly so that we could attend to *Sea Foam* as soon as possible, we now decided to postpone flying to Moorea until we'd gone into Papeete to see if anyone we knew was in port. "After all," Nancy observed, with a kind of logic that I understood, "when you're this close, there's no real hurry."

It was like coming home to walk down the quay, waving to friends who were living on boats tied up to the main street of a busy city. Our nostalgia was annihilated, however, when one of our more competent sailor-friends stopped us.

"What are you going to do about *Sea Foam*?" he asked, sympathetically. "Sell her, or try to bring her back?" So our bad news was commonly known.

"Jesus," said Nancy as he walked away, "I don't know if I want to go to Moorea, ever."

For a brief moment, the flight across the nine-mile channel that separated Tahiti from her smaller sister island, Moorea, pushed my troubles aside. From the air, granite peaks, clothed in green and skirted with coral, sat on a quilt of royal blue. Here and there the blue was appliquéd with a white sail, or embroidered with the silver thread of a powerboat's wake. Gradually the scene worked magic on my despondency, but nine minutes in the air was too short, and when we landed I still wondered if I had the strength to face our boat's condition.

The road from the airport followed the shore, and as we rode along in 'le truck,' a semienclosed, flatbed truck with wooden benches running along the side, we craned our necks to look at the cruising yachts anchored in the lagoon. There were two or three by the Bali Hai hotel; three more in Cook's Bay; two in Robinson's Cove; and three in the bight where *Sea Foam* was moored.

"Isn't it great to be back," Nancy mused, thinking, I was sure, of cockpit cocktails and moonlight suppers with friends.

"I hope you still feel that way after we've seen *Sea Foam*," I said.

From the shore, *Sea Foam* looked all right, exactly as we had left her, with two stern lines tied to trees on the bank, and anchors out to port and starboard. We slid our dinghy into the water and pulled ourselves along using one of the lines.

"See this," I said, pointing to the rat guard. "They gnawed through the plywood."

We climbed aboard. There were rat droppings all over the deck, but otherwise she looked OK—dirty, a little faded, but a pretty lady nonetheless, one that a bath and a day's scrubbing would put right.

But when I unlocked the padlock and slid back the companionway hatch, I knew immediately that Ed's letter hadn't exaggerated. The stench nearly made me sick, for the smell, it's true, but more because of what it foreshadowed. I took the hatchboards out and went below. Nancy followed. We both stood in the salon, looking around, unbelieving.

"Jesus H. Christ," said Nancy, and burst into tears. I put my arms around her and hugged and patted, the business of consoling her distracting me from my own feelings. Adding it up I thought I could see three to four months of intensive work in front of us. And we had just finished doing two months' work on *Lissa*.

"It's not fair," said Nancy. "It's just not fair." And then she was sobbing again.

"We never should have left," I said. "With nobody living aboard, an old wooden boat in the tropics goes to hell in a hurry."

"Why didn't Mark *do* something? He said he'd keep her aired and pumped out."

"He did keep her pumped out," I said. "Probably aired her out, too, but obviously airing wasn't enough. You have to fight mildew, even when you're living aboard. And he couldn't help the rats. As a matter of fact, he wrote that he'd set traps and killed a couple of them. But my rat guards weren't good enough. And there was no way he could have prevented a determined thief."

"Where do we start?" she asked, looking around the salon once more.

"For openers we'll move in on Mark and Anne—take them up on their invitation to live with them till the boat is ready to live aboard again. It could take months. By that time I'll have drunk them out of house and home."

"You mean *we* will," said Nancy, chin-thrusting.

The prospect of getting back at our friends encouraged us enough to start taking inventory of the damage, which was: carpet ruined because of mildew and rat shit; covers to mattresses, ditto; cushions, ditto; paint, mildewed and peeling throughout the galley, head, stateroom, and salon. A thief had broken in by removing the companionway sashes with a screwdriver, and had stolen: one quartz ship's clock, brass, brand-new, accurate to within one second per month; one large plastic toolbox containing all our small tools, plus countless small, irreplaceable bits and pieces; and one radio-telephone. The rats had eaten their way through a lazaret hatch and into one drawer, but otherwise had done little damage to the wood. They had, however, eaten holes in every plastic container on the boat, having learned, we surmised, that a fair percentage of plastic containers contained food. They'd shredded eight of our twelve life jackets; eaten holes in two of our four jerry jugs; eaten holes in each of our three fenders; eaten holes in all our bilge pump hoses; spread sunflower seeds, soy beans, peanuts, flour, and rice everywhere; had gotten into some of our drugs, and had eaten half a bottle of aspirin and a whole bottle of Ex-lax. The Ex-lax bit tickled me until Nancy pointed out that as revenge it was definitely two-edged.

If someone had come along that day and offered us a fraction of what *Sea Foam* was worth, we'd have grabbed it. Nobody did. Nobody would want her until we'd made her beautiful again.

Throughout the South Pacific we'd heard of cruising sailboats for sale for bargain prices. Many of them were like *Sea Foam*— as-is, where-is, rundown and neglected, shrouded in a fog of defeat through which few people have the vision or the energy to cut. As a rule, most of us want our purchases to have the enthusiasm built in so that our own fires will be fanned by it.

To wit: when we finally got *Lissa* to California after a 46-day passage from the Marquesas, she looked like a vagrant. The long, windward passage had peeled her paint and ravaged her varnish. We were tied up to a float in front of an elegant house in Newport Beach, and the contrast did even more damage to *Lissa*'s image. When we hailed a passing salesman friend who was demonstrating a brand-new, fiberglass, cruising cutter to a couple of dewy-eyed customers, he brought his proud yacht alongside, and the comparison of Weathered-Old versus Shiny-New totally destroyed *Lissa* as a viable boat.

"You going to junk her?" the tyro demanded after a quick inspection. Nancy and I found this so funny, we told the story everywhere. "What ninnies," we said, "with their eyes full of scales." But when another friend, a boat broker who'd been in the business for years, came to give us his professional estimate, we were reminded that it's not only the neophyte who judges by appearances.

"Well, the way she sits," he said, stroking his chin, "with the motor not working and all, we could probably get ten grand for her. Maybe twelve, if we hooked a real nerd." Two months later *Lissa* sold for $25,000—with no engine at all! (The engine was out for repairs, and the buyer didn't want it. We later sold it separately.) The difference? Some paint and varnish, new carpet, new cushions, and mattress covers. Tokens of TLC. Visible signs of faith in *Lissa*'s future. An aura of possibility. The fact that her new owner completely gutted her and redesigned her interior, thereby eradicating all the work we'd done, emphasizes the role cosmetics play in parting us from our money.

Nancy and I first saw *Sea Foam* when she was still in the yard, sweet-smelling of fresh paint and varnish. She was like a freshly minted doubloon, and much more than just a boat. There were many Justaboats we could have bought for less money—boats that might have served us well. But we must have known intuitively that our sense of magic needed support, and we passed all the Justaboats by. When we bought *Sea Foam*, we also bought a dream and a promise, and a year of shopping and reflecting had proved that we wouldn't settle for anything less. Now, five years later, *Sea Foam*'s cabin was soggy and stinking. Inside, her fungus-ridden paint was peeling and blistering. She'd never looked worse. But the dream and promise must have been still alive in our minds. Without them I don't know where we'd have found the courage to start down the long road toward bringing her back.

We began by taking pictures of *Sea Foam*'s interior. If, down the line, we should lose heart, it might be encouraging to see how far we'd come. The real beginning, however, was removing the carpets, cushions, and all the other gear, and parking the whole mess in a big pile by Mark and Anne's back door. From then on our milestones came at roughly one-week intervals.

End of first week: caught the last rat. End of second week: son Craig arrived from California, and we were three instead of two. Third week: our new gear arrived in Papeete from California. Fourth week: with bureaucratic red tape finally sorted out, we were allowed to bring our gear from Papeete to Moorea, where we parked it in a second big pile by Mark and Anne's back door. End of fifth week: finished painting salon. Sixth: finished head. Seventh: finished stateroom. Eighth: finished redoing all interior varnish. Ninth: installed new carpet, newly recovered mattresses, and cushions. Tenth: moved all our gear the four miles from Mark and Anne's house to *Sea Foam*.

Our plan for revenge on Mark and Anne never did work out. We lived with them in their two-bedroom house for 11 weeks, had the daily use of their car, and were included in their social lives. Mark taught Craig how to scuba dive. Not once did either Mark or Anne show impatience that our work was taking so long. Still, I think I would have tried to drink them out of house and home anyway, if our communal agreement hadn't specifically stated that we had to pay for our own booze.

A ton of work remained to be done, but *Sea Foam*'s interior was scrubbed, painted, varnished, and eminently liveable. Eleven months had passed since we had left to take *Lissa* to California, an interruption that nearly terminated our cruising life. Now, however, we were once more living on our boat and looking toward the future.

III / AROUND TAHITI

What's fun for a sailor is to go sailing. It's true. Most of the sailing that a cruising sailor does is done to get from *A* to *B*. While one is *A-to-B-ing*, moments of exhilaration or insight may take him by surprise—may leap out of the ocean of experience and nip him playfully on the ass—but to go sailing purely for the pleasure is all too rare an occurrence.

There are reasons. For one thing, if you live aboard your boat, going sailing requires a heavy investment in straightening up. There are those whose lives are always tidy, but ours was not. *Sea Foam*'s condition was gradually degenerative, neatnesswise, and if we hadn't gone sailing occasionally, we would have had to move off the boat, much as the Mad Hatter moved to the next place setting. Choked, finally, with the detritus of daily living, *Sea Foam* would have become uninhabitable.

For another thing, there is the anchor that must be upped. Upping an anchor that's been down for some time is a challenge, and in our case we would have to disentangle our lines from our quay neighbors' lines. Also, it's often a menial and humbling task as there is always in the tropics an accumulation of slime, grass, and coral on the rode, and mud on the anchor. The rode cleans up slowly, foot by foot, and on *Sea Foam* the job continually required more time than we allotted to it.

And then there's the dinghy: tow it or stow it? In some cases we left it on the anchor, thereby solving two problems at once. But it wouldn't have been too shrewd to leave it anchored out in front of the Papeete quay. Furthermore, we were moored on all chain, as usual, and leaving the dinghy to support that weight would have been risky—kids might sink it, and there we'd be, dragging for our gear.

Lastly, if the anchorage is crowded, as Papeete Harbor almost always was, there's the likelihood of losing your place and having to remoor in a spot that's more distant or less convenient, or risk the chance of being displaced entirely. There were only a limited number of spaces with both electricity and water, amenities for which some sailors would willingly kill.

And finally, in Papeete there was always the official hassle—the checkings-out and included in that, the fussy filling out of forms and, sometimes, the paying of fees. None of the above reasons were in themselves deterrents, but the combination of all of them usually was.

When you get right down to it, the reason we *Sea Foam*ers didn't go pleasure sailing very often is we were too damned lazy. But in Papeete in July 1977, our need was greater than our sloth. "We're off to circumsize the island," we declared to friends. (To circumsize an island is to sail around it while sizing it up.)

Circumsizing Tahiti is a project that only a few visiting sailors undertake. Perhaps it's because so many of the available anchorages are deep, or because the navigation is a bit tricky in spots. Perhaps it's because most of us tend to ignore what's under our noses. But here, too, the ultimate reason for *Sea Foam*ers was pure laziness. It is so much easier, and so much more likely to be rewarding, to go to the places that other sailors have raved about, than it is to go blundering off on one's own. But though success is less assured, the sense of achievement that goes with successful blundering is a pleasant change from always following the beaten wake. So we decided to gunkhole our way around the 85 miles of Tahiti's coastline. With notebook, camera, and snorkel we'd seek stories, pictures, and shells—a perfect mix of profit and pleasure. A changement d'air. The French attribute great curative powers to a change of place, change of pace, change of emphasis. A changement d'air does for me what shedding a skin must do for a snake. Prometheus's chains drop from my shoulders. The world leaps into my eyes and ears, touches me in private places, and afterwards I return to the mainstream of my life renewed.

Before we could leave, however, we had to find our sails. They were supposed to have arrived from Hong Kong a month earlier. I had been haunting both the customs and shipping agents' offices at the freight docks, but to no avail. Finally, months late, a copy of the bill of lading arrived from the shippers. Armed now with the proper documents, I resumed my assault on Bureauland.

"Ah yes," said the shipping agent. "They've been here for some time. Come with me, I'll show you."

We drove in his car to a huge warehouse full of large wooden crates, each of which was labeled 'Soyu'. Papeete must be the soy sauce waystation for the whole world. If everyone in French Polynesia were to eat Chinese food three times a day, it would take decades to consume all that sauce. And somewhere, deeply buried in this impregnable city block of soy, were our sails.

"How long before you'll move this stuff around so I can get at my sails?" I asked.

"No more than two weeks," he said. "Are you in a hurry?"

"What would be the point," I said, disgusted. And then, because it wasn't his fault, "Thanks for your time, anyway."

After talking it over, Nancy, Craig, and I decided to forget about our new sails until we returned. Our old mizzen had torn along the foot and a piece was missing, but we could still use it reefed in light air. The main and staysail had been patched and repatched, and the material itself had been weakened by seven years of sunshine; but with care they might last. The jibs were in good condition, and for the moment the engine was acting dependably. After all, we were only gunkholing. We'd be fine.

I was still feeling grumpy when we left. It was July 13, the day before Bastille Day. Called 'the fête' locally, Bastille Day has become a Polynesian Mardi gras. We had celebrated it with the French and Tahitians in 1974, and again with the Marquesans in 1976. But though we'd enjoyed ourselves both times, the fête wasn't what we were looking for now. What we wanted was peace and quiet and solitude. As we were leaving Papeete Harbor, we passed an eight-man canoe, manned by a Tahitian crew practicing for the races. Evidently the paddlers weren't putting their hearts and backs into it, and the coxswain was haranguing them mercilessly. As we passed, he counted to three, and eight inspired blades bit into the bay. The force of that first stroke sank the canoe, and the last thing we saw was nine Tahitians sitting in a row with water up to their chests. All, even the coxswain, were laughing. I thought of our buried sails.

"It's not polite to laugh," said Craig.

"I'm laughing about all that soy sauce," I said. Immediately I felt better, no longer burdened with exasperation. After all, we were setting forth on an adventure. As we proceeded south, gradually we would find more and more seclusion. Our problems would have to wait till we got back to Papeete. For the moment, the world was ours.

Nine days after we left Papeete Harbor we found ourselves anchored in the isthmus that separates the island into two unequal land masses, the larger named Tahiti, and the smaller bearing three names: (1) Tahiti Iti (Tahitian for 'Little Tahiti'); (2) Presque Île, (French for 'Almost an Island'); and (3) Tairapu Peninsula, (named for the easternmost district on the island). We had yet to have a day of nice weather. Craig had an old cold. I had a new one. We hadn't even come close to finding the number or quality of shells we'd expected. Lobster and fish had eluded us. The only thing we'd found that we'd hoped for was an absence of other boats. And after having raised the anchor a dozen times from depths of 60 to 90 feet, we were becoming acquainted (hand over hand) with why.

Yet we were enjoying ourselves hugely. Craig went shell hunting constantly, even in the rain, and came up only for meals, or to cough or sniffle. To aid in cleaning the shells he found, he and I invented a pressure water system. We first gathered together 50 feet of garden hose, a spray nozzle, and a nine-gallon jerry jug. Then we filled the hose with water so it would syphon, and affixed the non-nozzle end in the jerry jug. Finally, using the main halyard, we hoisted the jug to the top of the mast. Nine gallons didn't last long, and Craig did lots of hoisting and antihoisting; but a 50-foot head gave him all the pressure he needed.

Nancy and Craig often went shelling together, looking like crusading knights in matching, bright-colored wetsuits. The wetsuits, given to us by a friend in California, allowed us to stay in the water much longer without getting chilled. Nancy, who hates being cold, loved hers without reservation, except for one time when a shark shepherded her all the way across the lagoon back to the boat. "It's this damn day-glo orange," she said, referring to the color of her suit. "I felt much too delicious, in a red-snapperish sort of way."

One day some friends off another yacht introduced us to Fearless Ferdie, an octopus that had staked out its territory on a certain area of the reef. Ferdie delighted in enveloping any available ankle in his suckery embrace, while trying to rip anklemeat to shreds with his single fang. Nancy, who hates most slithery things, thought he was cute. While they all enjoyed Ferdie's antics as he hunted, changed color like the NBC peacock, covered rocks with his hoody membrane and nailed his victims as they darted out in fright, I remained for the most part cabin-bound, trying through encounter techniques to achieve greater intimacy with my typewriter. At the rate we were moving, ours was going to be the world's longest circumsizing.

However, anyone planning to spend time in French Polynesia might do well to consider spending some of it at The Isthmus. You have all the benefits of seclusion, and yet you can easily walk to either of two supermarkets or the post office. For the occasionally necessary trip into Papeete, you get up early (5 A.M.) and catch le truck, making sure not to miss the last truck back, which leaves the central marketplace in midafternoon. An outboard powered dinghy gets you out to the reef in short order for diving and fishing, but even this is not necessary. Depths of 20 feet and less make it easy enough to retrieve your anchor and take the yacht itself on day trips.

But we had to face the fact that the two weeks we'd allotted for our cruise were nearly up, and we were by no means even half way around the island. Thus, on day 13, in spite of the rain, we powered nine miles to the south inside the protected lagoon, out the pass and into the open sea. Our destination was Airurua Pass, around the southern tip of the island. There was little wind, and once again we were under power. In order to clear safely a hidden reef named Faratara, we were forced to stand off about three miles, and the rains were so intense that the sheer cliffs of the shoreline were often totally obscured. Therefore, when we finally rounded the southern tip of the island, I was at somewhat of a loss as to where the hell we were.

This time, however, the excellent French chart showed an inset drawing of the pass with the mountains behind, exactly as it appeared from the ocean. The topography was unmistakable, and my usual doubts were absent. We entered the pass, weaved through coral heads in the narrow but well-marked channel, and found anchorage in a delightful cove that was a mere 42 feet deep. The rain stopped. *Sea Foam* lay quietly in the cool, late-afternoon shadow of the mountain. Sitting in the cockpit and hoisting a few tall ones, Nancy and I were sumptuously entertained by the music of nearby waterfalls.

Nancy and Craig rowed to the motus (two islets on the coral reef itself) to look for shells, but with little success. As a result of the growing value of shells (a value that springs from the collector explosion), Tahitians have virtually exhausted their reefs. Craig, disgusted, gave up on shells temporarily and declared his new prey to be crevettes (freshwater shrimp). We'd been told of a river where they could be found, and Craig now needled me relentlessly to move *Sea Foam* to a spot nearby.

At noon the next day we got our act together and powered north about a mile to a river mouth named Valley Tomatoaloa. Out of a fork and a stick, we each made a five-foot spear with a head of several sharp tines. We readied a pressure kerosene lamp and a powerful flashlight. Then, having made a daylight reconnoiter, we settled back to wait for darkness.

After dinner we rowed ashore. The tropical moon was huge, full and golden, and hovered regally over the eastern horizon. We took the dinghy as far up the stream as possible and then proceeded on foot, wading in waist-deep water. An eel darted between Nancy's legs, eliciting a squeak of alarm. We were all a trifle edgy till we spotted our first crevette.

"Got him!" said Craig, excitedly, displaying a tiny, wriggling thing on the end of his spear.

"Huzzah!" said Nancy. Believe it or not, Nancy is one of those people who actually says 'huzzah'.

"All we need is another 99 of them and we're in businesss," I observed, deprecatingly. "We'll be here all night."

My sudden, cynical attitude had a reason. My middle-aged eyes, capable of seeing great distances, and able to function perfectly close at hand with the help of glasses, have an area between in which all is fuzzy. It was this no-man's-land focal length that was needed. Add to this the refraction that causes something under water to appear to be a few inches from where it really is, and it soon became clear that I wasn't going to be marksman of the month, shrimpspearingwise. After bagging 18 dead leaves and as many short sticks, I finally nailed one crevette. Craig, meanwhile, had speared 15, all considerably bigger than his first one. Cooked and eaten for a late-evening snack, they were tender, sweet, and made us feel pampered and spoiled.

The next day we powered to the extreme north end of the lagoon where we had heard that there were so many turban shells, they virtually blanketed the reef. Craig couldn't find a one. Never has a boy been misled by so many. To make up for his disappointment, we decided to invade the village. My mouth watered in anticipation of an icy Hinano, a luscious local beer. Nancy was sure she'd be able to buy one of the frozen, American chickens that were available in most stores at reasonable prices. Craig's radar was quivering, having picked up from a distance of a quarter-mile the subtle sounds of a scoop being forced through the glacial stiffness of ice cream. We rowed ashore and did our own things.

That night we departed for a small cove just opposite the pass through which we would escape when departing for Papeete. We picked that spot because it was near three fair-sized streams, all of which (Craig assured us) looked shrimpy. That night, armed and garbed as The Phantom Provider, he sortied alone into the darkness, to return in an hour with a festival catch of 17 good-size crevettes.

Saturday was a lazy day. The sun shone, its rays punctuated by the periods and commas of fluffy tradewind clouds. We swam, read, wrote, made *Sea Foam* shipshape for the next day's sail, and appreciated the perfect weather all the more because there had been so little of it. There was some criticism by Craig and me of good weather that stays away until the final day of one's vacation, but Nancy pointed out that the intermittent appearances of the sun had made it all perfect, as otherwise we might have had some sort of sick compulsion to varnish. Craig's and my complaining stopped immediately.

Sunday was another perfect day, but with light winds. We had to power nearly half the distance to Papeete before the wind came up enough to sail. Now, off Point Venus, we were sliding along briskly before 20 knots of wind, flying our tired old mainsail and a poled-out jib. God had turned down the rheostat, dimming the daylight with tropical suddenness. For a moment we were transported by the caresses of the warm wind on our backs, the musical hissing and bubbling of the wake, and the final flaming scar on the western horizon as it healed into darkness. None of us talked much, as each of us was peeking through his own knothole into immortality.

The sudden sound of tearing fabric brought us rudely back to earth. I'm willing to bet that any sailor, having imagined that particular sound in his more apprehensive moments, would recognize it immediately with a sinking heart. Craig and I moved quickly to the foredeck, where we saw that a fitting, which normally attached the reaching pole to a point halfway up the mast, had broken. The jagged end of the pole was working its way down through the fabric of the mainsail like a diabolical seamripper. Before Craig and I could lower the jib and retrieve the pole, the luff had been ripped along half its length.

Back in the cockpit I explained to Nancy what had happened. "The fitting we had brazed in New Zealand? It broke. Looks like it crystalized, weakened by the heat."

She looked at me. I looked at her.

"Thank God it wasn't the new main!" Said in unison, the line sounded as if we'd been rehearsing it all afternoon.

We powered into Papeete Harbor, riding the range lights on a compass heading of 149 degrees. The reef bordering the pass was marked with a flashing red light on the left, flashing green on the right. (Would I ever outgrow the urge to back into the harbor, simply because every place but the United States reverses the colors of channel markers as to which side they're marking?) Arriving after dark, boats were allowed to swing on an anchor along the western end of the quay. First thing in the morning we would have to move in beside the other boats—bow (or stern) anchor out, stern (or bow) lines ashore. For now, we anchored and rowed ashore to buy our supper from one of the kitchen trucks. Parked all along the quay, they filled the night with seductive savors. Our ritual required that we stroll the whole length of the quay before we chose among chicken, liver, goat, pork, beef, or lamb, roasted on skewers over charcoal embers.

"I'm glad to be back," said Nancy, holding my hand in both of hers.

"But I'm glad we went," I added. Which summed up an anomaly that I sometimes found puzzling, but which that evening seemed to sear its own brand of order into the flesh and sinew of our lives.

IV / MOOREA-BELLINGHAUSEN-SUVAROV

August 11, 1977. It's 5 P.M. and we're leaving the pass from Opunohu Bay, Moorea, and will soon be on course for Huahine. There's very little wind, but perhaps once we get out of the lee we'll get a breeze. For five days we've been waiting out a *miramu,* a strong wind from the south, and during today it died. The passage to Huahine is 80 miles, pass to pass, which for us means more than 12 hours sailing and less than 24. Because the pass at Huahine is neither lit nor marked with buoys, in order to reach it in daylight we are leaving in the evening.

We motor out the pass. We've been based in Tahiti/Moorea long enough to have become residents, and it's time to leave. On the other hand, we're leaving good friends and a place we've learned to love, and the way our lives seem to be pointing we may never come back. All this we know, and yet for two reasons much of the poignancy of parting goes unremarked. For one thing, we aren't leaving French Polynesia—we're only moving to another island in the same group. And for another thing, all three of us are busy trying to figure out why there's no wind.

"Maybe we're still in the lee," I say, hopefully.

"We'll be out in the open in an hour or so—I bet there'll be wind," says Craig.

The sky is overcast, the dead air oppressive. With too little wind to put up a sail, we are being rolled unmercifully by a four-foot swell out of the east. Why aren't the seas calm? There hasn't been wind out of the east for 10 days, but I am still too tuned to the land to read the signs correctly. When we finally leave the lee of the land we encounter not wind, but a three-foot swell out of the south, spoor of the 10-day *miramu* that has just finished. The combination of the swells from two directions, south and east, destroys the sea's rhythms and makes *Sea Foam*'s motions violent and unpredictable. Someone has made a drastic mistake and tossed us into God's Maytag.

"Jesus," says Nancy, "I'd just as soon go back."

"Too late," I say. "It'll be dark in half an hour. No moon, no stars. We're better off to keep going."

Twice before we'd felt our way into the unlit, unbuoyed entrance to Opunohu. Even with clear, starlit skies, finding the pass through the submerged reef was a nerve-wracking business.

"We could go back to Cook's Bay and go in on the range lights," she suggests.

"I don't see it. I mean, we're not in any danger; we're just uncomfortable."

"You mean miserable," she says. Craig leans calmly over the rail and throws up, but he's always sick when we first go to sea.

"Do you both want to go back?" I ask.

"Not me," says Craig, wiping his mouth with a washcloth.

"I guess not," says Nancy.

"OK then," I say.

Craig goes below and lies down, his only defense against inner-ear treachery being retreat into sleep. Nancy has the first watch, and I sit with her as she steers. Soon darkness becomes total, and Nancy's face glows eerie red in the reflection of the binnacle light. In the softness of the light I can hardly tell where Nancy leaves off and darkness begins.

"I love you when you're blurry," I say.

"I am *not* blurry."

"You're terribly blurry. I don't think anything can cure it, except maybe a cup of tea."

"Ah," she says, and smiles.

It is my lot never to get seasick. Well, hardly ever. I can depend on being the only healthy soul on board during the first three days of a passage. Nancy and Craig will never miss a watch or fail to do their share in sail handling, but the minute their duties are done, they withdraw into a chrysalis of misery. While they are sick I take over most of the chores, particularly in the galley, for which both Nancy and Craig claim to be grateful. But I often sense that they'd much rather I'd feel the way they do—plain lousy.

Once I did. It was off Mexico in the very beginning of our cruise. There were a lot of family aboard: Philip (20), Connie (20), Chris (19), and Craig, who was only 10. Conditions were perfect for seasickness: a dense, disorienting fog; large, rolling swells as regular as a pendulum; and a light wind from astern that kept a cloud of diesel exhaust fumes hovering around us.

"I don't feel well," I told Nancy, who was struggling not to vomit.

"I feel awful," she said.

Just then Chris leaned over the side and retched. Nancy and I looked at each other, trying not to get involved.

"Please take the wheel," I said. I went below and returned bearing two slugs of straight vodka. Nancy took one look and leapt for the rail.

"That was *not* the answer," she grated between barfs.

Nancy's vomiting brought me to the brink. Quickly I tossed down a vodka, quickly followed one with the other. The cure was miraculous. I've never had to resort to it since, perhaps because I know it's there. Nancy still hasn't forgiven me completely.

Now, using both hands for clutching and bracing, I go below without incident. Lighting the stove, however, is another matter. Burning alcohol spills from the priming cup and creates a lake of fire in the pan under the stove. I put the fire out with a cup of fresh water, but spilling alcohol has left too little in the cup to prime the kerosene burner sufficiently, and I must prime again. Blind rage calls forth the muse of obscenity, and dazzled by my own virtuosity, I forget my anger and am pleased when the burner lights.

Our little two-burner Optimus stove sits in a gimballed tray that I designed and built, and boasts fiddles—stainless steel railings that keep the pots from sliding off—which I also made. There is a particular skew to my handiwork that distinguishes it from the work of others. I call it originality, but Craig calls it weird. Knowing my limitations, Nancy saved me from failure by insisting that I didn't need to make the movable braces (also called fiddles) that lock the pots in place; she claimed she could do perfectly well with bungee cords. I use one now to secure the kettle over the flame and consider the operation a success, knowing that the hair on my hands will surely grow back.

When the boat is moving violently, the sensible procedure is to make one mug of tea, deliver it and return below to make another. No matter how many times I prove this, I insist on saving time by making both mugs at once. By slipping my forefinger through the two handles and letting the mugs press against the backs of my fingers, I can hold both mugs with one hand and use the other hand to steady myself. What I forget is that the mugs, filled with boiling tea, will become hot, and my fingers will be burned two ways—by the increasingly hot mugs and by the tea, which, because of my haste to deliver it before my fingers cook, will spill on my hands.

I sit in the cockpit once more, sipping my tea and brooding over my scalded fingers. Nancy interrupts my thoughts.

"I think there's a breeze. Maybe we could raise the jib. Go ahead and finish your tea first, though." Nancy revels in the power of being helmsperson-on-watch.

I go forward into smothering darkness. I can barely make out a shade of difference between the sky overhead and the ocean below. The horizon is indistinguishable. The boat is tossing and bucking in psychotic seas. Clinging with both hands, I make my way across the foredeck handhold by handhold, knowing that if I fall overboard Nancy won't miss me for several minutes, and that by the time she does, the chances of finding me will be zero.

Suddenly the boat lurches, and the port lifeline that I'm clutching with my left hand gives way. There is a split second of truth while I stare down Death's stygian throat and reevaluate my rejection of a safety harness. My right hand snatches blindly in the darkness with only instinct and memory for guidance. Miraculously my fingers close around the forestay. With a heave I pull myself erect and take the final steps to the end of the bowsprit, where I am safe in the 'U' of the steel railings of the pulpit.

"Are you OK?" calls Nancy. She can't see me, but she has sensed my close call.

"I'm OK," I yell.

Having raised the jib, I return to the cockpit and tell Nancy what happened. She's quiet for a minute, and I figure she's running a replay.

"I never would have found you," she says, finally. "What do you suppose made the lifeline break?"

"I don't know," I say, "but I'm not going back up there to find out."

Go back up I must, however, as an hour later our zephyr from the south switches to gale force winds from the east, and I finally realize the reason for the swells. Those from the south are vestiges of the *miramu,* while those from the east are precursors of the returning trades. The wind's suddenly increasing force sends me scurrying forward where, with nerves jangling, I lower the jib.

Even with staysail alone we make 4 knots, and I figure with a push from the current we'll have the island close ahead by dawn. I'm counting on this push because surface ocean currents, pushed by the trade winds, normally move from east to west. Sailing from Moorea to Huahine, the navigator can usually count on a favorable current of 1 to 1½ knots which, added to our speed through the water, should give us 5 to 5½ knots over the bottom. But the *miramu* that interrupted the trade winds has also disrupted the currents, and come daylight I realize we haven't made nearly the distance I'd expected.

The wind increases to 40 knots and the sea, a battleground for anarchistic swells, is chaotic and angry. *Sea Foam* is being pummeled so hard that I have no desire to increase her speed with more sail. As a result, it's late afternoon before we arrive, tired and out of tune, to drop anchor in front of the Bali Hai hotel.

All three of us inspect the broken lifeline. The stainless steel fitting that connects the lifeline to the pulpit has fractured for no apparent reason, and once again we're impressed by the treachery of stainless and its ability to break without the prior warning of visible clues. Later I inspect the rest of the fittings on the lifelines and discover no obvious flaws. We replace the broken fitting with a lashing of Dacron line, and decide that 'lifeline' is actually an insurance policy with unpleasant surprises in small print.

While we're at it, we rethink the steps that led us to our present position *re* safety harnesses. Except in the calmest weather, each of us wears a harness when standing a nightwatch alone at the helm. Sitting with legs in the cockpit and hands on a sturdy wheel is a secure position, but it's the odd chance of a rogue wave and the fact that the watchperson is alone on deck that makes the difference for us. However, in sail handling and other deckhand jobs, the harness's leash inhibits freedom of action and could conceivably cause as well as prevent accidents. On a clear foredeck the tradeoff might be worth it. But on *Sea Foam*'s foredeck with its deckboxes, staysail traveler, staysail, foot-high raised forepeak hatch, electric windlass, samson post, and 11½-foot bowsprit, the clutter makes the tradeoff too dear. Add to this the fact that had I been wearing a harness, the place I most likely would have clipped it to was to the lifeline, and you have our case: freedom from restriction is the best insurance.

It's night, and for some reason I'm wakeful. Without disturbing the crew, I make a cup of tea and go topside. Even in our cozy anchorage the gusts are angry. Herds of wild clouds stampede across the sky, in flight from demonic easterlies. I stare out the pass to the west. Leaving this protected place is as unappetizing as any prospect I've ever faced. I've lost my stomach for the sea, and I have no one I can turn to for help. It's true that if I told Nancy and Craig, they would try to buoy up my courage, but it's just as likely that I would sink theirs. So I keep my worries to myself. I know that in a few days I'll sail *Sea Foam* out that pass, but what will move me will be the momentum of all the work and effort that brought us to this point, and not any feelings of anticipation. For a moment I feel very much alone.

We are anchored near shore. Palm trees wave and beckon. Security sings to me in the siren tones. "But if Ulysses can pass you up, so can I," I urge myself. With such whistlings in the dark of my foreboding, I go below to bed and restless sleep.

We are two days out of Huahine on our way to Suvarov in the Cook Islands. I am steering. The gods have draped a moth-eaten cover over our earth-cage, and starlight is leaking in through the holes. The seas are moderate, the wind fair from the port quarter, and all is well. I am feeling like Job, biblical fall guy, this time because of our windvane. Diabolical instrument of my persecution, it broke today. Again.

A home brew, our vane has never worked properly. The first version was my very own design. It steered nary a mile. What it did do, when the wind reached 15 knots or better, was to vibrate so violently that the whole hull shook with ague. I sent home for a book on aerodynamic theory and began accumulating energy and optimism for another try.

A friend designed our second version. It steered *Sea Foam* perfectly, vindicating the design. Construction, however, was another matter. For economic reasons we had incorporated as much of my original vane as possible. The bracket that held the auxiliary rudder was weak, and broke after one day of rough weather at sea.

In Tahiti I rebuilt the broken bracket, which still seemed to be OK. This time yet another holdover from my original vane failed. The stainless steel pipe, spine of the auxiliary rudder, broke at a weld. "Shoulda had it annealed," offered a well-meaning friend on the radio. So we steer.

It's time to call Craig for his watch. He has pointed out that I sigh a lot lately. My pessimism is getting to the crew. Somehow I'll have to find a way to cheer up.

Nightwatch: Today has been a strange day. If you had told me this morning what I would later be a party to, I would have poo-poohed you right off the boat. I still don't believe it.

As a navigation check, we had wanted to pass within sight of the island of Bellinghausen, but at noon our latitude was so far north that I decided not to bother. The Sailing Directions said Bellinghausen was uninhabited. There was no pass into the lagoon. None of us felt the atoll offered enough promise to merit a detour. But in order to keep our sails full in a quartering wind we were steering south of our course, and as a result I was not too surprised to hear Craig say, softly in deference to his mother's nap, "Land ho!"

"Where?" I demanded, sticking my head up out of the companionway.

"There," said Craig, pointing.

"That is *not* land," I said. "How many times have I asked you to keep informational language as accurate as possible? The proper call would be something like 'Coconut palm fronds ho!' "

"Coconut fralm ponds ho," said Craig, agreeably.

"OKOKOK," I said. "But you have to admit it's only an *assumption* there's land underneath. How about 'Coconut trees ho'— 'Coco ho' for short?"

"How about 'Foliage ho,' or 'Foho'?" asked Craig.

"Don't be ridiculous," I told him.

We discussed how far away we could spot an atoll. In theory, according to Bowditch's tables of horizon distance, a line of sight from the eye of *Sea Foam*'s helmsperson (7 feet above sea level) to the topmost fronds of a 70-foot coconut tree growing on a 10-foot-high atoll will just clear the horizon at a distance of 13 nautical miles. But in practice the distance was much less. Except in a flat calm, fronds didn't appear feather by feather. We would scan, anxiously, an empty ocean. Then, *click*—a patch of foliage would pop into view. Craig spotted Bellinghausen's trees from nine miles away. Some atolls with shorter trees have remained invisible until we were within five miles.

"Don't tell your mother," I said when it was time to wake her for her watch. "We'll surprise her."

It was 15 minutes before Nancy, groggy from sleep, looked anywhere but at the compass or telltale. Then suddenly the shock of seeing trees dead ahead in what she'd assumed to be empty ocean elicited an unprintable version of "what's that?" She was even more explicit in responding to Craig's suggestion that she say "Coco ho."

I scanned the atoll with the binocs. A triangle in shape, the north side was in the lee.

"Looks calm," I said. "If you two want to go ashore, I'll stay with the boat." The appearance of the atoll had cheered us all, and I wanted to prolong the event, to make an occasion out of it.

Before they could decide, I spotted, through the glasses, three Polynesians in a dory powered by a British Seagull outboard. For an uninhabited island, Bellinghausen was jumping. When we drew closer, the young men came alongside. They proposed taking our anchor ashore to the coral reef, after which *Sea Foam* would lie in deep water, held off the reef by only the offshore wind. I had heard of this being done before. It had sounded risky, and I had never imagined us doing it. Correction: I *had* imagined us *never* doing it. So I was surprised to hear myself say, "Why not?"

After that moment of decision, events took on a surrealism like Alice's Wonderland. We anchored *Sea Foam,* boarded the dory, and headed for what looked like solid reef. On approach, however, we spotted a narrow, tide-ripped nightmare of a boat pass that led into the lagoon. One man, toes gripping the gunwales, balanced precariously in the bow of the dory, and stood ready to heave a line to another man who miraculously appeared on shore. In order to clear the coral heads that lurked beneath the surface, the man at the outboard was raising and lowering the racing propeller, using a cat's cradle of fishing line and wire for primitive but effective controls. Periodically an incoming swell engaged the outgoing tide in roiling battle, and I could see that for us to make it, split-second timing was essential. I looked at Nancy's saucer-eyes and saw that *she* saw that split-second timing was essential. But the young men caught an incoming wave just right, as they'd no doubt done a hundred times before, and in less than 20 seconds we plowed through white water into a pool of knee-deep calm. Even the 200-pound sea turtle, upside down in the bottom of the dory and facing a gloomy future as food, seemed relieved at the outcome.

"Get any pictures?" I asked a white-knuckled Nancy.

"P-pictures? J-J-Jesus!"

Ashore, Nancy and I were given a delicious, potent, home brew. Craig was given an exotic Sprite. We took their pictures and wrote down where to send them prints. They gave us shells, coconuts, and more home brew. We took more pictures, of mother and child, grandfather and child. The ride out the pass was just as wild as the ride in, but Nancy took pictures anyway. Back at *Sea Foam,* we made up a gift pack of several yards of material and some cans of food. Our hosts thanked us and retrieved our anchor for us from the reef. They smiled and waved. We smiled, waved, and sailed off into the setting sun. We'd passed through the looking glass for a mere two hours, but the adventure had accomplished a miracle. Instead of being on a grueling marathon, we were now on an "expotition." (To differentiate: an expedition is a journey with a purpose; but an "expotition," if you're not up on your Winnie the Pooh, is a happy journey whose purpose is hazy and whose goal is unrecognized, even when reached.)

An hour or so later I was below, reading a book and chuckling at nearly every page. Suddenly I put the book down, and, having flashed on a family joke, began to laugh uncontrollably.

WIFE: How was the golf today, dear?

HUB: Terrible. George died on the third tee.

WIFE: How perfectly awful!

HUB: Yeah. All day long it was hit the ball, drag George; hit the ball, drag George.

I laughed till the tears ran, my ribs ached. I laughed till Craig came to the companionway and looked below, wondering what the hell was wrong. I laughed till Nancy crossed the cabin and put a cool hand on my brow.

"What is it, Hon?" she asked.

"The windvane," I said, "the God damned windvane. In every port we'll refuse to leave without it working. I'll spend hours and dollars fixing it. The first day out it'll work, and then it'll break, and we'll haul it aboard and lash it down—useless cargo till we get to the next port, where I'll start all over again. With that stupid vane it'll be 'hit the ball, drag George,' the whole way around the fucking world." I started laughing again, but stopped, gradually, at the sight of Nancy's worried face.

"Never fear, Love," I said. "I'll fix it, I promise."

Relieved to see me return to normal, she smiled and returned to her book. But I knew what had really happened. The sluice of laughter had washed away the dregs of depression. Gone were the gossamer webs of fear. Encouraged, I was once more a free spirit, albeit, no doubt, *pro tem* . . .

Nightwatch: We dropped anchor in the protected lagoon of Suvarov at 1530 this afternoon. I woke up tonight for my watch, anyway. I always do for a couple of days. All I have to do is go topside to make sure we really are where we are, then go below and pump out the head a couple of times, and I feel better. Suvarov is perfect—a deserted island paradise. We are sharing it with three other boats. I don't mind. Had we arrived two weeks ago, the number of other boats would have been 14.

Last night was wild. About 2100 I was awakened by Nancy's squeaks. As she only squeaks when she considers herself in extreme jeopardy, I got up and went to the companionway. It was blowing a mean squall. Raindrops were pelting Nancy's foul weather gear. The waves were obscene. All I could see of Nancy was a windmill of limbs. Her right hand held the flashlight beam on the starboard telltale while her left hand spun the helm frantically, a frail but adequate defense against jibing or broaching. Sitting beside the wheel, as the starboard rail dipped, Nancy clung to the wheel, while her body, legs flailing, slid out to the limit of her short safety line. As the port rail dipped she slid back.

"What's the trouble?" I asked.

"What's the *trouble*?" she squeaked, "What in the hell do you *think* is the trouble?"

I thought. I was not going to wake Craig and order the two of us out on that slippery foredeck *in* the dark *in* the rain to try to take in a poled-out jib. I suppose I could have gone up and steered, but Nancy, though thrashing about, was doing a good job. The squall would be over soon. I came to a quick decision.

"You're doing fine," I said, and closed the hatch.

By the time it was my trick, the sky had cleared. The waves, which increased during each squall, had subsided. The stars were smiling.

"Have a nice watch?" I asked.

"Up yours," said Nancy, sweetly, "and good *night*!" She almost always says good night.

I watched *my* first squall approach from about five miles away. It closed rapidly. The seas increased. The clouds, giant sponges, wiped away all the starstains. Gusts of wind pummeled my back. By the time the rain came, I'd concluded that squalls make me lonely.

"Nan-*cy*!"

She appeared, sandy-eyed.

"What's wrong?"

Immediately, I felt foolish.

"You—you'd better close the hatch. It's raining in. And what time is it?"

She looked at me for a full 30 seconds, and intuition told me to be grateful she hadn't a weapon. Then, quickly, she slammed in the hatchboards, backwards, slammed the sliding hatch closed, and yelled something unintelligible, which I assume was the time. I'm not sure, however, as the next morning we didn't discuss it.

Today was sensational. The waves were huge. The wind was blowing 25 to 30 knots. Our first sun line showed that the squalls had blown us south. We had been advised never to approach Suvarov atoll from the southeast, as that quadrant is mostly reef awash. But the chart showed a tiny motu, a few trees, and visibility was perfect. If we were to get there with enough light to transit the pass, we'd have to take the chance.

"Let's go for it," I said.

"Why not?" said Craig.

"Shall we put up the jib?" I asked. "It'll give us another knot, knot and a half."

"Yes," said Nancy. We were already making six knots under mainsail alone. Normally she votes to reduce sail. Thus her priorities: more sail with a roller-coaster ride superseded heaving to overnight only a few miles from shelter.

Two hours later I was below, studying the chart, reading the Sailing Directions for the twentieth time.

"Land ho!" shouted Craig.

"What – did – you – say?" I yelled.

"I mean Coco ho," said Craig. Then, sticking his head down the companionway he added, "And I'll bet you $1,000 there's land underneath."

Even though I had renewed my faith in sextant, sights, and the science of reduction, I could hardly believe it. We had averaged 130 miles a day. Our best day was 143 miles. For *Sea Foam*, it had been a fast trip. I looked at Nancy. Nancy looked at me. No matter how delightful our visit to Suvarov might prove to be, it would only be a way station on a voyage that had made a new beginning. We swapped extravagant grins. Like the Phoenix, our dream had finally risen from the ashes.

CRYSTAL BALL DEPARTMENT: *The scene is Tarawa in the Gilbert Islands, months and thousands of miles later. The Crew has just dropped the Captain on shore where he stands, bent with burden. He looks very much like me, but older. The windvane, repaired and strengthened in Suvarov and re-repaired in Samoa, rests broken and akimbo in his arms.*

Crew (sitting in dinghy just off shore): *Go get 'em Tiger. Just hit the ball and drag George. You can do it, Herb. Hang in there. It's a piece of cake!*

Visibly encouraged, the Captain's posture straightens. He takes a deep breath, smiles, and waves at the Crew, then turns and strides purposefully toward the village where there is a welder. A few steps later he is whistling "Lucky Day," and there is even the hint of a skip in his gait. (fade)

V / SUVAROV - SAMOA

If there is one thing I've learned from being around Nancy, it's to evaluate a project as a whole, and not just by the result. Even if the goal wasn't reached, the by-products may have been of value. Specifically, Nancy taught me to take comfort from the gems I picked up on my way to failure.

One of our more costly mistakes began just before we were to leave Papeete. Nancy and I were having one of our fights. I was for filling *Sea Foam*'s tanks with diesel. She was for buying a minimum amount—just enough to get us to Suvarov, where we knew that a recent wreck of a Korean fishing boat contained hundreds of gallons for the taking.

"Look at it this way," she said. "Given the choice of 80-cents-per-gallon diesel and free diesel, and given the state of our finances, which would you choose?" The conclusion was inescapable, but I fought on, bravely.

"How do we know we can get it there for sure?"

"There's plenty left, according to Al." She was speaking of a friend, presently in Suvarov, with whom we talked regularly on the radio.

"Yeah, but what if we can't get it, or it's of such poor quality we don't want it? Or what if the weather's so bad we decide to skip Suvarov?"

"Then we can fill up in Samoa," she said. Nancy is an answer looking for an objection. I know, because she once told me that she married me for my objectionableness.

We sort of compromised. The way I compromised was to give her her way and then cheat. We agreed that 20 gallons would be enough, but when we got to the fuel dock I slipped in an extra 10.

"Safety factor," I said, when she caught me.

Soon after we arrived in Suvarov, we made a trip across the lagoon to the southern reef where the wreck was stranded. We'd gleaned two things from other yachts: that because there were several hundred yards of reef to cross to get to where the wreck was, we would need a dinghy to transport the diesel; and that success depended on catching the high tide. We followed our usual practice of getting a late start, however, and syphoning the diesel out of the wreck with a garden hose took longer than we'd planned. As a result, by the time we'd loaded the two dinghies with jerry cans of diesel for our second load, there was scarcely enough water covering the reef to allow us to drag, scrape, curse, cajole, and barge our way over or around abrasive obstacles of coral.

"Shit," I said later, inspecting the ravaging cuts and scars on the bottom of our nearly new inflatable dinghy. "It wasn't worth it." The wanton damage gave me a sick feeling in the pit of my stomach, partly because I knew that patience (come back at another tide for a second trip) or better planning (arrive early and get the full benefit of the high tide) or better execution (get started when we intended to) had all been deficient.

"We devalued our dinghy far more than what we saved on diesel," I pointed out to Nancy. She too was chagrined.

"Can't we patch it?"

"Yes," I said, "but you know as well as I do what a constant battle the patches are going to be." Before getting our new dinghy we'd spent years patching our old one, and had found that sun, water, and the inevitable scrapings of normal use will eventually de-patch even the most careful repairs.

"There's another way of looking at it," said Nancy sometime later. "How many times have we filled up *Sea Foam*'s diesel tank?"

"About 15," I said, ballparking.

"And which one stands out? I mean, when you get older and find yourself sitting in front of the fire telling tall tales to your grandchildren, won't this be one of them?"

The pluses and minuses didn't yet add up to a profit; but still, she had a point, and I was comforted. In my mind I could see it. The grandkids would sit spellbound through the whole yarn. In the telling I would play down our deficiencies, play up the adventure bearing in mind that the truth must never stand in the way of a good story.

"And we got line, hooks, swivels, stuff we can use, stuff we can give to islanders," I said.

"Stuff we'd never have bought, but we'll be glad to have," added Nancy.

"A gift. It's a gift from Providence."

"Providence indeed," said Nancy, in a tone that cast my ambivalence in concrete.

Our vane had broken its rudder post enroute to Suvarov, so while there we patched it up with the help of Dryrot John and a bandit. John was a kind and helpful person even though he lived on a trimaran. We called him Dryrot John because he'd named his dinghy *Dryrot*. When I told him what had happened to the windvane and how I intended to repair it, he coughed politely behind his hand and said maybe he'd drop by and see if he could help.

When John rowed over, he brought some resin that I'd asked for. He also brought a bandit. I had never seen a bandit before, and if one can be said to fall in love with a mechanical device, that's what I did. A bandit is a tool used to stretch and clamp steel strapping around wooden crates. John's bandit used stainless steel strapping, which made it perfect for making a splintlike repair on our vane rudderpost.

My jury rig worked beautifully, allowing the vane to steer us unerringly to Samoa, 450 miles down the line. It's true that the passage was benign, with steady winds and stormless seas, and that the repair might not have held up under great stress. But the pudding was proved, in that as long as we had enough wind to sail, nobody had to sit glued to the helm. Our emancipation was so welcome that I vowed to do my utmost to improve and strengthen our vane to where we would never again need to be without it.

"Vane hopes?" offered Nancy, when I told her my thoughts.

"God, I hope not," I said.

But I sometimes felt that my love of improvisation helped form my destiny. I welcomed problems that ingenuity could solve, and as a result maybe didn't place enough emphasis on repairing or building something properly in the first place. Modern tools and materials gave a certain technological authenticity to what was in fact a bailing wire, chewing gum mind, but as far as I was concerned, the passages during which something broke and I fixed it were achievements. If a passage went without anything breaking, what was there to talk about? What was proven? It's true what they say about an ounce of prevention. On the other hand, resourcefulness is part attitude and part skill, and can be drastically improved with practice. This was, for me, a horny dilemma.

Gradually, the shape of our lives became a house that Jack built. Flexible, it expanded to meet random demands but lacked overall design. When we left San Diego in 1973, our goal was a scenic trip to New Zealand, beyond which we had no plans. Then, because of a lack of money, we left New Zealand and headed for home. On the way we stopped in French Polynesia where I began work on the book that would eventually become *Blown Away*. At the time, I thought I'd discovered the secret of life—a beautiful, serene environment to live in, and a useful job to do. Then came the opportunity to deliver *Lissa*, make a little money, and visit home and friends—something we otherwise would not have been able to afford. But the trip disrupted my idyll, and when we returned to Tahiti my hopes of an advance to continue writing the book were dashed. Since then our master plan was patch as patch can, nourished by the fact that we were happy as long as we could keep on cruising.

We did have the loosely held objective of continuing around the world, but as far as I was concerned it was a passionless goal adopted merely to give our meanderings some direction. I didn't care whether or not we sailed all the way around. We were flowing downstream, third-stage Siddhartha stuff, bouncing off obstacles with a shrug and a ready willingness to change course. Our plans were constantly broken for economic reasons. Our purpose was jury rigged; the god of cruising wore tee shirts and jeans. We could be happy anywhere. It was our style that was important.

On our way to Samoa we lost our nameboards. They must have been struck when the windvane broke, after which the constant wave action finished the job. I was looking astern at the fish line, trying to will an entrée to take the lure, when I saw a crimson object in our wake. Leaning over the transom, I saw that both nameboards were gone. Who could know when we lost the first one?

If it had been up to me, I would never have turned *Sea Foam* around—if Fate wanted our nameboards that much, she could have them—but Nancy insisted. It required taking down our poled-out jib and, in order to retrace our course, powering back into the wind. It was a good drill, being the exact procedure we would have to follow in the event of a man overboard. Finding the first nameboard was no trouble at all. The red stood out against the ocean's blue like a candle flame in a cavern.

"Let's keep going back," said Nancy, once we'd picked up the one board. "Maybe we'll find the other one."

"We have no idea when we lost it," I said. "We'll just be wasting our time. For all we know, it could have come off hours ago, or even yesterday."

"Please?"

"You – are – impossible," I said. "But let's agree on a deadline, OK? Thirty minutes?"

"OK," she said. I know that the way Nancy negotiates with me is to agree and then cheat, but this time there was no need. Before the 30 minutes were up, Craig spotted the other nameboard a couple of hundred feet off the starboard bow.

"Not bad, for having come back three miles," I said.

I recalled a time when *Sea Foam* was new to us and we had taken a half-dozen friends out for a Sunday afternoon sail. Our cockpit cushions came in two colors: bright red and blue. It was a very blustery day, and one of the red pillows blew overboard. We came about and found it with no trouble, and during the four passes it took to retrieve the cushion we were always able to keep track of where it was. Later in the day the sky grew overcast, and one of the blue pillows went over the side. We searched for an hour, 10 pairs of eyes on the alert, and never saw it again.

"If you decide to fall overboard, please go below first and put on a red shirt," I told Nancy.

"It wouldn't match my life vest," she said. "Orange and red? Yech."

It was the pillow incident that decided us to focus our defenses on avoidance, rather than remedy. The attitude of a skydiver just before his first jump is without doubt different than that of a skier prior to his first efforts on gentle slopes. Falling overboard, we felt, should be viewed with the same awareness of calamity as a nonfunctioning parachute, and with the same sense of personal responsibility. Kidding about it ("if you fall overboard, I get your desserts") had the effect of keeping the danger alive and well in everybody's mind.

A certain sailing magazine once published an article that told of a man who fell off his boat at the mooring. It was October in New England, the man was overweight and had a heart condition, and in the frigid water he couldn't last long. Nor could he get himself either into his dinghy or back aboard his sailboat even with his wife's help. If it hadn't been for a nearby skipper coming to the rescue, the man would no doubt have died. "Now," the article said, "would readers please respond with recommendations for legislation that will prevent this sort of thing from ever happening again?"

My solution was to pass a law to prohibit anyone who was 10 pounds or more overweight from boarding his own boat between 1 September and 30 April unless wearing a survival suit and carrying a backpack with eight months' worth of food. That way, if he fell overboard, someone would be bound to find him in the spring. (I didn't win.)

Cavalier lack of caution versus precious overcaution—we discussed this often. There would have been no way to enforce our donning a red vest every time we came topside. In those days before we recognized the danger of sun-induced skin cancer, one of our fondest goals was a deep, all-over tan, and on a sunny day the uniform ranged from scanty to skin. No doubt a wardrobe containing nothing but orange tee shirts would have been one approach, but only if the quality of the life we wished to prolong was of no consequence. *Sea Foam*'s deck was busy with gear and provided handholds everywhere. Had this or any number of other conditions been different, perhaps we would have amended our approach to man-overboard safety.

In retrospect, the things we regretted most were the places we did not go. It was easy enough to forego places we chose to omit in order to visit someplace better, or to ignore places about which we could learn nothing inviting. But if an island looked appealing on the chart, or offered a promise of people, beauty, isolation, shells, or some other feature, we hated to pass it up simply because it took an effort to make a detour and investigate.

Rose Island was such a place—uninhabited, and with a sheltered lagoon. The chart showed depths that were iffy but possible. But a note on the chart said Rose Island was a wildlife sanctuary, and that one needed permission to visit there. Because we didn't have permission, and because by now we were impatient to get to Samoa to replenish our supplies, we didn't stop. It might have been just another deserted island with nothing special to recommend it; but on the other hand, it might have been a snorkeling wonderland, a sheller's paradise, and we'll never know because we didn't take the trouble to have a look.

Another place that later escaped us for a different reason was Canton in the Phoenix Islands. We passed up trying to visit Canton Island because the Sailing Directions said that westerly winds, which we were getting by the windbagful, would make the pass impassable. It wouldn't have been much out of our way to test this statement. Had we done so (we were assured later by a sailor who had been there), we would have learned that the pass was possible. More important, we wouldn't have had to spend Christmas at sea.

Two years before we had wanted to visit Rapa, an island in the southern Australs. When our radio, our only source of the accurate time needed for navigation, failed, we put the 600-mile sail out of our minds. By the time we got the radio working again, the delay had eroded our enthusiasm. When the iron was hot and optimism was high, the investment of energy required to bring off an adventure seemed a small enough price to pay. But when the iron cooled, the price in terms of effort seemed exorbitant.

The other side of the coin was that whenever we did go the extra mile (as in the case of Bellinghausen), we were rarely disappointed. For me, momentum is always crucial in making and carrying out decisions. If I'm moving from A to B I don't want to stop. Stopped, in a pleasant place, it takes a Siren's song (usually Nancy's) to make me move. Nancy's joie de vivre and Craig's knack of minimizing most problems have bullied me into more adventures than I'd ever have undertaken on my own, and I'm grateful for every one of them.

Just the same, I'm sorry we didn't stop at Rose Island.

Like the petals of a giant flower, the harbor at Pago Pago opened to the penetration of *Sea Foam*'s bowsprit. We anchored close to the dinghy dock for the sake of convenience, and by so doing suffered the uncertainties of anchoring in the world's worst holding ground. At the end of the harbor was alluvial mud, much better for anchors. But we had no outboard, and the regular exercise of a long row, though having merit, I considered more appropriate to the needs of others. So we anchored close in on a slippery shelf of coral, and when it blew, we worried.

One skipper friend had advised us via the radio to stay away from Pago Pago at all costs, as it was, in his opinion, a toilet. He saw the discarded refuse of U.S. package culture; feared the not-so-latent violence of racial tension; deplored the eyesore of listing rustbuckets that made up the Asian fishing fleet; and was repelled by the effluents from two canneries. He failed to react to the scenic grandeur of the mountains; to what the Sailing Directions call 'the best harbor in the South Pacific'; to U.S. postal service (complete with zip code, yet); and to cheap, cheap booze. He was a man whose beer can rarely ran over. Even when it was half full, he described it as being half empty.

It's easier to turn away from Samoa, to dismiss it as one more example of our (U.S.) incompetence in dealing with other cultures, than it is to confront the truth of it. Samoa was a perfect example of how often we tried to solve other people's problems with dynamite, bulldozers, concrete, steel, and money—even though these materials might have been inappropriate for the delicate web of the society in question. Long after World War Two our philosophy was still Seabee 1-A, the difficult we do instantly, the impossible takes a little longer. We reached into our bag and pulled out instant roads, electronic schools, a prefab hospital. Then, having supposedly solved for all time every important problem, we were somehow amazed at the social impact of our golden hammer.

There's a song from the score of *My Fair Lady* that always makes me smile. In the movie, Rex Harrison played a man who lives alone for many years in an ivory tower of wealth, bachelorhood, and a belief in male, English superiority. Suddenly the man is baffled by the behavior of Eliza, a woman who has disturbed the calm containment of his life, and his complaint is laden with delicious arrogance (so funny when one observes it in others) when he says, "Why can't a woman be more like *me*?" This summed up my feelings about Samoans.

"Scratch a Samoan and you'll find a savage," insisted a friend of mine who had worked in Samoa for a long time. He told me the story of a Samoan clerk who was fired for incompetence. When she found no one would hire her without a reference, she went back to her Caucasian ex-boss and demanded one. He refused, on the basis of the fact that although she might well be a child of God, she was worthless as office help. By the time his cries brought aid, the child of God had decked El Bosso and was choking the life out of him.

(Hey, man, what these people need is a jetport. We'll put it outside of town, near the new shopping center.)

Standing waiting for a bus one day, I watched a young Samoan man brutally beat up his younger brother. Kid bro submitted with the stoicism of an eater of just desserts. Big bro would hit him several times, stop as if he had done enough, then resume with a terrible, uncontrolled anger. Two dozen adult Samoans ignored the punitive bullying with apparent indifference.

(You know, by giving out yearly handouts of fifty to one hundred million dollars, we've put everyone on this island on the dole. What they need to be really independent is tourist business—a luxury hotel. We can throw one up in a jiffy, right over here. Throwupthrowupthrowup.)

A Samoan wife, on discovering that her husband was being unfaithful, would warn the other woman one time. If the hanky-panky continued, custom permitted the betrayed wife to cut off her rival's ears with a knife. Sewing ears back on Samoan heads became a specialty in the hospital we built for them.

Korean fishermen, clean, well-groomed, and subdued, would wander about in the evening spending their hard-earned money. Incidents were common. While we were there, a Korean fisherman was found one morning with a knife stuck in his chest. The death was reported obliquely as being due to heart failure.

(You know, we're not having much luck getting tourists to come here. Maybe it's because there are so many incidents of Samoans throwing stones at them. What we need is a real attraction, like a cable car that will take visitors up to the top of Mount Alava.)

Before the injection of U.S. supermarkets, Samoans got most of their protein from fish. A huge fish population was nourished by the living coral reefs that surrounded the island. In 1978, a serious invasion of the starfish known as 'crown of thorns' threatened to turn the rich fishing grounds into a wasteland by eating and killing the coral.

In an effort to reward the Samoans for helping themselves, the U.S. offered a bounty for each crown of thorns caught. Samoans, farsighted husbanders, knew that if you cut a crown of thorns in two you don't have one dead one, but like with angle worms you have two live ones. Therefore to sustain the flow of bounties as long as possible, they harvested halves and threw the other halves back. No Samoan discerned that once the reef was dead, all the reef fish would move away in search of food.

A couple of young partners, Americans, got a contract from the U.S. government to rid the reefs of the destructive starfish. After months of work they were successful. But when they went to the new Samoan governor he refused to pay them, probably because he'd followed the usual practice of dividing the money from U.S. grants among his family and friends. After many letters and a couple of trips to Washington, enough pressure was brought to bear that the Samoan government had to pay up; but not before a Samoan man had broken into the house of one of the young partners and cut off his nose with a knife. Fortunately, and perhaps because of their expertise with adulteress' ears, the U.S. doctors did a beautiful job of permanently reaffixing the nose. But the message—keep your nose out of our business—was clear.

Our visit convinced me that U.S. policy has damaged the Samoans heavily. Easy money and consumerism have seduced them and separated them from self-sufficiency. Though in their old world they were proud, competent, and free spirits, in their new world they act inept, dependent, and angry. There's no doubt in my mind that most and maybe all island cultures have suffered at the hands of Western benefactors, but in the case of Samoa the U.S. has proved that the concept of 'bigger and better' must include the messes we make.

(Why can't Samoans
Be more – like – *me*?)

In October we motored out of Pago Pago with the idea of sailing to Suva, Fiji, 650 miles to the west-southwest. Halfway out the pass we noticed that the transmission was slipping. Four years before, when we were coming down the coast of Mexico, it had done the same thing. By the time we reached Acapulco, the engine was barely moving us through the water. Now, barely out of Pago Pago Harbor, we were going to have to do something every sailor hates—turn back.

The momentum of leaving on a passage is an almost undeniable force. You've slowly built up anticipation to where it exceeds the desire to remain safely where you are. You've spent money for provisions. Maybe you've loaded up with ice and perishables, timing their arrival on board to the last minute so that they'll last as long as possible. You've said goodbye. Often you've pulled aboard, cleaned, and stored ground tackle that was filthy with mud and growth. You've loaded the hard dinghy on the deck and deflated the rubber one. You've paid port fees and checked out with customs, immigration, and the harbormaster. In other words, you've made a substantial investment of time, effort, and emotional gearing-up. And everything that's been laying around for living aboard has now been carefully stowed for sea. The last thing you want to do is abort the mission.

It's true that it was only 650 miles to Suva, which is not far as South Pacific distances go. But over half of it was among Fiji's eastern islands. Offlying reefs abounded on the route, and many were unmarked and without visible land to warn you away. It would be easy to stay out of trouble as long as the weather was clear, but horror stories were told by even experienced sailors who had been caught among the islands by bad weather. The bad weather season was upon us. I had no appetite for making the trip with an unreliable engine. Nancy and Craig agreed. With all balloons punctured, we slunk back to our old anchoring spot.

Our first task was to get some more money sent. If you want to get something done quickly and smoothly, you go to a professional, right? Thus benighted, off I went to the president of the Pago Pago branch of the Bank of Hawaii.

"What's the best way for me to get money here quickly from Maine?" I asked him.

"Wire transfer," he said, without a trace of hesitation. "Just have it sent right here, directly to the bank."

"Gee," I said, "it's great to deal with a pro!"

I went to the communications center and put in a call to my mother in Maine. After a three-hour wait I was told to take a booth, where I had half a conversation—I could hear mother, but she couldn't hear me. The trouble was she could *almost* hear me, so we tried for five minutes before I finally gave up. The cashier was pleasant enough. If I had come out right away, she told me, I might not have had to pay. But as it was . . .

I followed the phone call with a telegram, and backed up the telegram with a letter. A week later, almost all our cash was gone and nothing had been heard from home. I went back to my banker.

"I came to get my money," I said, brightly.

"It hasn't come yet," he said. "Have you tried communications? Sometimes they get a wire and don't bother to send it over to us for days."

My faith waning, I walked the three blocks to the communications building. Nope. No wires for me, or to the bank about me.

A week later we were penniless and had eaten our way through five days' worth of ship's stores. I went back to the pres.

"I came for my money," I said, hopefully.

"You'd better send a tracer," advised the pres. "No doubt someone in your bank sent the money to the wrong place."

"Gee," I gee'd, "I told them exactly what you said." Bankers are experts at moving money around, and when one of them passes the buck to an amateur, it shakes him up to have the amateur pass it back. Pres was indeed shaken.

"I'm sure it'll be here momentarily," I continued, pressing my advantage, "but we've spent all our cash. Do you suppose you could cash a personal check for a hundred, just to tide us over?"

Though there may have been a polite question mark in my tone of voice, my actions were strictly declarative. I had the check all written before he finished hemming and hawing.

"I suppose I could go a hundred," he conceded, shaking his head. I offered him my pen to initial the OK, but he preferred to use his own.

Back at the communications building I got through to my mother within an hour, and this time I really felt that she heard much of what I said. I could hear her quite plainly. Nevertheless, I decided to follow up the call with another telegram. Nancy, who never stops counting the expense no matter how bad things get, was furious.

"You've spent over $30 just to get $300," she pointed out, "and we're not getting *any*where!"

I didn't point out that yet to be counted were bank charges on the other end. Things were bleak enough as they were.

The following week I got a telegram from my mother saying that the money had been sent two weeks before and had cleared the correspondent bank in San Francisco.

"Now I've done all I can," I said, showing pres the wire, "and I think it's high time that the Bank of Hawaii make a search on the assumption that they received it and damn well lost it." So saying, I placed another personal check for $100 on the blotter in front of him, which he initialed without comment. I felt that I'd made definite progress by establishing the pres as a reliable source of a hundred dollars a week.

"I'll put a tracer on it from this end," said pres.

By now, everything was done on *Sea Foam* and we were hanging around solely for our money. Each day that passed brought us deeper into the hurricane season, making any move more threatening. As delicately as possible, I let the pres in on our problem. Pres, who by this time had a small but significant investment in our future, was concerned. Thus when word finally came from Honolulu that the main office of the Bank of Hawaii had indeed received my money, had held it for two weeks and had then sent it back to Maine, pres was desolate.

"Your bank can't have sent the money to Pago Pago," he said.

"I'm afraid it did," I said, showing him the copy of the telegram my bank had sent, a copy of which my mother had mailed to me. (Nancy had by now pointed out roughly 33 times that my modern, big-biz methods were neither cheap nor effective, and had we managed the affair by letter we'd have been out of here weeks ago.)

"Now what do we do?" I asked pres. "Start over?"

"Jesus," he said, pretty forcefully, I thought, for a banker. "Just write a check for the three hundred. I'll OK it."

As I was leaving the bank, he caught me at the door.

"You know, such a small amount—I'm sure a larger amount wouldn't have been lost."

"Oh, I'm sure," I said, generously, his cash in my hand. "As for the amount, it wasn't much—*but it was all we had.*"

Before he could digest the significance of my calculated confession, I left. From the safety of the street I looked back. Pres was still standing in the lobby where I'd left him, a thoughtful look on his face. To his credit, he didn't run after me, but instead he laughed—really laughed—before turning and striding back to the bridge of his ship of finance.

I had half a mind not to bother to ask mother to cover my overdraft. After all, bank presidents should have to experience some of the anxiety the rest of us do. But I did write, and my letter must have beaten the check. As for the pres, he still occupies a fond spot in my memory. Although his beloved system failed, he had, after all, come up with a jury rig that worked.

VI / SAMOA - TARAWA

Imagine that it is December 1977, and you are visiting Pago Pago for the first time. Unused to ascending precipitous heights in gondolas, you are nervous when you take the cable car to the top of Mount Alava. The gondola sways precariously across the harbor, buffeted by williwaws, while far below you the Korean fishing boats, cleansed and groomed by distance, are rafted together in orderly rows. Even the offensive canneries look industriously virtuous. The grandeur of the landlocked harbor, surrounded on four sides by heroic mountain sentinels, takes your mind off your nerves; but you are conscious again of your nerves as the gondola begins the nearly vertical portion of its ascent. Just before the summit the car stops, tenuously suspended over a sheer drop of 1,000 feet. "Oh Lord," you think, "they've miscalculated." But then the car moves slowly up the last few feet and stops beside the landing platform.

From your vantage point the ocean appears calm, even benevolent. You notice a sailboat leaving, heading out the pass under power. She is white, with a red stripe and a long, cocky bowsprit—a ketch, but with masts of almost equal height. Through the binoculars you make out a boy of about 15 on the foredeck, ready to haul on the jib halyard. A woman with short, curly hair of burnished copper, perhaps his mother, stands at the wheel. Stationed at a sheet winch is a man, bearded and behatted. You watch as the smart little vessel leaves the pass, turns right, and scuds westward along the southern shore of the island. If you, like some of us, have a restless spirit, your eyes might take on a faraway look as you think, "That's really it—sailing from island to island in the South Seas. Romantic. Adventurous. The stuff of which dreams are made . . ."

"What's wrong now?" I ask somewhat querulously as I stumble out of my bunk. It is Nancy's watch, and she has awakened me right in the middle of my deepest night sleep.

"I'm sorry, Herb—I put off waking you, but the wind's shifted and we have to do something."

"Damn," I say. And unfair, I think. When I went to sleep we

were sailing west to a 20-knot quartering southeast wind. Now it has veered to the northeast, forcing us, with our jib and main set on the port tack, to sail nearly south. What I'd planned as a simple maneuver has become a problem.

The island of Upolu (Western Samoa) lies west-northwest of the island of Tutuila (American Samoa). To avoid sailing wing and wing with a poled-out jib at night, we were going to tack downwind: sail west, and at a carefully estimated time, jibe and sail north dead center between the two islands. Anybody should be able to hit a 35-mile-wide hole, shouldn't they?

But these islands have another name, the Navigator Islands, a name born of irony and sired by the unpredictable currents that have led many navigators to disaster. I plot our position. Because we are socked in with a low, dense overcast, I draw a circle of possibility, somewhere within which we undoubtedly are. It has a diameter of seven miles. From its least advantageous point I lay a course to pass ten miles east of Upolu.

"Let's jibe and see if we can make it," I say, knowing that instead of running we'll be close-hauled. Damn!

We jibe. All's well—we can sail full and by. Allow for a five-mile set in five hours and we still have a five-mile offing, which is good, because a coral reef sticks out a couple of miles. Supposedly there is a light on it, but I can't count on the Western Samoans, newly independent, having maintained it. After all, *they* know where the reef is. Always have.

The rest of the night is a nail biter. The wind drops, making us more susceptible to the current, if there is any. And the overcast never breaks, making the world as dark as blindness. I whistle some, and talk to myself. Craig comes on watch, but I stay on deck and tell Craig to do the same, even though our windvane is steering well. Finally, after exacting repeated promises from Craig that he will wake me if he even *suspects* he sees anything, I go to bed and fitful sleep.

Dawn wakes me, and I go topsides. Upolu is about five miles behind us. Craig saw nothing as we passed it in the darkness, four miles off. There was no light. The island looks friendly in the daytime, a monument to carefree sailing.

By now we should be used to the vagaries of cruising. To wit: having arrived in Pago Pago on September 15, we had planned to spend two weeks before leaving for the Gilberts and Marshalls, islands not usually visited by the Pacific armada of cruising yachts. But when we'd learned that Tarawa in the Gilberts was hosting an epidemic of cholera, we'd canceled our plans. Then, having decided to spend the hurricane season (December to March) in Suva, Fiji, we'd had to cancel our plans again because of our slipping transmission.

That was November. Now we have changed our minds one more time. Rather than sail to Fiji, we will make a dash north to five degrees south, reputedly the line of safety from hurricanes, and then proceed in leisurely fashion to the Gilbert Islands. The cholera epidemic has receded. We've had shots (although we later learn that they are only about 50 percent effective). On December 3, we set our sights on Tarawa. Our ETA is a week before Christmas, give or take a few days.

By using most of our diesel fuel, we reach five degrees south safely and in good time. The first part of our plan is completed. Furthermore, we've passed the Tokelau Islands and are well west of the Phoenix Group. If we should hit strong westerlies, a seasonal hazard, we have some running room, a form of insurance we always seek. Of all the islands to the immediate east of us, only Canton has a lagoon, and this is (1) restricted to the use of the U.S. Navy, and (2) supposedly unenterable in strong westerly winds. If bad weather comes, we'll have to ride it out at sea.

Our problem in the beginning, however, is not too much wind, but too little. On December 14, eleven days out, we have made about 750 miles, over 300 of which are under power. The past two days under sail we made 80 miles. From our position at 2 degrees south, 177 degrees west, Tarawa lies 650 miles westward.

"Don't worry," I say to Nancy's query. "The Pilot Charts show a 90 percent probability of winds from the eastern sector. We should be running into a strong equatorial current in our favor. We'll be there in less than a week." This in spite of the following log entry for the same day: "Trade wind sky, trade wind clouds, trade wind seas, from the west-northwest! This can't go on. Perhaps atomic explosions have reversed everything and we're sailing on an antiocean toward negative Tarawa in a mirror boat. Still heading north looking for the *real* trades."

Steadfast me: believer in probability and statistics; reader of Pilot Charts and Sailing Directions; clinger to the illusion that thought and planning will triumph. White hats will win. Logic will prevail.

For the next few days, either we have winds so strong that we are under storm canvas or bare poles, or we have none. By the end of this time I've figured out that the current is flowing *east*ward at 50 miles a day, and decide that this reversal is the result of the continuous westerly wind. Such weather can't go on forever, I tell the crew. And when it changes, the easterlies will return, reversing the current and pushing us the way we want to go. Just like the book says. But in the meantime . . .

I work it out. *Sea Foam,* with her 13-foot 9-inch beam, has a problem going to weather, particularly when the seas are up. Periodically she hobbyhorses to a complete stop. In open ocean, the best course we can hope to steer is 60 degrees off the wind. If we sail 60 miles, theoretically we should make good 30. But in 15 hours of sailing to weather, sideslip costs us 10 miles of leeway. Add the 30 miles lost in 15 hours to a two-knot current and you arrive at the depressing sum of −10 miles made good (or, to put it another way, 10 miles made bad). And even though the wind usually comes from other points in the west quadrant than due west, thereby giving us an advantage on one tack or another, our prospects remain bleak. Either the weather must change, or we must spend the rest of our lives at sea.

I can remember having a catboat the summers when I was 10 and 11. Hard-chined and slow nevertheless my father and I shared the pleasure of racing it every Saturday. Our classless barge had no hope at best, but when we put our combined brains to strategy, the results got even worse.

One of my father's pleasures was to think up unusual ways to do things. Occasionally his ideas failed, a fact that had no effect whatsoever on his optimism. He was a delight to be with, but the fact that he was my most influential sailing teacher is proving to be somewhat of a hangup for me.

Time after time we would find ourselves dropping slowly behind as we tried unusual sail trims, egregious tacks. In a perfectly straight-forward, four-marker race, "I'll bet there's wind over by that island," would send us lonely miles off the beaten path. We compiled one of the most impressive racing records in the history of Casco Bay, Maine, and considered it a personal triumph if we crossed the finish line by dark. For us, the thought of actually beating the next-to-last boat was ambitious.

Thus my confidence in my ability to psych the wind has been impaired from square one. So I go by the Sailing Directions and the Pilot Charts with nearly the same quota of success. My encouragement to Nancy and Craig is cheerful enough, but it rings hollow in my ears.

For a few days we batter to windward in a westerly direction. I feel that maybe sailing north, to get over the top of the convergence zone, and maybe even going till we hit the northeast trades, might be a good idea. But childhood memories of misjudgment make me hold to the model of sailing as near to the mark as possible. However, after sailing mostly southwest, our resultant course is actually southeast. The log: "We cannot progress by dousing sail every night, but we could not have sailed last night— wind too strong. We are all terribly depressed. In addition to causing us to lose ground, the gales and the hard sailing to weather are wearing us to nubbins."

The rotten weather persists. One night we are lying ahull, the winds screaming through the rigging at better than 50 knots. *Sea Foam,* riding well, is cozy below, and the relative quiet gives us a false sense that we're safe and secure. We finish supper, and I retire to my bunk for a nap. The canvas leeboard covers all but the upper two feet of the edge of the bunk and gives me the feeling of lying in a cradle. I fetal up and drop off.

The next thing I know I'm lying on the cabin sole, a great egg forming on my head where it hit the mast. It takes Nancy and Craig both to get me to a sitting position, then to the settee in the main salon. I know I'm in *Sea Foam,* but that's all I know. I don't know where we are.

"Where are we?" I ask.

"We're in midocean, on our way to Tarawa," says Nancy.

Nothing is registering.

"Tarawa? What are we going there for?"

Even the nonamnesiacs have a hard time with that one.

"We left Samoa a couple of weeks ago. Don't you remember?" I can see that they really need to hear me say 'yes,' but the truth is, I *don't* remember. The most recent thing I remember is Tahiti— and not our recent visit, but our first visit four years ago. Craig, for whom the idea of amnesia is untenable, refuses to believe.

"Don't you remember Pidge and Dave?" he asks, naming two friends with whom we spent a good deal of time in Samoa. I do remember them, but from Tahiti, not Pago Pago.

"Where did we get charts? Do we have charts?" I ask.

"Jesus H. Christ," flaps Craig the unflappable.

Both of them see it's serious now. Little by little they lead me from earlier rivers of recall into the more recent but darker creeks of my mind. But it's two hours before I'm filled in completely, all the way up to the present. It's two hours before they can rest assured that I'm OK, and that my responsibilities are not going to be dumped on them at sea in the middle of a raging storm.

The situation isn't a bit frightening to me, of course. I'm just having a little memory problem. But I can see by their faces that it's scary indeed for both of them. So I work with them, more to cheer them up than for any other reason. It becomes a kind of game.

"I thought you were pulling some kind of joke," Craig says later. "Then, when I saw you weren't joking, I suddenly decided that I should have been spending more time learning navigation, like you keep asking me to do."

So there's good in most events, if you know how to find it. From that point on, Craig navigates some every day. Six months later, he is navigating right along with me, sometimes taking the first half of the day's work while I take the second half, and other times working at the same time I'm working. We never feel it's duplication, but rather a great chance to compare and practice. Soon Craig challenges me by becoming as good or better than I, and though my ego suffers, I'm comforted to know that if anything should happen to me, Craig and Nancy could sail *Sea Foam* wherever they wanted to go.

To brighten bleak days, Fate sends us Bird. A gannet, he arrives on a particularly funky late afternoon. Misled by role models the likes of Jonathan Seagull and the Red Baron, Bird is really a fugitive clown from a flying circus. His brown, scruffy feathers look as if fledgeling had feathered himself, God having been busy with other things. Bird is a cavalier scarecrow, a drunk from the set of *Those Magnificent Men in Their Flying Machines*. His whole manner radiates the impression that he has been far too busy taking Hero Lessons to bother to learn to dress *or* fly. As he buzzes our bowsprit, Craig and I climb out of our wells of gloom and wait for the chance to applaud. It is not long in coming.

After reconnoitering our plunging bowsprit, Bird decides to go for it. Circling afar, he makes some precise calculations, lines up a long, shallow glide, and crashes headlong into the side of the pulpit. Falling into the water, he is turned turtle and pushed aside by our bow wave. He self-rights and sits in the water for a minute or so, shaking his head and clearing his brain. Then he takes off and circles again.

Either his spacial perception is askew or his need is desperate. No way can that size bird come in with his wings spread and land on that pulpit. No way.

But there is one way. Bird stalls with perfect timing directly over the platform and plummets straight down, catching a wing on one rail and a neck on the other. Freeing his wing, for a moment Bird swings back and forth hanging by his neck, which is curved in a question mark over the rail. Finally, his neck gives out and he falls to the platform, a coincidence of pendulum and wave making it all work out. Whew. Bird is on *ferra terma* (leased iron) and he ain't moving. Ever. Till he's rested.

We watch Bird till dark. Like so many heroes, he spends a lot of his time preening. After an hour of pecking under his feathers, he pats his feet, ruffles his wings, draws in his neck coldpeniswise, and sleeps.

Nothing rouses him. Our necessary journeys to the foredeck, postponed out of consideration for fatigued flyers, eventually must be made. We needn't have worried. Bird sleeps through it all. And in the dead of night, when it becomes essential to raise the jib three times and lower it four (not in that order), Craig and I step over Bird, accidentally kick Bird, and nearly sit on Bird to no effect. He has decided where he belongs, has picked us as fellow tilters at windmills, and made himself t'home.

At dawn I ascend the companionway, camera in hand, just as Bird takes off into the gray dawn. Too late, I shoot a few frames at his disappearing back. But if Bird is only a flyspeck on my slides, he is a heraldic brand on our minds. We have a common enemy, the storm, but it strikes me that his battle is lonelier. Suddenly I feel better, and it's all the result of comparative moping.

The following day the vane breaks. It is the low point of our trip. That night, while Craig is steering, I crawl into the bunk beside Nancy.

"How long before we get there? Will we ever get there?" Her tone hints of tears barely dammed.

"If the weather system would do what it's supposed to do and turn around in our favor," I say, hugging and patting, "we could be there in a week. Maybe sooner." I don't mention what I think of our chances that this will happen.

"Oh, that's not so bad," she says, brightening.

"I have even better news," I soothe. "I've thought of a way to jury rig the windvane. All we need is a calm day."

"That's marvelous," she says, cheering up measurably. With that, she goes to sleep. I lie awake for some time, content that for once it was *I* who brought encouragement to *her*. It is good I don't know that it will be another 3½ weeks before we drop the hook in the Tarawa lagoon. Nevertheless I wonder, somewhat guiltily, how much I've deluded us all with the stuff of which dreams are made.

On Christmas day we cross the equator at 170 degrees west. Three weeks ago we left Pago Pago on a passage of 1,350 miles. We still have 1,000 miles to go. At this point, we give up the rhumb line course to Tarawa and head north, looking for a way around the bad weather.

You've probably met a few, talked to them—the macho skippers. They usually have thick necks, the redness of which rises osmotically to florid faces. Deep chested, they stand at the bar with elbows thrust out, shoulders hunched and threatening. "I never check the weather," they boast after several beers. "When I want to go, I go—and I sail the rhumb line." Most of us will divert to latitudes offering some hope for favorable winds. "Not me," is the assertion. "I always sail the rhumb line." The truth is, bravado can be as successful as prudence, if you can carry it off. But for now, we are working our way north.

With the still squally weather finally blowing us in the right direction, our tactics take on a pattern. During the very light winds, usually no more than six to eight knots, we put all sail up. Then, at the approach of a towering cumulonimbus, I consult with everyone as to how much wind they think is in it.

"What do you think?" I ask Craig.

"No problem—a piece of cake," is his standard opinion.

"How about you?" I ask Nancy.

"Doesn't look *too* bad," is her usual, worried reply. Then I take down at least some sail, often all but the jib. This is followed by Craig's grumblings that hint of perjorative opinions of my character, intelligence and courage. These mutterings become near mutiny when, caught with canvas down in a friendly, favorable, 20-knot breeze, I summon the two of them on deck in the rain to raise what they never wanted to take down in the first place.

"How can I develop foresight if I can't practice?" I plead to unforgiving ears.

All things end, and at dawn of our forty-third day at sea the stars put us 30 miles from the southeast tip of Tarawa. An atoll made up of a string of motus set in a reversed 'L' shape, our landfall will be the L's vertex. We'll then have to sail 15 miles along the foot, 4 miles north to the pass, enter the lagoon and find anchorage, all before twilight. It'll be close, but we have saved enough fuel just for this.

"Shouldn't we sail?" asks Nancy. "We've got wind."

"Yes," I say, "but it's not very strong, and it's flukey. And I want to get there today for sure."

The diesel starts on cue, and, with the wind astern, we cream along at about 7½ knots. We've got it made. On ice.

Our confidence lasts 30 minutes. With a roar, the engine speed suddenly jumps 1,000 r.p.m. My paranoia portfolio includes runaway diesel engines, and I reach the cutoff key in about two seconds, a spoor of gray hair marking my path.

"What did you *do*?" I ask Nancy, who was steering. I often ask her this when she's on watch, and it always infuriates her.

"Nothing, damn it—it did it to itself."

"Well, throttle down. Let's try it again."

The engine starts readily enough, but doesn't turn the propeller shaft even when it's in gear. I decide that the spring-loaded damper that links the engine to the transmission has finally broken. It has been giving me trouble, and though I'm pleased that I think I know the problem, there's no way I can fix it at sea. We have become a sailboat *sans* auxiliary.

But if the Lord taketh away, from time to time He also giveth. The wind freshens, and under full sail we raise Tarawa at 11:15. As we approach, the foliage changes from a bluish silhouette to a verdant richness, while the underbellies of ovine cumulus glow with an emerald reflection as they hover above the still-hidden lagoon. We schuss along the south shore, pushed by a three-knot current and sheltered from swell and chop. The calm seas, the brisk wind, the warm sunshine team up in a campaign to wipe the slate clean of the grind of our passage. Finally, we sweep around the southwestern end of the atoll and head close-hauled for the entrance buoy.

The lagoon is humming with activity. Here and there an outrigger canoe sail flits across the ocean chop. A pilot boat confers with a Korean trawler. A freighter leaves and steams north. A couple of landing craft motor busily about near the port. We are so absorbed with watching the action that we fail to notice we are making little progress north and a frightening amount of it west.

"We're not getting anywhere," points out Craig. "The marker's not getting any closer."

A couple of quick bearings prove him right. "Let's try getting closer to the reef," I suggest.

We come about, but it is plain that the port tack is as hopeless as the starboard. We are unable even to retrace our steps.

"Damned current's like a tiderip," I say. We tack again and sail north-northwest.

"Maybe we'll just have to heave to for the night," suggests Nancy, looking wistfully at the protected lagoon.

"Sure," I say. "We'll be swept 20 miles west and be in the same dilemma we were in for weeks—trying to beat back against wind and current. If that happens, we can kiss Tarawa goodbye."

"You don't *know* that," says Craig.

"Well, think about it!" I snap. I've gotten upset thinking about it, and I want everybody else to do the same.

"We could sail back and forth and maintain," offers Nancy, hopefully.

"Vetoed," I say. "The whole west side of the lagoon is a submerged reef. In the dark we could sail on it or drift on it with no warning at all."

To have our objective so close after so long only to have current and waning light snatch it away is more than any of us can cope with. Nancy goes below to lose herself in galley putterings. Craig lies down on deck and closes his eyes. I sit at the helm, lip-chewing.

"How about a flare," I say. "We'll get the pilot boat to tow us in."

"We have no white flares," says Nancy, "and we're not in distress."

"What do you mean, not in distress?" I argue. "Forty-three days at sea, three-quarters of our water gone, no engine, unable to get in the pass, and no harbor to the west of us for hundreds of miles—I say we *are* in distress!"

In spite of their tight-lipped dissent, I get out the flares. The first one works perfectly, a bright red ball soaring high above the boat. Of the five craft that could have reacted, not one does. We wait 10 minutes, then shoot off another. Zero.

"Good thing we're *not* in trouble," mutters Nancy.

"I just remembered," says Craig. "The Sailing Directions say that big boats sometimes anchor in sand, just off the reef in about 40 feet of water. If we could just get to the reef."

"Good idea," I say brightening. Our only hope, I think to myself.

We come about, and right away we can see that our luck has changed with the tide. The current is no longer sweeping us west, and the wind direction has bent 20 degrees in our favor. This tack will bring us to within 200 yards of the entrance. With the sun behind a cloud and sinking fast, we're in a race against time, but at least we have a chance of winning.

To enter the coral-studded lagoons of most atolls without good visibility is like playing Russian roulette with five chambers loaded. But two things about Tarawa are different: the channel is marked with buoys for large ships; and Craig, from the crosstrees, can see no ugly, brown blotches indicating coral heads—only varying shades of green, indicating sand. Entering looks possible, and so inviting we decide to go for it. A short tack and we are in the channel. Two more short tacks to dodge sandbars, so plainly visible that the buoys and our chart are hardly necessary, and we are close reaching for shelter. We drop anchor at 1815: 43 days, 3 hours; 1,350 miles made good; 2,500 miles sailed over the ground; 3,500 through the water.

Next morning Nancy and Craig assert that I celebrated late; that I drank with dedication; and that I finally arose from the cockpit and shouted, "I sail the *rhumb* line!" Shortly thereafter it is alleged that I slid down the companionway and toppled into the first available bunk. The story isn't true, of course, but it's hard to dispute even gross exaggeration when one's memory of the incident is hazy.

VII / TARAWA

Without an engine, we had decided not to anchor off the mole where the commercial shipping anchored. About a half-mile to the east off a beach was an old pier that had fallen into disuse. I could see no other cruising boats, and figured we would do better to stay out of the way of harbor traffic. We knew that no one would come to the boat to clear us the evening we arrived, but by eleven the next morning, with our first land in 43 days beckoning only a few hundred yards away, we began to get impatient.

Check-in procedures for yachts had varied tremendously from port to port. In Ensenada, Mexico, our first port of entry, no one came to the boat. It was up to the skipper to go ashore with his papers to the offices of the harbormaster and immigration. This was true all throughout Central America, where it seemed that the only officials who sought us out did so less for the formalities of checking in than for some thirst-quenching hospitality. Acajutla, El Salvador, was an exception. The only west coast port in El Salvador, Acajutla was geared to handling ship traffic. But at Playa Del Cocos, a supposed port of entry into Costa Rica, not only were we not boarded, but when we went ashore we could never find an official of any sort. And arriving after long passages at the Australs and the Marquesas, each a port of entry into French Polynesia, had we waited on board for an official we'd still be there.

Except in the major ports, then, and even in some of those, we were supposed to go ashore and seek out the officials ourselves. Now we'd been in Tarawa for 18 hours, our yellow flag had aroused no response, and I was beginning to wonder if that were the case here.

"I bet we're supposed to go ashore," I said.

"Me too," said Nancy and Craig, as if rehearsed. Preference, of course, had no influence on their opinion.

We rowed our Avon in to the beach and carried it up to the tree line. The sand caressed our bare feet, insinuated itself between our toes, and fried our soles to a crisp. None of us cared. I've always felt that kissing the earth was a little theatrical—nobody ever did it except maybe Italians. But if I had to name the landings where I was most tempted to become an earth-kisser, Tarawa would head the list.

The bubble burst, of course, when we arrived at the harbormaster's office and were told that we were supposed to have waited on the boat. Everyone was quite stern about it. I said that we'd go back, but did they have any idea how long we'd have to wait?

"Not to worry," we were told. "We are very busy."

"We've been at sea for 43 days," I complained, "and we'd like to get checked in as soon as possible."

"Just go back to your boat," said the official. "Someone will get to you eventually."

I detected a note of reprimand, and figured—correctly, it turned out—that if they had been in no hurry before, they'd be in even less of a hurry now. To make our waiting more bearable, on our way back we picked up our mail, three ice cream cones, some soft drinks, and some beer. Anything to ease the suffering of confinement.

Common sense should have told me that a port that is run by the British would be formal (stuffy) about the protocol of entering. There was also another factor; there was an extra charge because we'd anchored so far away, and they didn't want to lose that revenue.

Nine months later when we entered Tarawa again, the British were on the point of granting the Gilberts independence, and had relaxed their attitude about yachts. When we'd waited aboard *Sea Foam,* now anchored in the commercial anchorage, for a similar length of time, I rowed over to a nearby yacht and asked what the story was.

"I told them you people were here," said the skipper. "They said if they didn't get out to you right away for you to row ashore and check in at the office." So you just never know.

In Betio (pronounced Bay-see-oh), Tarawa's principal island, U.S. hardware from World War Two stood rotting and rusting on the reef. The story of that attack still sickens me. The reef was flat, and two thousand yards wide from lagoon to shore. The armored landing and assault craft that were supposed to transport marines all the way to the beach had instead gotten hung up at the outer limits of the reef because someone had been wrong in his estimate of the times of the tides. As a result, marines by the hundreds tried to make their way ashore on foot, wading in waist-deep water and dying like sitting ducks. The rusting halftracks reminded me of it daily.

As on most atolls, drinking water was mainly water that ran off the roofs and was caught in cisterns. All well water was brackish. Because of the cholera, all water was suspect, and even catchment water could be contaminated by birds. Rickety wharfs, legacies of Japanese occupation, supported public toilets that dropped untreated sewage into the lagoon, so that cholera, though no longer epidemic, would be endemic for the foreseeable future. Flies were everywhere. Eating seafood from the lagoon was risky.

The water in the lagoon itself was emerald and opaque, making Tarawa's lagoon the only one we ever saw where the water wasn't crystal clear. The phenomenon was caused by a colloidal suspension of coral dust in the lagoon. When you approach Tarawa and the light is right, the clouds over the lagoon glow faintly green from the reflection.

Betio was the only *motu* divided from the rest of the atoll by water. Australia offered to build a causeway that would allow vehicle traffic to serve all of Tarawa without recourse to the ferry. The causeway would also have inhibited the natural flushing of the lagoon and acted to contain the contamination of the public toilets. However, the engineers miscalculated. From a survey made, they thought there was plenty of sand available within dredge reach. With the causeway 20 percent of the way along they ran out of sand, and just to seal the project's doom, one of the bosses ran off with the money.

Betio's dogs would have appreciated the causeway. Two miles long and seven hundred yards wide at its widest point, Betio was the most densely populated island in the Gilberts, both dog- and peoplewise. In order to control the dog population, only male dogs were allowed on Betio. Occasionally, when the winds were from the east, about two hundred male dogs would take the ferry to neighboring Bairiki, the next island, for heterosexual exercise—at least those dogs would that hadn't taken up an alternative sex life—and return to Betio by the night ferry, tired but markedly less nervous. The dogs were never charged for the passage, as the Gilbertese viewed sex with the same amused approval as the peoples of Tahiti and French Polynesia.

Because Betio was flat and densely populated, young lovers really had no place to be alone. Houses were open and privacy was nil. As a result, the men who scaled the coconut trees to collect grog (an intoxicating liquor made from the sap of coconut flowers), would sing as they climbed the tree in order to warn lovers of the threat to their privacy. (*I* wouldn't have sung.)

It used to be that when a young couple married, the morning after the wedding night the groom would drive around the island waving a red flag from the back of a truck to signify his wife was a virgin. This was followed by an all-night celebration that included feasting, drinking, singing, and dancing. If it turned out that the bride was not a virgin, the groom had the right to give her back. Liberalization of sex taboos brought fewer and fewer red flags, fewer and fewer feasts. But by the time we arrived on *Sea Foam,* the worm had turned once more, and red flags were the rule, not the exception.

"Are there really more virgins these days?" I asked.

"Never let the truth stand in the way of a good party," was my friend's cryptic reply.

We went to the movies at the Betio Club, a building with a bar and the scene of great parties and dances. One night we sat through *Mandingo,* a story of slavery in the South. Cringing like wilting lettuce, we wished that if the U.S. must dramatize its own shame it wouldn't export it to where *we* were. The Gilbertese (at least half the audience were expatriates) thought the whuppin's were funny and yelled with glee at the explicit sex.

We met Willie, a Gilbertese who started a family in the Solomons and returned to his home in Tarawa without wife but with two sons. He'd lost one daughter in the Solomons, victim of the island custom of bubuci (the spelling is mine). Bubuci was the unbending custom that dictated that a good friend or relative could walk into your house and express a desire for anything you had, and you were obliged to give it to him. Willie had returned to Tarawa only to lose his oldest son to his aunt through bubuci. When we met Willie, he was looking for a place to go where bubuci-ing was out and keeping your own kids was in. If he stayed around, he'd soon be fresh out of children.

We were guests for dinner at Phil Wilder's house. Phil was a mixture of Gilbertese, Fijian, and European. He was also a radio nut, had a great deal of expensive equipment, and showed it off to me with pride.

After dinner, Phil picked up his guitar and tuned it with a quick, professional competence that made me hopeful. Even so, I was totally unprepared for the marvelous jazz that flowed from his fingers. We talked of music. Russ Garcia, a Hollywood arranger whose book on contemporary orchestration I had studied avidly, had visited Tarawa on his boat not too long ago. I mentioned having found, on a nightclub piano, a penciled manuscript of a song that Garcia had written called "I Lead a Charmed Life," a song that I loved and played for years. In a decade, only once had I heard it played by anyone else. Phil played the whole thing, flawlessly, and what's more he sang the words, which I had never heard.

I mentioned to Phil that the guitar which I had on *Sea Foam* was out of commission because one of the nuts (the screws that tighten the strings for tuning) was broken. A son-in-law went to one of Phil's cupboards and brought me a set (they come in sets of three).

"Like this?" he asked.

"Uh-uh," I said. "Mine are a little different."

He produced a different type.

"Yes, like those," I said, amazed.

"Why don't you bubuci them?" asked the son-in-law.

I was tempted. But Phil had already been generous with his hospitality, and we'd established a rapport with radio and music. Tough as a rubber nail, I couldn't do it.

Phil's house was attractive by Betio standards, but it needed a new roof. At one time he had bought and assembled all the materials, but his cousin had immediately bubuci'd them. (The word 'bubuci' may well have derived from the fact that if you had anything desirable, it was a booboo to let relatives see it.) Phil was just waiting for the money and the appropriate moment to try for a roof again. Meanwhile, when it rained he resorted to pots and pans, using rusty ones that wouldn't be likely to be bubuci'd. We left Phil with our thanks for entertaining us. For his part, he was totally content, having unexpectedly retained possession of his guitar nuts.

We met Brian, a delightful teller of tales who had 14 children by three wives to whom he admitted, and God knows how many more children by wives to whom he did not. Brian claimed that there were two kinds of people—those who were Irish, and those who wished they were. And we met Peter and Roseanne, English, on a three-year hitch running the shipyard; Doug and Jan, New Zealanders, doing a three-year hitch as teachers; Trevor, an Australian engineer who specialized in back rubs; Jack and Molly, English, he an expert in labor relations and a champion half-miler in his youth; Bob, an Australian who fixed our radio; and George Fujiyama, the yard engineer who guided me through all my mechanical repairs. For being at what I would call the end of the earth, Tarawa was a trove of hospitable, helpful friends.

Our passage to Tarawa had been grueling for both us and the boat. About two-thirds of the way through our trip, our list of things to remedy when we made port had numbered 72. By the time we dropped anchor in front of Betio, it numbered 100.

"We cruising folk are merely sailors with a compulsion to work on our boats in a string of constantly changing anchorages," said Nancy. "Sometimes it seems like that's all we ever do."

I thought of our head, sold to us secondhand in Tahiti with the admonishment that we should rebuild it once a year. I hadn't touched it for three years and it had worked faultlessly. Now, however, it was blending, homogenizing, and recirculating everything we put into it, and I was going to have to face the reality of an overhaul.

"You know," I said, "I think a marine toilet is a thing of duty that annoys forever." Nancy made a face and didn't speak to me for five minutes.

Getting intimate with a marine head is very much like dealing with toilets on land, except that the cramped spaces on most boats make the job much like mud wrestling in a phone booth. I like to imagine myself dealing with life wearing silk gloves and using tongs, but now I must roll up my sleeves for an arms-in experience. And when I'm done, no matter how thoroughly I wash, I'm convinced that for days I give off the aura of a mobile septic tank.

Sea Foam's decks—two-inch, laid teak—persisted in leaking, and I decided Tarawa was as good a place as any to recaulk. I had all the materials aboard: caulking cotton, masking tape, and three gallons of two-part, black, polysulfide compound. Polysulfide was marvelous stuff, but it was tormenting to work with. There were two kinds, and we tried using both. The first kind was one-part, came in tubes, and took three to four days to cure. The second was two-part, set up within 45 minutes, and cured completely overnight (unless you failed to add enough catalyst). Both kinds were designed to stick to anything forever, and *Sea Foam* acquired many jet-black daubs of testimony to the goo's perniciously adhesive character.

Caulking the deck was a bit like repairing a roof. We had to decide how much of the deck we could do in one day, as it would have been disaster to leave seams open all night on the strength of a prayer that it not rain. As a matter of fact, the consistency with which such prayers were denied has, over the years, lent philosophical credence to the theory of the existence of God's sense of humor.

The work was tiring, particularly in the hot, summer sun. All the old, black polysulfide had to be taken out of the seams, and the sides of the seams scraped clean. We had to make our own tools for doing this, using suggestions we'd read about. Then the seams had to be cleaned of all dirt, sawdust, and crumbled cotton. In our case, most of the old cotton was still good; but where it wasn't we had to remove the old and tamp in new. A vacuum cleaner would have made the cleaning job so very much easier. We didn't have one, and made do with a small, stiff brush and a dustpan, a seemingly endless chore doomed to imperfect results. Then the sides of each seam had to be taped with masking tape, in the forlorn hope that we could control where the black goo would end up.

By the time I finished this segment of the job I was usually exhausted, hands battered and bleeding from battling with my homemade seam-reamer, and every muscle bitching from having had to work in an inhuman, Michelangelically contorted state for hours. Now, when I needed my coolest head, clearest eye, and steadiest hand, I had to cope with an aching body and a crippled disposition. Like the last of the day's ski runs down the mountain, fatigue and haste were the compost for a rich harvest of disaster.

I believe that somewhere there are people so totally organized that frustration rarely enters their lives. I can even imagine myself playing such organized and adequate roles. But the introduction of two-part polysulfide assured us of a script in which the element of success was barely discernible.

Originally we would just caulk that part of the deck that seemed to be leaking. For this we'd use the one-part stuff. Always before the three days required for curing had passed, one of us (or a guest) would have stepped on the gooey seams and tracked a trail of ineradicable black footprints. When I learned about the two-part stuff that set up quickly, I welcomed it as a panacea. But 'panacea,' like 'effective' and 'adequate,' lives only in the world of concept. Two-part polysulfide had its own built-in drawbacks.

The first challenge was to guess accurately how much to mix up. Too much, and it went off before we had a chance to get it all into the seams, leaving us with a perfect, rubbery, *expensive* black lump the same shape as the coffee can or whatever mixing container we'd used. But too little was a drag, also. Each mixing required clean tools, containers, and extremely careful measurement of catalyst to basic black goo. If we'd had a raft of dixie cups, measuring spoons, and disposable gloves, the job would have been far easier. As it was, we had to clean up our measuring and mixing tools with each batch, using expensive and limited supplies of acetone for the job. (Presently there is at least one polysulfide product that cleans up with water, a quantum leap of progress that was too late to be of use to us.)

Furthermore, we were used to the consistency of the one-part stuff: thick, stiff, and puttylike. It came in a tube, and was applied like toothpaste from a caulking gun. The two-part stuff was of thinner viscosity—Nancy dubbed it 'devil's diarrhea'—and we tried several different ways of applying it. The first time we applied it with a spoon, a method so absurdly inadequate I refuse to describe it further. The second time I used a one-pound coffee can whose rim I'd bent to a sort of spout. Given the necessary haste and a hand unsteady with fatigue, this too resulted in getting far too much goo in areas best described as unseamy.

The third method—Nancy's idea—worked best, and once we'd tried it we used this method exclusively. In California, Nancy had bought 500 heavy-duty, clear plastic bags from an industrial supply company. Folded flat, they measured 18 inches square. We used them for storing anything we wanted to keep dry, and they were a godsend. For deck caulking jobs, we would fill one of these bags with goo that we'd mixed up in another container, twist the mouth of the bag shut, and squeeze the goo out a small hole made by cutting off one corner of the bag with a pair of scissors. (Evidently this is how pastry cooks who can't afford guns ice their cakes.) Getting the hole the right size was accomplished about one time in five, but other than that the system worked well. I'm happy to report that the toughness of the bags was enough that one never broke. A full bag breaking would have required a prompt and flamboyant suicide. Some disasters just aren't worth surviving.

Having filled the seams, the final chore was to remove the yards and yards of masking tape. This had to be done before the goo hardened when it had just begun to firm up. If we were too late, the tape wouldn't come up and we ended up spending hours removing it inch by inch with a chisel. If we were too soon, the goo was still too runny and uncontrollable. And then the wind, whose cooling breath made the tropic sun bearable, suddenly became the enemy, blowing the goo-covered tape into a fluttering, streaming, Medusan nightmare. Dealing with both the goo and the tape stickum reminded me of a cartoon sequence with Mickey Mouse and some flypaper, except that when it was happening to Mickey, it was funny.

Maddening as this whole task was, I remember it with much pleasure. We were anchored in a protected lagoon of unqualified beauty. In the evening, friends sailed up, dropped anchor, and invited us over for tea. They joined us on *Sea Foam* for dinner. We sat up late musing under voyeuristic stars, pleasured by caressing breezes. Everyone has experienced the miracle of transformation that time and memory can effect. But memory is also perverse, and I will never understand why I can't remember one detail of our serious and sober conversation that night, yet cannot forget one detail of the day's dealings with devil's diarrhea.

VIII / MAJURO

Majuro, we'd been warned, was a slum, a place to stop as briefly as possible for mail and supplies. We had planned it to be a mere way station on our journey to Maloelap, the atoll where Nancy's brother, Dan, served in the Peace Corps. Get in, get out, get on with it. What in fact happened was that we stayed there for 5½ months.

As always, there wasn't just one reason for staying there so long, but several. One of them was *Sea Foam*'s engine. The vibration damper that had been welded in Tarawa as a temporary measure had broken again, and we awaited a new one. We also needed a new alternator, and needed to repair our starter and our leaky exhaust system. Before we could start on all these projects, we had to wait for money.

I had sold some stories, but most of the money we were waiting for depended on a contract with SAIL Books for my book. In the constipated communicatory wilderness that was Tarawa, we had heard no word from editors, and had just about despaired of future cruising. We'd been down to our last dollar so many times, I often wondered why we didn't get used to it, but we never did. We'd actually decided, one rainy Friday, that we were going to have to head for home and jobs. But that same morning a letter came with word that my book outline had been dragged from its file and reconsidered, and that SAIL was now offering to give me an advance to finish it. Brinkmanship economics being what they were, the sound of "WHOOPEE" was heard in the land. Promises, however, were one thing, whereas grinding out the details of an agreement proved to be another. So in Majuro, our breath baited, we waited.

Finally, and by no means last in order of importance, we stayed because of the friends we discovered there.

"Hon, how'd you like to go to someone's house and take a real shower?" It was Nancy, back from a shopping trip to the supermarket. "The nicest woman just came right up to me, at the checkstand, and invited us. Her name's Robyn."

"What's she like?"

"Oh, I don't know—tall, pretty. But Herb, she laughs – out

loud!"

We'd been talking about how it would be great to get to be with Americans again, who'd laugh at the same things we did, who would enjoy laughing. Robyn, however, turned out to be Australian, but was married to an American, Don. They had two young daughters, Jennifer and Alissa. Don and Robyn had arrived in Majuro five years ago, having sailed their 40-foot yawl, *Landseer,* from Australia via New Guinea. But Alissa was a baby and Robyn was pregnant, and the voyage had convinced them to settle down in Majuro till the children were bigger. They got a job running a division of a company that ran raft trips down the Colorado River, and that now offered fishing/diving/swimming vacations on a remote Pacific atoll. Vacationers would be met at the airport and taken 12 miles across the channel to Arno, where they'd be put up in tents, fed ice-cold martinis and prime steaks (thanks to a kerosene freezer and refrigerator), and exposed to two weeks of roughing it in the tropics. Just before we came on the scene, the Arno operation was discontinued. Don had bought up all the boats and equipment, and was presently making his living by chartering and fishing.

They lived in a tiny house right on the beach on the ocean side of the atoll. An open air shed served Don as a shop, in which he maintained the dozen or more outboards that powered his fleet. Robyn, a former nurse, raised pigs, chickens, children, and hydroponically grown veggies. Their doors (front and shower) were always open to us.

It was in June, when we had been at anchor in the same place for four months, that Craig dropped his bomb. He had just left to row ashore, to get off the boat, and had said he was going over to see Don. Nancy and I were sitting in the cockpit, watching shooting stars and sipping after-dinner coffee.

"This afternoon, Craig told me that he wants to go home to the U.S.—live with his dad and go to a real school," said Nancy.

"Perhaps he should," I said. "He's at an age when maybe he should spend some time with his real father." I was very insecure in my role as stepfather, with tremendous guilt feelings about divorce and how it had affected the children. Nancy's and my falling in love had caused too much spinoff distress as it was, and if Craig wanted to live with his dad for a while, I wasn't going to stop him no matter how much Nancy and I would miss him.

"His dad's life isn't set up to have Craig live with him perma-nently," Nancy insisted. "I just know he's better off with us."

It was Robyn, with Don's help, who led us out of our dilemma.

"He's bored," Robyn said. "He doesn't really want to leave. He just needs to be challenged—and to have some things to do that are his alone, and not all three of yours. Offer him some expanded horizons and he'll forget about going back to the U.S."

Don helped by taking Craig fishing with him, returning him to us exhausted but full of excitement and tales of battling big tuna on handlines. Robyn suggested that Craig dive with O.K. Davis, who ran a fish-procurement business for U.S. pet stores that were currently selling a lot of tropical, saltwater fish. So we got Craig a scuba tank for his birthday. Then Robyn got him invited to give a talk to the local school about what it's like to grow up on a cruising sailboat. Less than a month after declaring that he wanted to leave, Craig informed us at dinner that he'd changed his mind and would like to stay. It was all his decision, it was wholehearted, and it did not result from a laying on of 'shoulds'. In other words, it was the best kind of decision possible. But without the Cole-mans' wisdom and friendship, I'm convinced he would have left.

Another couple that became close friends were Jim and Barbara Winn. With Jim, I shared a love for jazz, and he had a stereo and a great record collection. With Barbara, both Nancy and I shared a love for bridge, and whenever we could, we played two or three times a week. For the only time in my life, with Barbara as my partner, we bid and made seven notrump, doubled and redoubled. When the Winns left the island for a 10-day vacation, Nancy and I house-sat for them, luxuriating in all the goodies we'd left behind in order to go cruising: air conditioning, daily showers, a real (as opposed to our primus) stove, ice and jazz on demand, a washer, a dryer, and TV.

TV on Majuro consisted of one station that showed month-old, taped programs from the U.S. networks. We drank it all in like camels at an oasis. One night when I *wasn't* watching, the pro-gramming ended as usual at 10 P.M. The girls who ran the station were entertaining their boyfriends at the studio, and around 1 A.M. decided to run an X-rated videotape for their private view-ing. What they forgot to do was throw the switch that cut off the transmitter. For some reason I cannot explain, a couple of dozen Majuroniacs had left their TVs running, and were thus treated unexpectedly to 30 minutes of hard-core porn before the station manager, aroused from sleep by the police, could get to the station and turn off the transmitter. The damage was done, however, as thereafter nearly everyone on the island watched electronic snow from 10 P.M. till the wee smalls, hoping, hoping . . .

The Marshallese sometimes named their children (and sometimes even legally renamed themselves) with whimsically appropriate names. There were people named Pencil, Television, Charter Balloon, Cement, Pepsi, Rester, Oilcan, Greaserack, and Borrower. Two men, born during U.S. military presence during World War Two, were named Souvenir and Boo-Boo. And the two young Marshallese girls who were the constant playmates of Don and Robyn's daughters were named Quarantine and Marina. Quarantine had already planned her future family. Her children's names would be Scarlet Fever, Hepatitis, and Prickly Heat. Marina, a lovely child, wanted a small family too, but Nancy had an idea that due to Marina's beauty and vivacious sense of mischief, her family will be bigger than she expects. I can just see Marina naming her kids: Gas Dock and Launch Ramp, followed by Slip One, Slip Two, Slip Three . . .

It was Robyn who first told us about the Love School. Accounts varied, but either the married women took all the teenage boys to a remote island and taught them what was (or wasn't) up; or they took all the teenaged girls to the same remote island and instructed them in the facts and arts of wifely love. Both Nancy and I decided this was a great idea. Imagine how much fun lovemaking could become if we all actually got good at it. For a while, all I could think about were the labs.

I once had to make an emergency evening run into town. I'd worked all day trying to dismantle, patch, and reinstall *Sea Foam*'s exhaust system, and had continued right through till 8 P.M. in order to get the job done and the boat back into some sort of liveable shape. For the last two hours I'd kept going by fixing in the forefront of my mind a vivid image of an iceberg floating in a sea of gin. But when I went to the liquor locker, the cupboard was bare. At that particular moment the importance of strong drink was, through deprivation, magnified out of all proportion.

"Are you going into town this late?" demanded Nancy.

"You'd better believe it," I said. "You said it's an hour till dinner, so I've got time."

"Are you going looking like that?" she asked.

"I don't have time to clean up," I said, "and anyway, I'm just going to the store."

Taxis into town cost 10 cents. They acted like buses, stopping to pick up passengers until they were full. There was only one road, essentially, so everyone was going in one direction or the other. The trip in was quick—I had the cab all to myself. But standing by the side of the road trying to get a ride back, with my unbagged bottle of gin in my hand and my skin and clothing smeared with exhaust-pipe grime, I couldn't get a cab to stop for me. I suspected discrimination, and when one finally stopped to let off a passenger, I leaped in before the driver had a chance to take off without me. Once in, I saw that I was sharing the cab with three pretty Marshallese girls, the oldest of whom was 16— maybe. She was the one in the *front* seat. The one beside me was about 13. The minute I got in, the cab was filled with giggling and bubbling conversation, all in Marshallese. And though I couldn't understand a word of it, there was no question that its content was both sexual and explicit.

Suddenly I was very conscious of the gin bottle and, embarrassed and not knowing what else to do, stuck it on the seat between my legs and put my hat over it. I also was suddenly aware that I smelled like a grease pit on a hot summer afternoon. Far from cringing, however, before we'd ridden 300 feet the girl beside me had put her arm around my shoulders and was hugging and patting, a constant stream of Marshallese tumbling from her lips.

SELF: (Woodenly, with weak smile) Hi.

GIRL: (Softly, with hugs and pats) Hi.

I tried to maintain an air of nonchalance, as if this sort of thing always happened to me when I dressed like this, but I failed. No cool course of action occurred to me, and I became an inarticulate lump. The girl beside me hugged and patted tirelessly. The other girls talked continuously, giggled at me, talked some more. Finally, after a journey that seemed endless, we pulled up in front of a house. The girl beside me disengaged her arm and made the teenybop, circular motion with her palm out, as if wiping fog off a windowpane. There was more than a touch of mockery in her smile, her "'bye." I feebly wiped some fog in reply, and the girls decabbed.

"Jesus," I said to the cab driver as we pulled away, "she was only a baby, for Christ's sake."

"Yeah," said the cabby, chuckling, "but she sure knows how to do it. She *really* knows how to do it."

I told Nancy when I got back to the boat.

"I wonder what she'd have been like if she'd graduated from the Love School?" she asked, giggling.

"I suppose she'd have learned better manners," I said. "She didn't even have the courtesy to get rid of her lollipop."

IX / HONOR THY SEXTANT

After 5½ years of navigating around the Pacific, I was convinced that navigation is a simple matter. Start at point *A* and proceed to point *B*. Perform rituals with sextant and tables, keeping constant check on progress and position. Proceed according to a pre-thought-out plan and make minor adjustments as celestial feedback indicates. Arrive within reasonable parameters of your ETA. Logical; routine; so simple. But in actual practice there are always surprises that confound logic and interrupt routine, and you are left with a task that is more gristle than cake.

Take our trip from Majuro to Tarawa. We left on August 15, a Tuesday afternoon. When we had made the 370-mile trip north from Tarawa five months previously, we'd sailed the rhumb line, a straight course that kept plenty of sea room between us and the string of atolls that lay between the two points. This time, however, we planned to stay close enough to sight each island, as we needed to maintain all the easting we could against wind and current. Our first landfall would be Mili, 65 miles from Majuro to the southeast.

We intended to leave on Saturday, but last-minute repairs cost us three days. In exchange we received a fair wind and perfect weather. Friends came down to wish us bon voyage. We sailed down the lagoon toward the pass, the wind on our starboard quarter. As we neared the pass, a runabout sped toward us from one of the uninhabited *motus*. Leaving his charter party swimming and snorkeling, Don Coleman was coming out to wish us well. After he turned and headed back to his customers, only the delusion that we would all meet again someday kept us cheerful. A cold beer or two, consumed as we went out the pass and sailed toward the west end of the atoll, helped to maintain my attitude.

The sun crashed in flames of brilliant orange, searing red, and was replaced by a cool, waxing, three-quarter moon. Stars blinked myopically across galactic distances. Squall clouds had taken the night off. As we rounded the end of the atoll I noted with satisfaction that you can see a palm-studded island for at least four miles in the moonlight. We set the vane for our course to Mili. Full sail. Beam reach. I tried to come up with an omen that wasn't good, and failed.

Nancy woke me for my watch at 11:30. We were still in the lee of Majuro and its eastern neighbor, Arno, carving our way through a millpond ocean at six knots. Conditions were so benign and the pleasures of easy sailing so ineffable that my usual anxiety refused to function. I could find nothing to worry about, and this alone should have triggered a warning in my mind.

We sighted Mili at nine the next morning. I had taken a sun shot about an hour before we sighted land, and as a result had hardened up more to the east. I had misgivings that the sun line position indicated we were farther from the island than we really were, but I couldn't be sure. The difference could have been as much as five miles; but with the course change, drift, possibly an inaccurate estimate of our speed, and the angle of our approach, there was no conclusive check. We sailed south along the lee, again enjoying 20 miles of flat ocean and a 12-knot, reaching wind. Leaving the lee, we hardened up slightly and headed for our next landfall, Butaritari (mistakenly called 'Makin' on U.S. charts), northernmost Gilbert, 180 miles to the south-southeast.

Mili was a conveniently constructed atoll from our point of view, in that the islands were nearly continuous on the western side, the side we approached. Butaritari was another story. A crescent of islands like the letter 'C' lying on its back. The opening that faced north was 11 miles across and all submerged reef. We hoped to raise the atoll on the afternoon of the second day. I foresaw no difficulties. All we had to do was travel 180 miles in 52 hours, averaging a speed of 3½ knots, and I was prepared to power if necessary.

Winds and current were a problem. Our passage south would take us across the boundary of the northeast/southeast trades, a line which fluctuated, but which normally lay around two degrees north, just to the north of Tarawa. Northeast trades were notoriously flukey at this season, anyway, and we were lucky to have had them for a full day. We fully expected the wind to swing gradually south of east and head us. Our passage also would in all probability take us across the Equatorial Countercurrent; but for all we knew, that current, which also fluctuated in latitude, could lie north of us and have no effect on our position. We couldn't be sure, however, and had to allow for the possibility of being pushed eastward, though the probability was that we'd be pushed westward. We knew we might have to fight for easting against the wind and a current that could reach speeds of 50 or more miles per day, but so far we had had to fight neither.

In the afternoon the wind did swing, forcing us to steer west of south. But at dawn the wind dropped, and we started the engine. A line of position from my morning sun shot was convenient, as it was virtually congruent with our desired course. To hit Butaritari, all we had to do was power south-southeast.

At 11:30 the engine stopped. We were still having trouble with algae in our fuel, and although I had flushed the fuel tank several times and added Biophor, an algicide, the filters were clogging up after only 24 hours running. I changed the filters. Whenever the engine dies of fuel starvation, as it does when the filters clog up, it's necessary to bleed air from the fuel lines, a painstaking process at which I'd become more adept than I ever would have wished. When I tried, however, I realized that in Majuro I'd assembled the starter wrong. The Bendix wouldn't stay engaged. It was enough to start the engine under normal conditions, but air-bleeding the lines required continuously turning over the engine. Three hours later, I'd fixed the starter and gotten the engine running again. However, I'd broken my resolution not to drink a cocktail before sundown.

We powered all night. At 8 A.M. the next day the wind came up, and we were able to sail full and by on course; but the noon shot showed that no way would we sight Butaritari before dark. Current, leeway, engine breakdown, and the fact that I hadn't been able to keep up our average speed, all contributed to our failure.

Still, I wasn't nervous. Clear skies guaranteed a star fix. I was confident I could pinpoint our position at sundown and set a safe course to pass the atoll at night. I prepared for the sights carefully, worked out the stars' probable positions and altitudes so that I could identify each one, and took my sights quickly. All went like clockwork until I plotted the lines. The result was a total screw-up. Although the mess indicated we were safely to the west of Butaritari, my confidence was badly shaken. In such clear, calm weather, I should have had a pinpoint fix. Instead, all I could depend on was that we were somewhere in a circle whose diameter was 15 miles, which told me only that we were somewhere between 2 and 17 miles northwest of the island. For a veteran, this was shameful. I rechecked the math, procedure, and plotting, but there were four things I couldn't verify: my sights; my reading of the sextant; the sextant's accuracy; and Nancy's reading of the time. My disorientation had begun.

We passed Butaritari in pitch darkness somewhere around 9 P.M. It was unmistakable. In olden times, Marshallese and Gilbertese navigators sailed these islands successfully for decades by properly interpreting wave patterns. The navigator, always an older man, often lay in the bottom of the canoe so as not to be distracted by anything other than the waves, and would direct the helmsman from there. Now the lee of Butaritari was so evident that we must have passed the atoll at a distance of between five and eight miles: no less than five, because even with a full moon we never saw it; no more than eight because the lee was so pronounced and lasted approximately the length of the island. It was so obvious, I considered putting away my sextant and spending the rest of the passage lying on the cabin floor.

Before we reached the lee, however, I suffered a couple of hours of apprehension. If I could be that far off, or the sextant, or whatever, there was really no telling *where* we were. My imagination conjured up sailing right into the opening of the crescent and onto the reef. This would have taken an almost inconceivable combination of circumstances; but when I felt things were going wrong there was no limit to my imagination. Nightmares, they're called—and I had them when I was awake.

We were now in the area of the strongest and most capricious currents. They could be north, south, east, or west: strong, weak, or nonexistent. Unpredictable, we could only rely on my sights for feedback; and they, in my opinion, had become unpredictable too.

We sailed close-hauled, roughly due south, and I did not expect to sight Abaiang, as with leeway and probable current we would be pushed too far to the west. My 7 P.M. star sight was far from excellent, but it was passable for yacht navigation in waters that had roughened considerably, and I was heartened. We were 15 miles west and a little south of Abaiang, approximately where my dead reckoning put us. I decided that we should continue south to the same latitude as Betio, the southwesternmost *motu* on Tarawa, after which we'd tack and head east-northeast. Tarawa is 16 miles long in a north-south direction, and with such a target I figure we'd be bound to hit some part of it. At 3 A.M. we tacked and were able to maintain a course only 10 degrees north of true east. If things went according to my plan, we'd raise Tarawa sometime before noon. So much for optimism.

At 9 A.M. we spot the fronds of coconut trees in the distance. Ninety minutes later another tiny islet appears on the horizon. I think I can identify Betio, our destination, and the islet as Bikeman, the inner range for the entrance channel.

"I can't believe it," I say. "We must have had a little push to the south—maybe three or four miles. I hate to be too optimistic, but it looks like we'll be at anchor for a late brunch."

Nancy and Craig are both cheered. My uncertainty has disturbed them; but now that land is in sight, all's right with the world. Nancy is glad not to have to make a breakfast in the rough sea that's running, and I'm excited enough to ignore my own hunger.

But as we approach, I begin to realize something is wrong. Tarawa, government center and port of entry for the Gilbert Islands, is a fairly active port. We should begin to spot some boats. The breakwater and the port complex should be coming into view. My heart sinks as I realize that it can't be Tarawa. No doubt, however, it's Abaiang, only five miles north of the tip of Tarawa. Betio can still be ours before nightfall.

The ocean calms as we approach the lee of the atoll. The wind has been gradually heading us for an hour, and is now coming conveniently from the east. We tack and head for the southwestern tip.

"What if it isn't Abaiang?" I ask Craig, half joking. "How can you explain the fact that after sailing eight hours nearly due south and eight hours nearly due east that we are now *north* of our last night's fix?"

Craig shrugs his shoulders. In the morning, with land in sight and clear weather, there is really nothing to worry about, even if you don't know where the hell you are.

"We should be able to see the north tip of Tarawa from the south tip of Abaiang," says Craig. "It's only separated by five or six miles." Five or six miles is a sure thing for raising an atoll in clear weather. We've raised our still-unidentified atoll from more than 10 miles away.

We reach the boundary of the reef and now Craig, standing on the pulpit rail and looking south, should be able to see any palm-covered island for 15 miles. Nothing.

"It can't be Abaiang," he insists. "Both Gary and Peter told us, last time we were here, that you can see Abaiang clearly from the north tip of Tarawa. So you should be able to see Tarawa from Abaiang." Craig's logic is superb.

I read the Sailing Directions. Again. There's no way, from the description, to positively identify Abaiang from Maiana. One coral atoll looks much like another. Abaiang is 5 miles north of Tarawa. Maiana is 15 miles south. We have no small scale charts of either—only lower Tarawa and its entrance. From the large scale chart it's difficult to be sure of the shapes and relationships. I suddenly feel that either place is possible. I snapped a quick sun shot, ignoring my usual practice of taking three sights as a check, and the line that I plot shows we might be south of Tarawa. This, plus Craig's insistence, makes me fly in the face of logic. Besides, if the current could push us 30 miles north, it might alternatively have pushed us south instead. Having suddenly accepted the possibility of the latter, I become confused.

"We could sail north for an hour, and if this is Maiana, we should definitely spot Tarawa. If we don't see anything, we'll turn around and head south again."

Craig looks at me with misgiving. "OK. But if this is Abaiang, why can't we see Tarawa?"

We come about. I'm feeling discouraged. If my decision to head north is wrong, it means another night at sea—a night of heaving to off Betio light and the nervous frets that current and reefs will be sure to engender.

"It's almost time for the noon shot," says Nancy.

"For whatever it's worth," I reply, glumly. "I'm at the point where I want to *see* something. I have no faith left in sun lines."

But I take the noon shot anyway. I sit for 20 minutes, making sure I catch the sun at full height. I worked the ridiculously simple math. It places our latitude at 1 degree 56 minutes north, right at Abaiang. And – still – I – head – north!

"I think you should believe the sextant," says Nancy.

"Why couldn't we see Tarawa?" I ask her. "And what about the shot that showed we might be south of Tarawa?"

"I think you should believe the noon shot," she says.

I have to agree. No matter how inaccurate the sextant or its user, it stretches credibility to entertain an error of 50 miles. And *still* I head north.

"If we don't see something in an hour, I'll turn around. The only way I can believe it's not there is to prove it."

"I think you should believe the sextant," says Nancy, and rolls over with her book, ending the conversation.

I rework the math from my earlier sun shot, the only indication (other than Craig's point) that we might be south instead of north of our goal. There's an error. When replotted, this line, too, puts us north of Tarawa. Craig, on the bowsprit, can still see nothing to the north. Finally convinced, we turn south and start the engine, power sailing at 7½ knots, hoping to make Tarawa before dark. We've wasted 3½ hours.

I can only attribute my irrational behavior to extreme disorientation, something I'd read about but never experienced. Back in the early days of aviation, pilots used to tell of actually flying upside down, but feeling so strongly that they were right side up they disbelieved their instruments. Those that survived were adamant in describing the overwhelming strength of their feelings. The moral of each of these tales was: trust your instruments. And yet instinct, no matter how often wrong, can be compelling.

Other factors that contributed to our dilemma: inadequate charts; failure to check the sextant thoroughly from a known position; misreading the stopwatch (Nancy on at least one occasion became confused by the minute hand which, on our stopwatch, is very small and difficult to read); and a brutal northerly current of well over two knots that made any conclusion regarding our position— even the correct one—seem illogical.

We did have a proper chart, we discovered later, which we'd xeroxed off a friend's chart nearly a year before. We had glued the 9-by-11 pieces in their proper relationships on the back of an old chart we no longer needed. We then rolled it up and forgot we had it. There is some sort of karma in this.

We steam past Abaiang's southwest corner and see another cause of our confusion. The reef, which from the northern viewpoint extends due east as far as we can see, is revealed to bend southeast and continue for 10 miles. It's from the southeast tip that Tarawa can be seen. Hours earlier, if we had continued south for another 20 minutes, our situation would have been plain. There is karma in this, also.

Now we know where we are, a great leap forward, but it's obvious we'll never make the Tarawa pass before dark. At last light we pick up the islands on the far side of the Tarawa lagoon, but it's 9 P.M. before we raise the Betio beacon. (A Betio resident later told me that quite often the beacon isn't working due to power failure, but I refuse even to think about that.) By 11 I raised the lights of the waterfront and estimate that we are three or four miles northwest of the beacon. I heave to, wake Nancy, and tell her to wake me in three hours or when the light has nearly disappeared, whichever comes first. At 2 A.M. she wakes me. The light is only visible on the swells, bearing east-southeast.

I decide that the safest thing is to power due south. After an hour of apparently holding my own, I realize the light is gradually getting farther away. Current must be pushing me west. I come about and power-sail east on the starboard tack.

Now I'm heading straight at the 17 miles of submerged reef that is the western side of Tarawa atoll. I lay a sector out on the chart, within which I'll be in safe waters. As long as the light bears no further south than 150 degrees magnetic, I'll be well off the reef. Still, it takes every ounce of self-control to continue. The light comes closer. The shore lights come into view. Over and over I check the bearing and persuade myself that I have to trust my piloting, even if it does only depend on a fragile card, swinging lethargically in liquid and glowing red in the cockpit. My instinct screams warnings that we're getting close to the reef, that I should come about. The compass says "keep cool, you've plenty of distance off yet." I neither come about nor keep cool, but continue toward the reef, sweating.

I'm still sweating it when dawn comes. No need. We're three miles off the reef and four from the pass. I wake Craig and Nancy. Neither has any idea of what I've been through, my personal war, and I'm too elated to tell them. Although neither of them like me much when I'm depressed, they consider me impossible when I'm manic. I suggest a rum punch breakfast, which is vetoed. Never mind. I have enough natural high for us all.

Soon after our arrival in Tarawa I spent an entire afternoon on the end of the Betio breakwater. I had my plotting board and instruments with me. With a useful horizon to the west, I was able to take shots every 45 minutes, thereby testing the sextant throughout its arc. My worst shot was four miles off. All the rest were within two miles. As far as I could see, the sextant was accurate.

I discovered that I had developed an idiosyncrasy in shooting, however. Navigation students are warned that the most common error in sighting is to bring the sun too far down, sinking it into the horizon. I discovered that I was overcompensating, not bringing it down far enough.

But the most important thing the afternoon accomplished was to renew my confidence in the sextant's accuracy, and my ability to use it properly. I have to be wary of becoming too casual and overconfident in taking the sextant's reading though. To guard against Nancy's confusion, in the future she will use two watches, one for the minutes. At sea I have always checked our compass frequently against the rising and setting sun (the compass, a Danforth White, was a superb instrument), and will now make it an equal priority to check the sextant from known positions. Suddenly distrusting the sextant at sea is what led to my disorientation, a mental purgatory I hope never to revisit.

After my long night hanging off the Betio light, I decided to try to find a place to anchor in Betio's tiny boat harbor. The harbor was manmade and was entered through a long narrow channel between two breakwaters. The channel opened up into an enclosed square-shaped area containing maybe two dozen small runabouts, four small tugs, four small ferry launches, three large landing craft, several cargo barges, usually one or two 150-foot inter-island steamers, a resident catamaran, a 40-foot work boat, and various strays. There was room for two visiting yachts, if the skippers were flexible and accommodating. When ships were anchored outside in the lagoon the harbor was a beehive of tugs, barges, and shoreboats, all added to the regular traffic. On this morning, three ships were being unloaded and the place was a madhouse.

We steamed into the channel like returning prodigals, confident in familiar waters, and realized immediately that it was far too busy and too crowded for us to find a spot. Maybe, we thought, we could row in later and talk to people, work something out; but for the moment we'd best go back outside into the lagoon and anchor in the stiff, easterly chop.

Sea Foam, like many sailboats, had a mind of her own in reverse. The technique for turning her around in a small space was to go in reverse as far as room permitted, and then apply strong throttle ahead with desired rudder. This would turn her quite a way before she gained much forward motion. Once she got going forward, the trick was to reverse and repeat the procedure.

I put her in reverse. We were going backward at about two knots and were within one boat length of the resident catamaran (a homemade mutant that aesthetically deserved to die, but knowing and liking the owner-builder, I had no desire to be its executioner) when I put *Sea Foam* in forward and applied power. There was no braking effect, no reassuring swirl churning in our wake. Instead, our speed backward actually increased. I put the lever in neutral.

"Something's wrong!" I yelled. "We have no 'forward'. Come help fend off!"

For some unaccountable reason, *Sea Foam* took a hand in her own (and the cat's) salvation. We curved gently to port, missing a violent collision by less than an inch. But we were continuing backward across the channel toward the opposite breakwater with no reduction in speed.

"Drop the anchor!" I yelled to Craig. Fortunately he was standing by, ready to drop it if we could have moored in the tiny harbor. He asked one question.

"Here—in the channel?"

"Yes, God damn it, here and *now*!" My tone of voice convinced him.

Though this had never occurred before, somehow I had an idea what had happened. I dashed below and tore aside the companionway ladder. A pin had come out of the control linkage, leaving the transmission in reverse. No matter which way I accelerated, all I got was more reverse. The pin, which could easily have dropped into some inaccessible recess of the bilge, was lying in full view on the top of the transmission.

Trying to insert a pin into a close-fitting hole while under duress leads to fumbling. I heard the anchor chain take up and grab. Plenty of time. Calm yourself. There!

Now *Sea Foam*, in neutral, moved back across the channel. Dragged forward by the weight of the anchor chain, she accelerated rapidly toward the other breakwater. A tug, entering the harbor, was coming toward us at speed as if nothing was wrong. A second tug towing a barge was trying to leave.

"Reverse!" yelled Craig.

I reversed. Our forward motion slowed, came to a stop. Craig quickly retrieved the anchor, and I backed out of the way of traffic.

The tugs and the barge passed within five feet of our bowsprit.

We had entered, nearly wiped out the fleet, and were on our way out the channel in less than five minutes. I didn't dare look around for local reaction. Doubtless the event was noted with no more than a raised eyebrow by the easy-going Gilbertese. Nevertheless, the fact remained; in spite of an unpolished performance in all phases of the passage, *Sea Foam* had arrived.

X / TARAWA - FIJI

We've been out of Tarawa eight days. It is 0130, a dark, squally night with winds to 25 knots and confused, messy seas. I am pushing *Sea Foam* to weather, keeping the jib up longer than I like. But *Sea Foam* will not go to weather without the jib—she virtually heaves to and stops—and I am determined to make progress. The wind is forcing us to sail a course 100 miles west of Fiji anyway, and I am worried about how we're going to make easting against the trades when it comes pay-up time.

I'm steering because the vane linkage has come apart, and a part fell overboard. Perhaps I can make a new part tomorrow. It's been an interesting watch. Earlier I spotted the red running light of a ship, somewhat ahead and to the west of us. The sky is overcast, with only an occasional patch of stars, and there isn't much else to look at. The other ship is moving at about the same speed we are—at least it seems that way. For an hour it maintains its same position relative to us, keeping the distance between us at three to four miles. Another vessel is an exciting event, affirming that we *Sea Foam*ers are not really all alone on the planet. On some passages we see several boats, usually only their lights at night. On some passages, we don't see even one.

Suddenly we are hit by a squall—rain and gusts of wind up to 30 knots. I hear a crack, something breaking, and I grab for the flashlight. The cheekblock for the mizzenmast's port running backstay has broken—crystalized bronze has done its surprise trick—and the wire stay is flapping wildly. Luffing quickly into the wind, I set the other mizzen backstay. (We aren't using the mizzen sail, so setting the leeward running back poses no problem.) With the backstay set, I fall off and resume course.

On *Sea Foam* the jib hanks to the headstay, which runs from the tip of the bowsprit to the tip of the mainmast. Aft support for the mainmast tip comes from the spring stay that leads from the tip of the main to the tip of the mizzen. From the tip of the mizzen, running backs lead down to cheekblocks fastened to the aftermost part of the deck. This makes the running backs essential whenever we fly the jib in a stiff breeze, and losing the port mizzen one is the start of what is to become a bad day.

Sea Foam, a thirty-six-foot Sea Witch ketch built in 1952, under sail in Tahitian waters

A small child guided Herb and Nancy off the beaten path to see an ancient stone tiki in French Polynesia.

Sea Foam's crew makes underwater repairs in Robinson's Cove, Moorea, French Polynesia.

A Marshallese child scrambles up a coconut tree in Maloelap.

It is a Polynesian custom to give flowers to a departing friend. If the friend then throws a flower into the sea, she is sure to return. Nancy, however, could not bear to part with her gardenias and orchids from Ovalau, Fiji.

Craig scans the horizon for a pass through the reef as *Sea Foam* leaves Tahiti.

Fijian village boys stormed *Sea Foam,* but Herb invited them aboard and peace was achieved. Below, wave action eroded this lava rock passage until it resembled an eerie Hobbit land. Craig snorkels near the dinghy as *Sea Foam* waits at anchor in the distance.

Paulini and the other women prepare for a Fulangan feast in Fiji.

Sea Foam at anchor in Tahiti-iti's lagoon. Coral heads and deep-water channels are clearly distinguished by their colors. The larger island of Tahiti can be seen in the distance.

The boat I spotted earlier is now showing me both red and green running lights, which means she's heading right for us. I check *Sea Foam*'s running lights to see that they're working. The other boat isn't closing fast, but she's definitely closing. What with the squalls, the confused seas, the backstay failure, and now the approaching ship, I'm beginning to feel picked on. I'm sure the other boat, whose behavior to date has been somewhat erratic, is well aware of our presence, and that she's drawing near on purpose. To what purpose? I wonder, suspiciously. But our speed of four to six knots doesn't allow me many options for evasive action and none at all for flight, so all I can do is continue on course, be predictable, and keep my eye on the other vessel with the (feeble) hope of being able to do something at the last minute if it turns out she's after me.

Eventually she crosses our wake no more than two hundred feet astern, moving very slowly, obviously curious. About 150 feet long, she could be a fishing boat, but she doesn't look like any fishing boat I've ever seen. I finally guess her to be an interisland steamer. But what, I wonder, is she doing poking around in mid-ocean as if she were looking for something? She never does turn her spotlight on us. Eventually we pull away from her, after which she continues slowly eastward and disappears. But she lingers in my mind, and my imagination refuses to stop inventing possible scenarios for her behavior.

There was one other time when I encountered a mysterious boat on my nightwatch. It was on our trip from Samoa to Tarawa. We had been at sea in bad weather for over two weeks, a condition that other skippers have told me can leave you highly susceptible to hallucinations. Earlier I had seen something which, given the rainy overcast, could not have been more than a mile astern. It could have been a meteor, or it could have been a missile. My first reaction was that it must have been a missile, because it was moving horizontally at an altitude of not more than 1,000 feet. All that I saw was a trail of green flame in the sky. I only saw it for a few seconds, and though I kept looking astern for an hour, I never saw anything else unusual. Because we were way out in the middle of nowhere, I eventually discarded my missile hypothesis.

Later that same night I spotted the dull red glow of the 360-degree masthead light that Japanese vessels use. I began to feel as if we were the only people left on earth, so I altered course to pass by as close as I could. If it turned out to be a trawler I knew I'd have to avoid coming up astern of her, but she lay broadside to our course. I was just wondering if there was any practical way to make contact when the ship, whatever it was, steamed off at no less than 20 knots. It was as if the captain didn't want me coming close. In 43 days at sea, she was the only vessel we saw. Intriguing.

At 0300 I turn the helm over to Craig, tell him about the broken backstay, and go below to sleep. *Sea Foam* is sailing balanced on double-reefed main and jib, and requires only intermittent attention. Everything seems to be going well.

About 5 A.M. I'm awakened suddenly by a change—I feel the boat righting itself as the wind spills from the now-flapping sails. I rush topside.

"What's going on?" I ask.

"We've got a bit of a problem," says Craig, pointing. The tension on the starboard mizzen backstay has pulled up part of the deck, breaking three planks—teak two-by-twos—in the process. Once again the jibstay is straining at the unsupported tip of the mainmast, and there is a great hole in the deck besides.

"We'll have to get the jib down, fast!" I say, heading for the foredeck. With no support, I wonder what kept the tip of the mainmast from breaking. But it didn't break, probably because Craig promptly spilled the wind. I get the jib down, after which I put up the staysail. We don't do as well to weather, anywhere near, but by falling off 10 to 20 degrees we can keep moving.

"Just do the best you can," I say to Craig. "I have to get some sleep. We'll see if we can fix it later."

Of course I don't sleep well, my mind full of what we'll do if the winds stay fresh and we have to beat another 600 miles. So when Nancy gets up for her watch at 6:30, I get up too. Groggy and grumpy, I try to cure my disposition with six cups of coffee. It doesn't work.

Nor does it help when Nancy points out that the strain on the jib sheet block has, during the night, actually pulled the bulwarks inboard a couple of inches, indicating hidden problems of rot or rust with which I have far too few psychological resources to cope.

"The God damn boat's falling apart. Again."

"You'll fix it," says Nancy serenely.

Her faith stirs my dormant optimism. I drill new holes and move the jib sheet block further aft to a part of the bulwarks that seems more solid, and try with a crowbar to pry the damaged section back to its normal position. A sudden lurch of the boat dislodges my purchase, and although I don't go overboard, the crowbar does. With it goes my sense of humor.

"It's – not – my – day," I say between clenched teeth.

"Bad things come in threes," says Nancy. "Windvane, backstay, and jib sheet block. Your ordeal is over."

"And crowbar makes four," I mutter, gloomily.

Craig gets up, and together we make a new part for the windvane linkage out of copper tubing. Freed from steering's servitude, all our dispositions improve. I then transfer the unbroken cheekblock from the torn-up starboard side to the port side, giving us at least one mizzen backstay. No problem. On the port tack we're all set. On the starboard tack, we're OK as long as we don't use the mizzen.

"See," says Nancy. "I knew you could do it."

In the evening the saltwater cooling pump on the engine refuses to pump water, and we can no longer run the engine to charge our batteries. From now on we'll have to be stingy with our electric lights, our one profligacy on a passage.

At dusk, the binnacle light goes out for the second time. The previous night it went out and I fixed it by taking off the cover and playing with the bulb; but not this time. It will have to wait for daylight, and for tonight we'll have to check our course with a flashlight.

Sometime around 3 A.M. the wind dies with the suddenness of assassination. *Sea Foam* slows and wallows in the still-substantial seas. Before I recover from my feelings of gratitude for a respite from the strong winds and realize what the sudden calm might mean, *Sea Foam* loses way, stalls, and the vane rudder slams a mightly slam against the transom. When I check with a flashlight, I see that the trimtab has broken off and fallen into the deep. Gonzo.

Binnacle light (twice); backstays (both); windvane (twice); bulwarks pulled in; loss of crowbar; and a failed water pump. Nancy is right—troubles do come in threes. She just didn't figure that there are three of us on board, each with his own ration card.

Losing the engine virtually cripples us as a weatherly boat. The use of the engine and the sails together is what keeps our boat going in the seas, gives it much-needed extra drive and a better angle on the wind. In situations where the chop and seas bring *Sea Foam* to a dead stop under sail, the engine's power becomes a necessity.

In the beginning when we had a windward goal, we used to try dropping all sail and powering straight into the wind. But when the swells are up and the chop is severe, 55 horsepower just isn't enough. Far more effective is to use both sail and power, tacking as we would under sail alone. That was our plan for making the last leg to Fiji, until it was so rudely interrupted . . .

"How hot should the engine be?" asks Nancy. She is sitting in the cockpit, soaking up sunshine, steering over mirror water and sporadically monitoring the engine instruments.

"One hundred eighty degrees, plus or minus," I yell. *Sea Foam* under power is reminiscent of a small foundry.

"I think it's too hot, she calls. "About 210?"

"Throttle down," I shout, leaping for the cutoff switch. I raise the companionway and have a look. Steam is escaping from various apertures, and the engine is hissing and seething in recrimination.

"Too hot to see what's wrong—we'll have to let it cool down before we can find out."

The cooling down takes an hour and is a reminder of one of the hells of sailing. We have been powering with main and staysail up. The minute we shut down the engine, our forward speed slows, the apparent wind drops to practically nothing, and the heavy swells roll us like a log in the troughs. The gaff and boom slat no matter how tightly prevented, so we drop all sail, which eliminates the slatting spars. But as there is no longer a damping effect from the sails, *Sea Foam* now rolls flamboyantly. Calms are preferable to storms, but they bring a misery all their own.

So as soon as the engine cools, I'm eager to find the trouble. It's not hard to diagnose. We start the engine and check the exhaust.

"Dry as a bone," says Craig, claret-faced, having hung by his heels from the taffrail to inspect it.

The engine's salt water pump had failed intermittently on our last passage. I'd managed to coax it to continue to operate by removing the faceplate and greasing the surface traveled by the impeller, but I knew at the time it was only a stopgap measure. Once we reached Tarawa I removed the impeller and found that the blades were badly worn on one edge. Reversing the impeller returned the pump to service, and as there were no impellers available at the Tarawa shipyard, we left. Now I dismantle the pump and see that the impeller has lost three of its six blades, and that the others are cracking and about to go.

The cooling of our engine is accomplished by using both fresh and salt water. Fresh water is circulated through the engine in a closed system like that of an automobile. In a car, air flows around the radiator and keeps the water cool. But on a boat, the usual means of cooling the fresh water is to pump cold salt water from the ocean through tubes in the fresh water reservoir—a device called a heat exchanger. Thus, when the engine is running, the cooling depends on two pumps—the one that circulates the fresh water through the engine, and the one that pumps raw sea water through the heat exchanger. It is the salt water pump that has failed, so if I can figure out a way to cool the engine's fresh water, we'll be back in business.

My first idea is to secure a large jerry can on deck, rig a syphon, and have Craig keep the jerry can filled by means of a bucket and a funnel. It would be easy to run a syphon to the heat exchanger, and nothing is more reliable than a gravity feed. The reliability of Craig, however, is in question, particularly when I'm treating him like a galley slave. Craig has grown large enough to stage a sizeable and maybe even a successful mutiny so although my syphon idea would be fine for short jobs like charging the batteries or entering a pass, it's impractical for the long haul.

Five years before when we were outfitting *Sea Foam* for voyaging, I had been nagged by the same question that confronts most tyros: what spares and equipment should I buy? Space and budget were both limited, and even experienced cruisers have difficulty predicting what items are most likely to fail, what extras are most likely to come in handy. Ask any yachtie who's been at it for a while and he'll tell you that what fails will be the thing you've run out of or never put on board in the first place, whereas many of the most handy devices will be those you passed over as white elephants. At best, prediction is a murky business.

Magazines and books were helpful, but we also found that looking through marine catalogues sent our thinking jogging along the right road. It was a catalogue that caused us to buy a Jabsco Water Puppy, a little auxiliary 12-volt pump. "Use it to transfer diesel," said the blurb. "Yeah," vibrated our psychic center in agreement. "Use it to fill your water tanks." "Yeah, yeah!" vibed our PC. "Use it to wash down decks and anchor chains." "Yeah, yeah, yeah!" we vibed. "Use it for an extra bilge pump in an emergency." "Ulp," we ulped; but yeah, that too. We bought, shelling out gladly.

During our whole cruise we used the Water Puppy to transfer diesel once. And once we tried using it for a salt water deck washing system, and subsequently an anchor washing system; but with the abundance of young crew, buckets were faster and less hassle. We never found a pump to be convenient for transferring water— either it came aboard through a hose from a spigot, or we horsed it aboard in jerry cans. And so far, knock on wood, we've never needed an auxiliary bilge pump. As a result, for five years our purchase has lain unused in the forepeak, an area that for one reason or another has seen its share of raw, green ocean. Might it still work, even after all this time? I send Craig to fetch it.

"You mean this?" he asks, after one of those searches that involves pulling out mountains of junk and finding what you want at the very bottom. The pump, covered with rust and corrosion, is a Great White Hope with Ring Around the Collar.

I hook up the leads to the battery. The pump motor runs, but it no longer purrs like the quiet, smooth-running machine it once was. Now it bounces and clatters like a garbage disposal devouring a teaspoon.

"It'll go for a while, maybe," I say.

With two sizes of hose and some hose clamps, Craig invents a reducer that should leak but doesn't. We bypass the engine pump and put the Water Puppy in line. Wired to the ignition switch, it will operate only when the key is turned on.

During the first hour we check the pump several times. It is cooling the engine nicely, but the pump motor is nearly too hot to rest my hand on. Even the fuse that I wired into one of the leads is hot to the touch. I'm sure that the pump will burn up in a matter of hours. However, it will allow us to charge our batteries, and it might even last long enough to give us a few miles on our power-sailing windward leg to Suva.

Perhaps Fate decided we've coped with enough, that it's time to smile; or perhaps she is off busy messing up the lives of other sailors. Whatever, when we finally sail far enough south to make sailing east a necessity, the wind goes stone dead, the ocean becomes a millpond, and we're able to power all the way to Suva. Not only does the engine run cool the whole way, but we continue to use the Water Puppy for the 10 weeks it takes our new impellers to arrive from the States.

The night before arriving in Suva, I was listening in on the Maritime Mobile Ham Net when I heard a call that there was a message for Craig. Don Coleman, who hoped to sail *Landseer* to Australia to sell her, had his crew of two Marshallese decide at the last minute that they didn't want to go. Don would single-hand *Landseer* as far as Tarawa, but wanted to know if Craig would fly back to meet him and help him bring his boat south to Fiji.

It's one thing to successfully complete an ocean passage on a sailboat. It's quite another to arrive at your destination only to hop a plane back to your starting point and do it all over again. When Craig heard the message come over the air, he was understandably reluctant to make a snap decision.

"Tell him I'll give him an answer on tomorrow night's net," was his answer.

Nancy and I pointed out that he was under no obligation to go back if he didn't want to, and God knows there were plenty of reasons not to want to. But if he did want to, Nancy and I wouldn't object.

Craig was quiet most of the day, but as we approached Suva Harbor the next evening, just as the net was coming on, Craig said he wanted to do it. It was all his choice, and when I passed it on to Don on the air, there was no mistaking the relief and gratitude in his voice.

"At age 16, it was a big decision for me," Craig wrote later. "I knew as well as Herb and Mom that I didn't have to go. But Don was a good friend whose crew had deserted him, and since he wanted to leave right away, there was no chance of finding anyone else. Also, I'd get a chance to polish up my star navigation and see if I could consistently get a reasonable, three-mile triangle."

When we arrived in Suva it was the start of a holiday weekend, and customs and immigration didn't check us till the next afternoon. We barely had time to get Craig on the plane. All our money was in American dollars, and the banks were closed till Tuesday. (The airline was firm about not selling us a ticket for U.S. money.) We did the only thing we could think of—row around to the boats of friends and say, "Hi, glad to see you, it's been a whole year, and how about lending me all your cash?" No one refused, and Craig was able to catch his plane.

Their passage was totally different from *Sea Foam's*. Instead of sailing down the meridian, as we had done, Craig and Don island-hopped their way down the Kiribati-Tuvalu chain. Cursed with nothing but calm weather, their route allowed them to refuel twice, without which they'd probably still be out there waiting for wind. Then, on leaving Funafuti, they ran into a gale that forced them to heave to for two days, during which they were set 120 miles to the west. When they finally raised the Yasawas (the high islands of western Fiji), Craig was much relieved to have the two passages over and done.

But as he told me later, the trip with Don was a good experience for him. First of all, he enjoyed the chance to sail with a skipper other than me for the first time in his life. Secondly, he had the chance to test his celestial navigation (Don let him do it all) without me looking over his shoulder. Thirdly, he had a chance to see two islands that Nancy and I missed, a stroke of one-upmanship that pleased him immensely. For my part, I was glad that he had made the trip too, for all his reasons, but also because there's nothing better for a young man's self-confidence than to be needed by a friend, and nothing better for his character than to respond to it.

XI / PARTS

A number of people have suggested that we went cruising to escape reality, but this is pure nonsense. Reality is a coin with two sides. Sure, there were times when we spent glorious afternoons broad-reaching under velour skies and cotton clouds, had evening picnics on lonely golden beaches, or stood watches under guardian stars. But also there were difficult days when we faced economic uncertainty, weathered storms, or wrestled with emergencies. And if, as some say, reality is learning to deal with ordinary, day-to-day frustrations, we paid our dues there, too, in our struggle to maintain our boat.

When we first left California, we put aboard as many spares as we could afford and had room for. Some, after six years, we still had. Many had been used up, given away, lost, or had deteriorated into rusty shadows of their former selves. The result was that now, instead of merely reaching into a locker for a spare, we had to (A) make it, (B) shop for it in whatever port we were in, or (C) send home for it. Choosing A, B, or C resulted in a Test of Ingenuity and Endurance (TIE).

Our early TIEs were in Tahiti, where we absorbed a full measure of Papeetian shopping lore. The first requirement was to keep enough money on hand to take advantage of bargains. Papeete shopkeepers used a pricing system based on a percentage markup. If subsequent wholesale prices increased, only new inventory was affected. On the dusty, remote shelves of many stores, old inventory that wasn't affected by shelf life represented handsome bargains. I once bought a dozen U.S. fuel filters at half the current U.S. price (one-third the Papeete price). Even though we had little spare money, we never regretted it. We also left Polynesia with over 100 sheets of wet-and-dry sandpaper. The price in some shops was 50¢ a sheet. We bought ours for 15¢ a sheet. At a time when my sweat and toil was bringing in $15 a day, we had just saved (earned) $35.

We learned not to get too hung up on what we would or wouldn't find. A hopeless quest, I thought, would be an impeller for our marine bilge pump. I found one. But I never could find a simple sparkplug for our portable generator, even though the generators themselves were sold new by at least two different stores. At one place a quart of white spirits (paint thinner) was 85¢; at another, $4. A couple of U.S. magazine editors were surprised when I submitted stories on newsprint offcuts, given to me by a friend at the *Tahiti Bulletin;* but the only typing paper available cost $13 for 200 sheets. One day, on the strength of a rumor, I borrowed a bicycle. Two miles outside of town I found the only store in Tahiti that carried our engine's size fan belt. The same store sold nine-gallon jerry cans (which had contained acid) for $3. With four of them dangling from me and the bike, I wove my way back to the boat through rush hour traffic. It was necessary to shop with strong legs and an open mind.

Our persistence in dealing with TIEs was sometimes productive in unexpected ways. Recently in Suva, Fiji, I found I needed a repair kit for our engine's fresh water pump. After days spent in parts stores, I finally took my problem to Johnny the Indian, the owner of a small auto parts store who had taken a personal but ineffective interest in my previous parts-hunting safaris. Johnny was a short, round man of about 40. His cheeks were fat, as if full of acorns. The young men who worked for him were tall and thin. Due to remodeling, the store was a shambles of displaced inventory, but as usual, Johnny's spirits were overflowing.

"Just bring the pump in—I'm sure I've got a repair kit for it," he assured me.

My pump leaked but still worked, and because of the threat of hurricanes I wasn't eager to remove the pump and be a sitting duck without an engine. There was no help for it, however. I'd already learned that there was no correspondence between my parts manual and the Australian or English ones, and that my only hope of success was to bring in the old part. "Like this," I would say, and would wait patiently, trying not to sigh while they rummaged for hours, and failed. Johnny the Indian exuded confidence, however, and I lacked my usual premonitions of nonsuccess. So much for prescience. After an hour and a half, Johnny turned up empty-handed.

"Never mind," said Johnny. "I know who's got one." We adjourned to Johnny's car, a zippy, yellow Honda that he drove with a cheerful disregard for caution. We visited machine shops, garages, new-engine dealers, and parts stores all over Suva. Johnny's grin, litmus to failure, was absent as we departed each store, but was regenerated by screaming revs, screeching tires, and careening challenges to kinetic consequences, and we would arrive at our next destination with his grin in full bloom. We never found a kit, but we did find a seal that would tide me over till a kit could be summoned from the States. Johnny presented me the gift of the seal in a little ceremony in his office that involved his staff, a mirth-ridden account of our quest, and a bottle of rum.

If parts-hunting in foreign ports was challenging, ordering things from the States was even moreso. Not only were there the added problems of communication and shipping, but there was no way to shop around, or to seek out places that carried rebuilt or second-hand items. The best solution was to impose on a friend who, at least for a time, would be happy to be our proxy.

Once, however, I asked a friend to send me a rebuilt alternator. Rather than hassle with shopping around, he picked up the phone and had a brand-new one sent, and refused to accept the difference in price. This made it difficult to ask him for another favor, but somehow I managed it. From Majuro I wrote him for a couple of new impellers for our engine's salt water pump and asked him to send them to us in Fiji. We arrived, but no impellers. I decided that we'd worn out this particular friend, that he needed replacing, but a quick search through our address book confirmed my fears: after six years of cruising we had exhausted the vein of friendships, and must now strip mine among acquaintances who, on reaching my signature, would probably ask "who the hell is Herb Payson?"

We had no choice but to order the parts from Osco Motors, the manufacturer of our engine. At the same time, I wrote to Jabsco, the manufacturer of our pump, on another matter, and merely as an aside mentioned our trouble in finding parts for our pump, a discontinued model. Osco filled my order promptly; Jabsco sent some parts *gratis;* and a few weeks later a whole passel of parts arrived from my friend, having taken months to come by ship. We suddenly had enough impellers and seals to keep our pump running for 30 years.

The best way to have stuff shipped to us in the South Seas was by air parcel post rather than by air freight. In Tahiti, for instance, if it came by mail, we went to the parcel depot, declared that the parcel contained parts for a yacht in transit (and was thus not subject to duty), paid a $2 handling charge and collected our package.

But if it came by air freight, we had to go to the airport and pay an import agent $12 to fill out declaration forms, and three days later we could come back to get our package. Usually the paperwork hadn't been done and we were forced to make a third trip.

Air freight had a minimum charge, so that parcels less than the minimum weight cost considerably more than they would coming via air parcel post. When I complained to one U.S. parts manager that the four-pound parcel he'd sent me had cost me $45 in shipping charges and would have cost only $15 by air parcel post, he replied that air parcel post was only 60 percent reliable. (We found this to be true in Mexico and Central America, but not in the South Pacific.) His letter also implied that if I wanted overseas service, I'd have to pay for it. I logged the $45 under 'tuition'.

Not only was air parcel post cheaper than air freight, in Suva it was infinitely more convenient. We could usually spot a yachtie in port because he'd most likely be laden down with parcels like a Mexican donkey. When distances were great, the affluent used cabs. The rest of us used buses. A bus from the Tradewinds (15¢) or the Royal Suva Yacht Club (9¢) let us off downtown only two blocks from the post office. The air freight office, however, was way out in Raiwaqa (Rye-wang-ga), a 30-minute (12¢) bus ride out the other side of town.

A TIE that I almost flunked began when we got word that our new jib had arrived at air freight. I phoned and asked if it could be sent downtown to our mailing address at the Bank of New Zealand. No way. We must pick it up out in Raiwaqa. Exuding tolerance for foreign foibles, I climbed on a bus. Raiwaqa buses are of two kinds: those that go to the air freight depot in a straightforward fashion, and those that don't. Before I learned to tell the difference, I was treated to instructive, relaxing, but ultimately boring detours through endless residential districts. The only bright spot was a small apartment building where, from a window, a lovely young Fijian girl shot a smile at me every time we passed. (Eventually I realized her target was the driver.)

I arrived to discover that yes, the jib had arrived, but the bill of lading had not. I would have to come back. I returned to the Tradewinds Bar to renew my optimism. Back in Raiwaqa the following day, my cheerfulness was dissipated by the news that, although I'd made a point of giving my address as Me, c/o Bank of New Zealand, the Stateside senders had shipped it to the bank, attention

Me. I must return to town and get a note from the bank releasing the parcel. By the time I'd bused in and sifted through a dozen bankers to find the one man authorized to release the parcel, it was noon. Air freight was closed till 1:30, and having nothing else to do in the city I decided to retreat, regroup, and reattack on the following day.

The next morning I busted my ass to get an early start, bused downtown, rebused to Raiwaqa, and finally bustled into the air freight office in a whirlwind of Western Efficiency. Papers were signed, money changed hands, and I proceeded to the customs desk.

"The duty will be $30, sir."

"There shouldn't be any duty—it's for a yacht in transit."

"A yacht? Then you must get a release from the customs boarding officer. He's located on the main wharf downtown . . ."

"I know, I *know*, I *KNOW*!" My childish impatience made me realize that I still had room for personal growth.

Back I bused into town to get the release. By the time I finished with the formalities it was the beginning of a rainy rush hour, and I decided to return to *Sea Foam* and strong drink to fuel up for tomorrow's foray.

The final day was an anticlimax. The Raiwaqa bus driver greeted me by name, and I was welcomed at the freight dock with friendly smiles of recognition. The scene ran with a potential for sentiment equalled only by my high school graduation. Suffused with the mixed feelings of achievement and nostalgia, I was hard put not to scribble a squishy, yearbook-style message beside my signature on the receipt.

"That'll be 50¢ for storage," said the clerk.

"Huh?" Equanimity drained from the bathtub of my being, leaving a ring.

"Fifty cents. Storage. The package has been here over a week."

A flash of foresight momentarily blinded my mind's eye. I saw that I would argue, cool at first but progressively warmer, until I became a boiling cauldron of protest. Then, having unburdened myself to deaf ears, I would slam down the coin and stomp offstage. I'm an optimist, but I know futility when I see it. By quietly paying the 50¢ I traded a crisis of high blood pressure for the chronic festers of sufferance.

There were times when we had to deal directly with companies without the aid of a friend, and surprisingly often, things went well. I once sent a letter to Exide complaining that a new battery had failed to work in my camera during a passage, causing me, a photo-journalist, an irretrievable loss. The quick reply was apologetic and included two new batteries, neither of which worked. I rewrote. Back bounced a reply with three new batteries that looked like the others but bore different numbers. They worked. My letter of thanks included a picture of *Sea Foam* and a pledge of allegiance.

Texas Instruments made a durable and accurate wrist watch, which I bought in Pago Pago for $12. I used it, abused it, and loved it. But because it had a virtually impregnable back, I sent it all the way to the factory for a new battery. (There has been some question in the minds of skeptics as to the self-sufficiency of a round-the-world sailor who can't replace the battery in his watch all by himself; but they never had to deal with *my* watch.) The watch came back with new batteries inside, a new strap, and the advice that it was still under guarantee (it wasn't).

The difficulty arose when a real effort was needed to save money. A friend would often do this, but a busy parts manager couldn't be bothered. In Suva when I needed to repair my fresh water pump, I ordered a rebuilding kit directly from Osco. "Sorry," came the reply, "no more kits for your pump—it's been upgraded." A friend would have found a kit ($20) and sent it to me air parcel post ($15). The parts manager shipped me a brand-new pump via air freight for a total of $125, and in a letter pointed out that though it was expensive, at least it was quick. Tuition was going up.

It was bad enough when I felt that the intentions of the company were good, but it was ulcer-making when I felt they were dealing shabbily with me because I was far away and helpless. In New Zealand, the owner of *Lissa* had installed a brand-new, Bukh diesel which he'd bought for a bargain price. Months later when we were delivering *Lissa*, the engine froze up, and I was stunned by the U.S. agent's price of replacement bearings. The judicious use (or threat) of letters and/or publicity got the price reduced by half, and my friend found himself in the anomalous position of being happy to pay only three times the cost of domestic bearings.

The lesson, that a low purchase price isn't the whole story, was hammered home when our portable Honda gasoline generator broke. We had bought it while in the U.S. on our *Lissa* delivery, and loved it. It recharged our batteries, ran our power tools, and eventually would power Nancy's promised new sewing machine. One night in Majuro I left the generator on deck during a shower, and thereafter it refused to put out full voltage. An electrician diagnosed (for $25) the problem as a faulty voltage regulator. As the device was sealed in plastic and couldn't be repaired, we would have to buy a new one.

A dealer in Hawaii quoted me $80. I was both shocked and angry—the price of the whole generator, brand new, was under $300. I wrote the factory in Tokyo, who replied that $80 was high but not out of line for Hawaii. I then wrote California to the dealer where I'd bought the generator. His answer: $68 for a regulator. But taking the sting off the still-incredible price were copies of four pages from the shop manual that showed how I could test to make sure it was the regulator that was to blame. This consideration impressed me, and after further tests we ordered the part.

We waited and waited. Three months later I got a bank statement showing that my check had cleared eight weeks ago, and I decided I was being shabbily treated. I wrote the dealer again, telling him that while I might be tolerant of unavoidable delays, I became unstable when overlooked and schizoid when ignored. My parts came by return mail, along with a letter advising me that I'd been neither overlooked nor ignored, but misplaced. My feelings recovered, but my wallet remained in intensive care for months.

A happy ending would be pure fiction. In spite of our careful diagnosis, the new regulator did not fix the generator. Our power tools remained useless, and Nancy stoically cranked her electric sewing machine by hand. Our pumps all worked, however, which meant I was batting .500, not bad for me. I basked for a while in the sunlight of this statistic, just to dry out dampened spirits. Then, one afternoon, I dropped in on Johnny the Indian. He was glad to see me. But he'd had a bad day and his spirits were low, so this time *I* brought the rum.

XII / NGAU

Nineteen seventy-eight to 1979 was a banner season for cruising-types to visit Suva Harbor. We were 1 of 30 boats that had chosen to summer (Northern Hemisphere winter) in Fiji, and although all 30 boats were never in Suva at the same time, rarely were there more than 10 of us out gunking in the hinterholes. Sheer numbers meant that the best spots to anchor always had boats in them. If you had to take your boat for water or fuel, it was wise to leave your dinghy on your anchor. Otherwise your spot would be snatched up immediately by a skipper who had been waiting in the wings, covertly coveting.

This was our second visit to Fiji (we had spent five weeks here in 1974). Sailing into Suva Harbor, we not only had the comfortable feeling of coming home, but we also had a clear mental picture of the lay of the water, and the particular ambiance of each area. Essentially, there were three anchorages. One was in front of the Royal Suva Yacht Club. The RSYC was a great watering hole, as the bar prices were the lowest in town. A money-conscious sailor could spend hours weaving sea tales around gin and tonics without fretting too much about denting his budget.

Another area was the quay, or sea wall, at the Tradewinds Hotel. This was upper class suburbia, anchoragewise. The bar prices, though not outrageous by other hotel standards, were double the prices at the RSYC, and only the wealthy or the profligate drank there. The Tradewinds had a pool, and with the excuse of a healthful swim, people would gather around the pool from after lunch onward, having only an occasional beer or Bloody to ease the stringencies of the rigorous pursuit of an athletic life.

The third place was behind Mosquito Island, out of sight but only a short row from the Tradewinds dinghy dock. There was room for roughly five boats, and we tried as often as possible to be one of them. It was more protected than in front of the RSYC, and far enough from cheap drink to make the blandishments of self-indulgence out of oarshot, if not altogether out of mind. The disadvantage was that the buses that ran between the Tradewinds and town ran more seldom and quit earlier at night than those that ran to and from the RSYC. This made shopping and nightclubbing more difficult, a good thing, we thought. So the only time we went someplace else was when we were desperate for a change of scene.

But when we first arrived, we chose to anchor in front of the yacht club. We had lots of business to attend to, store prowling to do, and the added convenience of being closer to town tipped the balance. We joined the RSYC, bought a RSYC tee shirt but eschewed the burgee, and settled in for some conviviality.

Thursday night was movie night. Movies were cheap and sometimes godawful, but you could smoke, and the bar was right there, and if the movie was ghastly you could shoot pool during the second reel. Few of us missed the movies.

Sunday night was BBQ night. Great braziers were lit out on the lawn between the club and the bay, and everyone could line up and buy his preference at bargain prices—steak, hamburger, or hot dogs—and cook his meat himself, just as he liked it. Liquor flowed from the inexpensive bar, and as sea stories tend to get better and more colorful with the addition of good food, friends, and booze, some of the best sea stories I ever heard were told at the SNRSYCBBQ.

Two delightfully debilitating recreations peculiar to Suva were Lucky Eddie's, a disco, and Indian restaurants. Lucky Eddie's featured early evening jazz on Mondays, usually a pleasant quartet with a featured singer transvestite who sounded like Anita O'Day; but the late evening disco assaulted the ears. Getting up to the bar at Lucky Eddie's was a test of shove-and-smile diplomacy. Bouncers doubled as waiters, 'waiter,' in this case, meaning one who makes you wait. Rather than pester you with aggressive frequency, they'd let you die of thirst. So you went to the bar.

As for the Indian food, it assaulted the stomach with fiery pleasures. Cheap and delicious, it stuck with you for at least two mornings afterwards. The bus schedules made innovators of us all, and Nancy and I would occasionally take in a movie *followed* by dinner, a routine that usually got us to the depot in time to catch the last bus. If no bus, we took a cab, usually remembering (as with cabbies everywhere) to agree on a price before we got into the car.

Papeete, Tahiti, was our most recent port of call with any cosmopolitan pretensions, and Suva, Fiji's capital, in spite of its diesel-fume-laden atmosphere, was a breath of fresh air. The streets teemed with Indian women dressed traditionally in kaleidoscopic saris, bright red marks of caste on their foreheads; with lovely

Fijian girls wearing afros and ready smiles; with policemen dressed in white skirts (*sulus*), a uniform that is totally appropriate for the setting and not at all, as someone suggested, like L.A. Ram linemen in drag; with young, dark-skinned boys selling the *Times* or the *Fiji Sun;* with proper Britishers dressed in walking shorts and knee socks; with bewildered tourists wearing dark glasses and carrying Nikons; and with an ever-growing number of yachties, most of whom were readily identified by the long-suffering mien of those who walk everywhere, carry everything, and are always required to pay cash.

The pièce de résistance, however, were the picnics on Mosquito Island, marathons of pleasure which significantly tested human endurance. They lasted all day and most of the night, and when the caretaker of the island finally would throw everyone off, celebrants would migrate to somebody's yacht to help him annihilate his liquor supply. Mosquito Island picnics never ended, they petered out; and on one record occasion, four determined revelers carried on for a week, the point at which they ran out of credit.

When we first got to the Royal Suva Yacht Club we went around telling everybody we wanted (hoped) to cruise the Lau Group of islands. A cruising friend in Tahiti had told us that the Lau Group was "the best Goddamn cruising in the whole world," and his enthusiasm had been one of the main reasons for our return to Fiji. However, the responses from our yacht club friends were discouraging. "No one can cruise there any more. The Lau Group is closed to yachts."

But long ago we'd learned that the 'you can'ts' were often less rigid than they appeared, and so we held high hopes in spite of ambient pessimism. These hopes were given substance when a skipper told me of a certain boat, *Naomi,* gaff-rigged, bowspritted cutter that had recently gotten permission to visit by applying to the Bureau of Fijian Affairs. *Naomi*'s captain and crew were an amiable but scruffy-looking lot, just as their boat was an adequate but scruffy-looking boat, and I was sure that if they, apparent hippies, could wangle permission, we *Sea Foam*ers with our mom-and-pop respectability could certainly do so. Besides, I, a writer, would apply my golden pen to the cause. Cinch. Good as done.

Nancy and I dressed in our most conventional clothing (which required digging to the very bottom of our lockers), and took the bus to the Fijian Affairs office downtown. The regular minister was on vacation and a Fijian subordinate, a generic gov-employee type, was sitting in. His name was Joe.

"Joe," I said, smiling my most winning smile, "my wife and I and our son have sailed thousands of miles because we've heard of the beauty of your fair islands in the Lau Group, and now that we've arrived, we find they're closed. I understand, though (wink, confidential), that a *few* boats are being granted permission, and I wondered if we might be considered." Christ, I was *shame*less.

"Write me a letter," said Joe, "telling me the names of the islands you want to visit, and why you want to go there."

I beamed. Write? A letter? We were *in*.

"How do you feel about our chances of getting a 'yes'?" I asked.

"I should think they were very good," Joe assured me.

I wrote the letter, mentioning that we were a family, that I was a writer, and that we wanted to visit certain islands, which I specified. As Joe suggested, I checked back in a week. No Joe. No answer. Nobody in the office even knew of our request. Another week saw me back again. Nothing. Finally I received a letter in the mail saying that my permission had been denied, and that this was a matter of policy to which there were no exceptions. To us, that meant there was no hope.

I made one more trip to the bureau and learned that Joe had gotten in trouble for giving *Naomi* permission, that he'd been banished to one of the country's more remote posts, and that the director of Fijian Affairs was absolutely adamantly altogether against visitors to the Lau Islands. N – O.

"Oh well," I told my amused friends, "it would be pretty silly to sail that far from Suva during the hurricane season, anyway. We'll visit the nearer islands. It'll be just as much fun." But their snickers told me I hadn't convinced them, and Nancy's long face told me I hadn't convinced her, either.

Connie wrote. She'd reached a time in her life where she needed a quiet place to collect her thoughts, and could she come live with us on *Sea Foam* for a while? Whoopee, was Nancy's reaction. Mine too—I just wasn't sure how much quiet Connie'd find in Suva.

But with Connie and the hurricanes definitely on their way, if we wanted to see anything beyond Suva Harbor, we had to get moving.

So as soon as Craig arrived on *Landseer* and rejoined us, and we had celebrated a reunion with Don, Craig, Nancy and I set sail for Levuka, on the island of Ovalau, to visit friends who lived there. Their house overlooked the bay. As we sat in their airy, open living room, we could look down on *Sea Foam* nodding at anchor. At that point, sipping an icy gin and listening to Oscar Peterson and Ray Brown's driving rhythms, the Goddess of the Cruising Life strode stage center, wearing a golden toga, her aureole cocked jauntily over one brow. It was the first time in months she'd seen fit to wear anything other than jeans and a tee shirt.

I told our friends about having been denied permission to visit the Lau Group, and how we were trying to decide on some other places to visit.

"That's ridiculous," they assured me. "We see the local official socially. We'll just stop by his office tomorrow and have a chat with him."

The official, a Fijian, had no qualms whatsoever about granting us permission, and even wrote a letter requesting the island chiefs to give us hospitality.

"In this government," said the official, "the right hand never knows what the left hand is doing anyway. Just stay away from Lakemba, the prime minister's island." I got the impression that one of the main reasons for refusing yachts permission to visit the Lau was not, as we'd thought, because of the disturbing impact of Western customs on the simple lives of the islanders (including nudity, boozing, and pot smoking, as well as wealth and technology). Rather it was because the prime minister wanted to guard his privacy without specifically singling out his own island as off-limits; and because he certainly didn't want an admitted writer, for God's sake, making observations about the motel and golf course he'd built there since becoming prime minister.

Our friend also taught us a few Fijian words, and instructed us in the protocol of visiting a Fijian village.

"You must present *sevu-sevu*. That is, you must bring the chief some yangona root. It's a symbolic, not a utilitarian gift. And be sure to wrap the yangona root in newspaper—that's the accepted way."

I was amused at the various inroads of Western culture. Yangona root in newspaper was only one. Another was the ubiquitous biscuit tin—a huge tin that once contained cabin biscuits but which, when empty, became a drum and one of the principal instruments in their rhythm sections.

On our way from Levuka to the Lau Group we decided to stop at the island of Ngau, as we had spent a week anchored off one of the villages, Waikama, in 1974. The ceremonial aspect of *sevu-sevu* can be sweetened with practical additions such as tobacco, cans of corned beef, or, as in our case, with two, 15-pound *mahi-mahi* that we caught as we approached the pass. If the chief picks up the *sevu-sevu* (which you've laid on the ground or the floor in front of him), he has accepted your presents and your presence. As a guest, you are welcome to roam the village, to take fish or shells from the lagoon, and to come and go as you please. If he refuses, which is unlikely, or if you fail to make the gesture, it is within his purview to order you away from the village, or, in the extreme, to tell you to leave the island.

We were glad the gift of *sevu-sevu* was symbolic. Ngau grows most of the yangona root that is used for kava making throughout Fiji. Large drying racks laden with yangona root were everywhere. No doubt the roots we brought with us had been grown here and shipped to the Suva market, where we in turn bought them and carried them back. Our goals to Newcastle were accepted gratefully, however, as within the memory of the Waikamans, we were the first yachtsmen ever to conform to the custom. The small trouble was infinitely worth it, as thereafter every house opened its door to us.

Whenever we visited a village, we were always a curiosity. There was always a certain amount of possessiveness, too. Waikama was 'our' village, and if another yacht had sailed in to share it we would have had to shuffle our deck of ownership cards. Among the other villages on Ngau, we were 'their' visiting yacht, and any gifts or privileges that came from us should justly accrue first to Waikamans.

We had anchored *Sea Foam* nearly half a mile from the cement pier in the hopes that we'd be far enough away to cut down the constant stream of visitors that always flowed through our boat when we anchored close to a village. Not that we were feeling antisocial, but Craig was still putting in two to three hours of studying per day, and I was spending each morning writing. Also, we had maintenance chores that always seemed to hang over our

heads, so that the constant interruptions of hosting would sometimes become a pain in the neck.

So we had a choice. Either we put aside all routine activities
and devoted our full time to intercultural intercourse, or else we
removed ourselves and our boat for a certain part of each day.

We had not removed ourselves far enough, however, as soon a
fleet of bamboo rafts arrived, manned by village youths who poled
and paddled, then boarded and invaded, claiming us as theirs.
There was no point in remaining irritated by the intrusion, so we
just put aside adult pursuits and took up childish things. Break out
candy and cocoa. Explain each thing a dozen times. Sit through
long, grinning silences. And finally, ask them to please leave so
we can get some work done, but to be sure to come back
tomorrow.

A flash of Nancy's genius finally saved us: 'open boat.' That
evening we rowed (and *rowed* and *rowed*) ashore and told the
villagers that we were going to bring *Sea Foam* to the pier the next
day, and that everyone was invited to drop down and come aboard.
(Not all villages offered the convenience of piers with deep water,
but Waikama was Ngau's port for the whole island—consisting of
a pier and a storage shed.) Several dozen adults and scores of
children—over half the village—showed up, swarmed, and left us
dizzy with questions, but intact. Thereafter, the privacy of our distant anchoring spot was respected.

One day we hitched a ride on the island's sole vehicle to the
north end, where we visited a Fijian schoolteacher and her re-
cently-become-chief husband, friends from our previous visit.
James and Polly's thatch roofed house boasted the village's only
(kerosene) refrigerator, and all day long people entered and left,
depositing and withdrawing from their food accounts, playing
what looked to us like musical fish. On our last visit we met William, James and Polly's son, who was slightly younger than Craig,
but big for his age. William was away in Viti Levu visiting his
grandmother. We promised to try to return to Ngau later in the
year, a promise we would not be able to keep.

The driver of the island's one truck had told us that he made one
trip a day to the village of James and Polly. We started walking the
five miles back toward Waikama and *Sea Foam* in the gathering
clouds, the spitting rain. We'd gone maybe a quarter of a mile
when the truck appeared. The driver wouldn't admit it, but there

was no question he'd made a special trip just for us.

Arriving in Waikama, we went to one of the houses where a group of elders were listening to the radio. Fiji weather was forecasting winds of up to 40 knots, possibly increasing.

"You'd better move your boat to the other end of the bay," we were told. There was more than a little justification for this advice. In the first place, the wind was blowing out of the south into the opening of the bay, and the resulting fetch of over three miles allowed a severe chop to build up and to which *Sea Foam* lay exposed. In the second place, recently during a similar blow another yacht had anchored where we were anchored and had dragged up onto the shore at the north end of the bay.

This presented us with a tough decision. The south end of the bay was full of hazards, and we'd never explored it. In the darkening overcast of later afternoon, we wouldn't be able to see any coral heads, and of course none were marked. Furthermore, although we were exposed to the wind where we were, if it should shift we'd be sheltered. In our present spot we were exposed to a narrow sector. In the south end of the bay we would be vulnerable to a much larger sector. Finally, we had tested our anchor and knew that it was dug in securely, and that we had plenty of swinging room for all the scope we might need. In spite of my respect for local wisdom, I thought of this as a case of "better the devil you know." We decided to stay put, much to the disapproval of our obviously concerned friends.

We put out a second anchor, ate a nervous supper, and stretched out with intent to sleep. Sorry, Charlie. The wailing of the wind in the rigging and the pitching of the boat made sleep impossible. Pitching, of course, is the most worrisome of anchoring situations, as the up and down motion of the bow is literally acting to snatch the anchor right out of its grave. Fortunately, toward 2300 the wind veered to the northeast, putting us in the lee, and the pitching subsided. Nevertheless, the wind increased, and at one o'clock in the morning the jib tore loose the stops that secured it, furled, to the lifeline. The fury of flogging fabric sent Craig and me scrambling topside, like a fire drill where everybody shows up in pyjamas, except we weren't wearing pyjamas. While relashing the sail, the two of us were subjected to the acupuncture of stinging rain, watery pins and needles driven by gusts which reached 60 knots.

I've been more nervous in less wind. Here, at least, we had

plenty of swinging room. Being the only yacht in the bay, there was no danger of another boat dragging down on us. Our anchors were well positioned, and holding. Even so, we put in a sleepless, anxious night.

By morning the wind had shifted even further into the northwest and had weakened considerably. I was tired—we all were—but we suddenly realized we'd been given a statistically improbable fair wind. As it would have been ungrateful not to use it, sunset found us powering out Ngau's northern pass and heading around to the eastern side, where we set a course for Matuku, 65 miles to the south. During the night the wind, having shifted full circle in 24 hours, ended up blowing out of the southwest. When daylight came we discovered that by trying to hold to our course we had pinched too close to the wind and made very little progress. We would have a tough time getting to Matuku before dark, even if we used the engine. But because it didn't matter to us which Lau island we visited first, and because we were now the lucky donees of a perfect wind for sailing east, we changed our destination to Ongea, easternmost of the islands we wanted to visit. We never got to Matuku, a thing not done and therefore regretted. What we did not regret, however, were two weeks of the finest cruising we have ever had, and a whole village full of new friends.

XIII / ONGEA - FULANGA

The wind remained brisk and fair, pushing us along at six or seven knots, so that by noon we were approaching the wide, safe channel leading through Ongea's fringing reef. We were passed as we entered by a fleet of 10 outrigger canoes that were outward bound for Fulanga, an island five miles to the west. The 20-knot winds were gusty, and all crews were totally occupied with the tasks of sailing. We later learned that one canoe tipped over in the open ocean. Because Lau canoes are made of *vesi,* a Fijian timber that approaches the density and specific gravity of granite, they barely float when swamped, and are impossible to right at sea. Thus the crew abandoned their craft and were taken aboard another canoe, convincing me that (A) local boat-building must be flourishing; (B) it's good that the Fijians sail in groups; and (C) there really *are* obstacles to worry about when sailing at night.

Ongea was made up of two large islands and inumerable small ones. The land at sea level has been eroded by the waves, so that the islets looked like spectral mushrooms with unruly topknots of scrub. We anchored in a cluster of these small islands, completely protected. Each night at the cocktail hour, the western sky became inflamed with the rash of sunset. Suddenly the sky would be darkened by a great cloud of bats, flying north to wherever they feed. The mushroom islands, the solitude, the flaming sky and the bats bewitched the lagoon, and a feeling of expectation made me both surprised and disappointed that there were no leprechauns or hobbits darting in and out of the bushes. The hurricane season would not reach its peak until the months of January, February, and March, but we were in November, and hurricanes had been known to hit as early as September. So one of the first things we did was to look around for a place to hide, should one be forecast. A cove on the south end of the island would have been lovely and protected, but when we investigated it in the dinghy, we found that the channel leading to it was too shallow for *Sea Foam*, even at high tide. Another cove on the west side of the island had barely enough water at the entrance to allow us to pass. But inside there was seven to eight feet, and landlocked protection. If a storm threatened, that would be our choice.

We spent three days snorkeling, shelling, and exploring. There was a village, but the men had all left to go to a religious conference at Fulanga. We paid our respects, then anchored several miles away. Except for one visit in an outrigger by some teenaged boys, we had one whole end of the lagoon to ourselves. The weather was gentle-trade-tropical, the sky an everchanging pastiche of Rorschachian cumulus, the water clear, the reefs varied and inviting. We were loaded with food and water, and could have stayed for weeks. Instead, after three days, we felt restless and in need of a change. We had a lot to see. Time to move on.

Serenity, the big 'S,' is supposed to be so desirable. There are specialists—Zen gurus, for instance—who devote their whole lives to achieving the big S. The itch of restlessness is something to be got rid of, a sort of Herpes of equanimity, the shameful shingles of dissatisfaction. Siddhartha's final stage, where he sees himself as a molecule in the river of life, is supposed to be the penultimate S. The object of life is to go with the flow. Gentlemen don't sail upwind. Relax, accept, whatever, why not?

I've often peeked out from the bastions of Western attitudes into the greener pastures of Eastern thinking, and nursed a yen for Serenity. A Zen yen, if you will. It was one of the things I thought I might find by going cruising. But serenity for me was not the 'nothing' of Zen. It was the right thing to do in the right place at the right time. Thoreau, at Walden, was busy as hell, not only taking care of shelter and food needs, but working out ideas and setting them down. The most serene time that comes to my mind was when we were anchored in Robinson's Cove, in Moorea, and I was hard at work on *Blown Away*. I needed to be an actor, not a prop. If there were times when the script called for the actor to do nothing, so be it; but if there's too much nothing going on, the audience is going to go home.

Ongea was as beautiful a place as I have seen in this world. Not too long ago, the fact that I didn't want to stay there forever would have bothered me. But we had savored it, had tasted its sweetness, and just because we liked it didn't mean we had to eat the whole thing.

Having enjoyed our brief period of isolation in Ongea, we decided to anchor in front of a village in Fulanga. We presented *sevu-*

sevu (it was accepted) and were immediately taken under the wings of Paulini and Ted, a brother and sister in their twenties, both of whom spoke very good English. They told us that *Spirit,* a yacht that had visited Fulanga for six months in 1974, had successfully ridden out hurricane winds of 160 knots in a protected hole in the northwest corner of the lagoon. Because the hole is too small for swinging room, and because the holding ground in these islands is often only a thin layer of sand over a shelf of coral, *Spirit* ran lines to shore. The force of the storm is witnessed by the fact that all the houses in the village are newly built, replacing those that were blown away. I was reassured that we had a good place to take refuge if we should need it.

In order to balance privacy with gregariousness, we made it a practice to pull up anchor in the late afternoon and motor two miles up the lagoon to an uninhabited island with a picture postcard cove and beach. This insured undisturbed supper and sleep, and meant that in the mornings Craig, Nancy, and I could do our work. School done, we would power back to the village, refreshed and ready for more social doings.

The high point of our visit was a feast that the village gave in honor of the departure of their much-loved priest. The day before, most of the villagers went fishing. We took Ted, Paulini, and several younger boys and girls out to the reef on *Sea Foam.* Ted, exuberant and optimistic, claimed he would win the competition by catching the most fish. Paulini and the girls brought back a whole dinghyload. Craig speared a dozen. Ted caught only one, and the ribbing he got from the girls failed to diminish his cheerfulness, which he turned around into laughing praise for Craig's day's catch.

The feast lasted all day. The men sat around drinking kava, which they call grog. Kava is what they make from the yangona root. After hours of continuous drinking, the dedicated could achieve a state of relaxed drowsiness along with thoroughly flushed kidneys. I tried, having discovered that the taste was not quite as repulsive as I remembered, but all I got was the flush.

Most Europeans find native food palatable but not particularly appealing. Yams and kasava (tapioca root) are cooked in earth ovens until whatever moisture these starchy foods contain is driven out, after which it is served without benefit of butter or sauces. Fish is cooked in the same way, moisture evidently being a culinary anathema, and served whole—scales, skin, spines, eyes, and all. For dessert there was a pudding made from tapioca that had been whipped to a thick, glutinous mass. To this they added coconut, sugar, and coconut cream. We were served heaping platesful, did our best, and were unable to eat even half our helpings.

Ted and Paulini told us that attending a feast is the other occasion at which a visitor is expected to present *sevu-sevu*. In addition to the symbolic gift, Nancy had made an onion casserole, and we also brought three cans of strawberry jam. Jam is not the usual potluck contribution, but we thought it was one of the few things we had on board that might conceivably be shared by 70 or 80 people. Fijians love cabin biscuits, and we figured they'd put the jam on them. Not so. All the children lined up, each was given a teaspoonful, and soon the landscape was dotted with smiling children licking jam out of upturned palms.

The men sat together under a lanai-like shelter. A portable radio played music broadcast from Suva. Long silences were punctuated with laconic remarks. The checkerboard went the rounds, challengers challenging the champ. From time to time, one of the men would doze. It was, as a party, about as laid back as you can get.

Nancy sat with the women. Shrieks of laughter accompanied the Fijian women's earthy, extensive, and explicit conjectures about Craig's attributes, and it was finally moved (Craig opposing, Nancy abstaining), that he would remain in the village and marry one of the younger girls. And if he would like to impregnate more than one, he would be quite welcome.

The women put on a *meke*, a hand-dance performed in costume while sitting. They were accompanied by male and female singing, and by percussion produced by hitting split logs with sticks. One man, as always, beat time on the traditional biscuit tin. Craig had been instructed to walk down the line of dancers and sprinkle Johnson's Baby Powder on the women's hair and cheeks, but he missed his cue, and we never found out the significance of the baby-powder ceremony. We did learn that although the feast was in honor of the priest, the dance was done especially for us.

Ted was cheerful and friendly, as were most of the villagers, but Paulini was special, one of those remarkable people who bubble with warmth and good humor. When we first arrived, Paulini was our first visitor, poling her log raft out to where *Sea Foam* was anchored. Her dress, which reached to her ankles, had gotten completely soaked, and she laughed at herself delightedly. Nancy gave her the bread recipe she asked for, and on our return to the village the next day, Paulini presented us with two warm loaves of freshly baked bread. Nancy and Paulini exchanged gifts, material, patterns, and together one afternoon they cut out a dress for Paulini. When we left she hugged Craig, shook my hand, and embraced Nancy in an emotional parting of close friends. We had known her for three days.

We left Fulanga and spent two days in the Yangasa cluster, both nights in uncomfortable, roly anchorages, where we looked for elusive nautilus shells, and got chased out of the water by sharks. The morning of the third day we sailed to Kambara, and at 3 P.M. dropped anchor in the open roadstead off the main village. We rowed ashore, paid our respects to the chief, walked through the village. The chief walked with us, an old man using a cane. He asked if we could spare some cans of corned beef.

We went to the co-op store to buy a kava bowl, a large bowl with legs, the whole thing carved out of one piece of *vesi*. Among other items, on the shelf of the store was a big stack of cans of corned beef.

"How come you want corned beef from us?" I asked the chief. "Your store has loads of it."

"Ah, but I am a poor man," he said. Status but no dough. He was wearing a yellow shirt, and his smile showed heavy attrition from a lack of dental care. I rowed out to the boat, collected four cans of corned beef, and picked up a frisbee for the young boy who had guided our tour of the village.

On returning to shore I approached the co-op where we'd last seen the chief. Leaning out of the window was an old man wearing a battered smile and a bright yellow shirt. I handed him our gift.

"Pretty rusty," he said, inspecting the cans critically.

"They're fine," I said, peeved. It had been a long row in a stiff chop. "We had a can of it just last night."

"Oh, well, OK." He took the cans reluctantly, as if he was doing me a favor.

"That's not the chief," whispered Craig into my ear.

"Huh?"

"I said, that's not the chief."

"Oh Jesus," I whispered. "Are you sure? What do I do now?"

Nancy later pointed out that I should have left him one can. She is always right about these things, but she was off somewhere else and my composure had been shattered. I took all the cans back, apologizing, my face burning.

"They're not for you," I said. "I thought you were someone else. These cans are for the chief."

The laughter of the children, a pack that followed us everywhere and watched every move we made, was merciless, and whether it was directed at me or my hapless victim was hard to tell. I stumped off to the chief's house to finish my now-hated errand. Perhaps it was noblesse oblige, but when the chief looked the cans over, he didn't seem to think they were too rusty at all . . .

Impatient, now, to get back to see if we had word from Connie, we left Kambara that evening and arrived in Suva 32 hours later. Waiting for us was a letter from my mother who, having lost the sight of one eye three years before, had just lost the sight of the other one. Craig should be thinking about college, if he was going to go. I wasn't keen to sail *Sea Foam* around the world without him—taking on other crew was an option, of course; but our cruise, which till now had been a family affair, would then become something else. And if Nancy and I were to do it alone, I wanted a more simply rigged boat. The reasons were piling up. Perhaps, after the season, we would not point our bow west after all.

XIV / DECK LEAKS

Some boat problems can never be solved. I don't mean cosmetic work, which is demanding but which, if the results are good, can be infinitely satisfying. I mean problems that are ongoing—they can be dealt with for now, if you're lucky, but you know they'll recur forever. They have a way of wearing away the soul the way the wind erodes the mountain. Problems like this that Bug And Recur Forever are known to nautical analysts as BARFs. They appear simple, as if any dolt should be able to cope with them, and yet they resist permanent solution with the swivel-hipped elusiveness of Hell's halfback. BARFs have caused the most heroic sailors to become obsessed with the picayune, have made seagoing philosophers nasty and impatient, have turned brave men into wimps. BARFs, one of my pessimistic friends insists, are salts in the wound of Life.

There are many kinds of BARFs. High on the list is the Pernicious Irritating Nightnoise (PINs). PINs are more than just noises that occur at night. They are the noises that, as you lie in your bunk picking out the sounds around you, refuse to be identified. *There—that clicking's the vane rudder, a little sloppy in its gudgeons. The creaking—that's got to be the gaff, swaying in these light winds. The gimbals on the stove are making that squeaking. Maybe put a bit of grease on them tomorrow. But that knocking, what the hell IS it?* The knocking seems to grow louder, etching its waveform into my brain. Sleep is impossible.

"Nancy, do you hear that knocking? Any idea what it is?" *How can she sleep?* "Nancy?" (Nudge.) "Nancy!"

Nancy wakes up and murmurs something about how it's probably coming from the galley, but before we can discuss it she's rolled over and gone back to sleep. I am momentarily distracted from the noise while I construct a thumbnail analysis of people who can sleep, unaffected, through PINs, but having finished I'm once more captured by the insidious knocking. Thunk-thunk, thunk-thunk. (Pause, long enough to engender hope.) Thunk-*thunk*. Soon I am up, flashlight in hand, crashing around in the salon until I find the source. In this case it's the swing-out metal wing that supports the leaf of the salon table. With the leaf in the 'down' position, the wing swings to and fro about an inch, hitting the wooden leaf that amplifies the knocking like a sounding board. I wrap a rag around the wing and return to our bunk. Nancy, infected with my excess adrenalin and the profane search it provoked, has the light on and is reading. My attempts at conversation fail to win a response, and soon, in self-defense, I am reading too.

PINs rarely occur when the yacht is heeling under a steady breeze, and only show up when you're going downwind, or when it's calm enough that the boat is rolling from side to side. The children of a friend of mine, whom I'll call Marty, nearly drove their martinet-father crazy. During a downwind passage, each night the boys put a marble in the overhead between the liner and the deck. In the morning they'd remove it. Some accoustical phenomenon disguised the source of the sound, and Marty spent many a fruitless night trying to track it down. At breakfast, tired and irritable, Marty would demand, "Didn't either of you hear that noise last night?"

SON I: What noise, Dad?

SON II: Yeah, Dad, what noise?

Marty became sullen and uncommunicative. By grabbing short naps during the day he was able to conserve his strength for the night's hunting. Success always seemed to him to be just within his grasp, yet it remained elusive. He lost weight. His face took on a haunted expression. The sons were delighted, and the torture might have continued indefinitely had not Marty suddenly made an intuitive leap. From then on, whenever the noise occurred, he would wake up his sons and force them to join the search. Two nights of this and the noise ceased, inexplicably, forever.

Irritating as PINs are to certain kinds of people, mysterious topside leaks are even more disruptive. In his book, *Two On a Big Ocean,* Hal Roth dwelled on a deck leak with such insistence that in spite of the fact that his voyage was both colorful and adventurous, this pernicious but harmless (not life-threatening, anyway) leak remains uppermost in my memory of his book. Various efforts to find and cure the leak were described in successive chapters until it became obvious to me that this particular BARF was really challenging the Roths' equanimity. Experienced and intrepid sailors they surely were, but that didn't make them immune to the torture of dripping water.

There's a special type of leak which is noted in the "Yachtsman's

Guide to Psychological Attrition." It's known as the Stubborn Leak Over the Bunk (SLOB). In his book, *Song of the Sirens,* Ernest K. Gann revealed himself to be a nautical traditionalist and confirmed ascetic when it came to comfort or amenities at sea. Having admitted that he had a SLOB aboard his 115-foot yacht, *Albatross,* he went on to describe lying in his bunk and watching a can sway back and forth over his body. The can was suspended by a harness of marline. Drips that otherwise would have fallen on Gann, fell into Gann's can instead. Every hour and a half the can filled up, whereupon Captain Gann would arise, carry his can to the sink, dump it, and return to his bunk. For an indefinite period, at no time during wet weather did Gann get more than 90 consecutive minutes of sleep. Since reading his book, certain impromptu stopgap remedies aboard our boat have been dubbed "Gann Solutions." And it was Craig, I believe, who coined the phrase, "If you can't fix it, Gann it."

I've found patience to be the key to the treatment of a SLOB, particularly when it's on Nancy's side of the bunk. On *Sea Foam,* Nancy and I slept in a stateroom just forward of amidships. The size of our bunk was roughly a 120 percent single, speaking jibwise. But by fitting our limbs into a carefully planned pattern we made it serve as a double. When we first started cruising, during the night one of us would have to wake the other up to change positions. But this was finally worked out with a system of options: from position Y we could change to X or W without disturbing partner; to go to position S or T required a gentle shove, such as one might use to stop an enduring snore. All other changes required the wakeful cooperation of us both. Thus I was surprised and a little irked to be jostled awake one night to find Nancy still in position Y, having exercised none of her X, W, S, or T options.

"What's the matter? I just got to sleep."

"There's a leak," said Nancy, "and it's dripping on me."

It was the rainy season. We were anchored in Suva Harbor, and the skies had been dumping on us steadily for two days. There had been no sign of a leak before now, and in my grumpy sleepiness I was sure Nancy was making it up.

"Where?" My tone was that of he-demanding-proof, rather than he-concerned.

"There," she said, taking my hand and putting it under the cornerpost of the trunk cabin. ('Put' is such an amorphous verb. Actually she slammed my hand up against the mahogany trim.) There was no question. Clinging to the wood were several threatening drops.

"Seems warm enough," I said, rolling over and closing my eyes.

During the next half-hour my sleep was interrupted several times by Nancy crawling over me (it was her month to sleep next to the hull) on her way to and from the linen locker to fetch towels, which she draped scientifically over the lower section of her body. The next morning we exchanged only that information which could be conveyed in grunts.

The rain continued. I began to get an inkling that Nancy's and my relationship was deteriorating when she crawled into bed that night in a full suit of oilskins, knowing full well that I find both the texture and smell of slickers unromantic. The following night I came to bed and found that our pillows had been switched, and by the tilt of her chin I knew that even though her month wasn't up, we had definitely changed sides.

Two more nights passed before the rain stopped, during which I slept comfortably under a plastic dropcloth that I'd found in the lazarette. As soon as the deck was reasonably dry I went topside to find the leak. It was amazingly easy to find. There is a molding around the trunk cabin at deck level. Behind the molding were several tiny pinholes in the bedding compound. It was there, obviously, that the water was finding its way in. I made the pinholes large enough to fill with some polysulfide compound, flooded the deck with water and went below. No leak. Triumphantly I exchanged pillows, putting Nancy once more next to the hull.

"What the hell do you think you're doing?" Her eyes were flashing and her hands were on her hips, but I was grateful for the words that made up the first complete sentence she'd spoken to me in five days.

"Not to worry. I fixed it. I fixed the leak. It's fixed."

"Oh," she said, mollified. During the day her attitude toward me gradually thawed, and at cocktail time she displayed a mien that could almost be described as friendly.

In Fiji in the rainy season there are seldom many days between deluges. Two nights later I was awakened by the sound of a torrential downpour punctuated by unprintable oaths spoken in the mezzo-soprano range. I managed to fall asleep again, only to dream I was being stomped by a herd of buffaloes. I awoke to find Nancy crawling over me with a certain lack of consideration, her arms laden with towels. The rain continued throughout the following day, and that night I discovered that our pillows had once more switched positions.

Dry weather eventually returned to Suva, and I attacked the SLOB with thorough and determined logic. There was no way water could be getting in around the lower molding now. I could see that all the seams were intact. Therefore it must be leaking somewhere else. The seams in the foredeck had needed recaulking for a long time. The water must be getting into one of those seams and running downhill and aft until it could fall on either Nancy or me. I resolved to recaulk the whole foredeck and, at the same time, renew all the plugs. Two days later I exhanged the pillows again.

"Oh no you don't!" said Nancy.

"But it's fixed," I said. "We're incapsulated in wood and synthetics. I have virtually rebuilt the entire section of deck that could have any bearing whatsoever on water getting into our stateroom. Technology has joined with cool reason to triumph against encroachment. Our days of bondage are ended. I have emancipated us from the SLOB. We're free."

"We'll see," she observed, but left the pillows as I'd arranged them.

Meteorologigods obliged with a true test in the form of heavy rains that night, and I was awakened by a determined Nancy.

"Get the dropcloth," she said. She left no room for either misinterpretation or debate. By the time I'd returned with the dropcloth, the pillows were rearranged, and Nancy was dozing on the nonleak side. As I crawled over her into the wet half I thought I heard her mumble, "Sleep well, Emancipator," but I might have been mistaken.

Logic having failed, I decided to use a sort of Zen-ESP amalgam of my own design. I went to the SLOB area. I emptied my mind of mundane thought and allowed it to fly beyond the bounds of cause and effect. I closed my eyes. Occasionally in my effort to free myself from the chains of natural law I moaned a little. Days passed. I explained to Nancy that I was seeking inspiration on a mystical, quantum basis; and, quanta being unpredictable by definition, it might take me a long time. (This earned me a shrug.) I finally arrived at 'GO' by means of a combination of Western and

Eastern thinking. If the water is not entering through a logical place, I reasoned, it must be entering through an illogical place. (Sound of trumpets, French horns.) I went below and got some masking tape and laid out a series of lakes or reservoirs on deck, using the tape to make the banks of the lakes. I filled each lake in turn with water and went below to inspect. No leak.

I went topside again and sat on the cabin top. Suddenly I had it. The corner of the trunk cabin was a quarter round post, and the sides of the cabin were rabbetted into the post and the seam sealed with caulking compound. I had inspected these vertical seams and could find no fault, but there was an upper molding around the top edge of the cabin house. Could the water have gotten in there, run behind the molding to the vertical seam, and thence down *behind* the seam compound to the bunk below? Excited, I searched the upper molding for a sign of a leak. Sure enough, there were some small voids, which could be the culprits. I could hardly believe they were, however, as they were at least two feet from the corner post. But I was grasping at straws. I caulked the voids, but this time I refrained from bragging of success, nor did I change the pillows. My personal SLOB had humbled me; and besides, Nancy's month was over and it was my turn to sleep next to the hull. Of course this time the leak was truly fixed, and I was accused by Nancy of getting down to business only when it was in my own self-interest.

Some weeks later, we were joined in Suva Harbor by *Sea Witch*, *Sea Foam*'s sister ship and hull #1, owned by a family of five bent on world cruising. The owner-skipper was a man of strong opinions, high standards, and his vessel was gleaming, as Bristol as if he had just sailed her off the showroom floor. Identical to *Sea Foam* and several years older, *Sea Witch*'s appearance was such as to make me feel like a seagoing Pa Kettle. I was invited aboard. Handsome family, handsome yacht. Below was just as shipshape, just as spotless. Intimidated though I was by her condition, I was nevertheless interested in the variations of interior layout. When I got to the stateroom I noticed that it was exactly like ours, but with one difference: over the bunk and under the corner of the trunk cabin was a funnel hanging in a marline harness, and from the base of the funnel, a small, plastic tube led down the side of the bunk and into the bilge. My friend saw me looking at his handiwork and grinned. He pointed out that he used to have a can there, à la Gann, but that he'd had to get up every 90 minutes or so when it was raining just to dump it, and that disturbed his sleep. The can, furthermore, was subject to unsightly rust. One night he had awakened from a sound sleep, his lower regions soaked because the can had lurched with a wave, and had an inspiration. This new arrangement was the result. All plastic, it solved the problem simply and economically. I complimented him on his ingenuity, and he actually preened.

The next day I caught a bus into Suva and bought several items that I stored on *Sea Foam* in a very accessible place. Never again do I wish to suffer the domestic purgatory caused by an untraceable leak. When the next SLOB strikes I'll be ready with funnels and backup funnels, and plenty of plastic tubing. With apologies to Mr. Gann, I'll always be grateful to my friend, the skipper of *Sea Witch*, for showing me that not all of the answers to cruising problems are to be found in cruising books. There are some things you just have to work out for yourself.

XV / HURRICANE

One of our main reasons for spending the Southern Hemisphere's summer in Fiji was to stick close to a hurricane hole. We could have gone to New Zealand, which lies south of 90 percent of the danger. (We had already spent nearly a year in New Zealand and loved everything about it but the winter.) Or we could have stayed north in the Marshalls and weathered their winter westerlies. We chose Fiji because 'hurricane hole' sounded cozy and safe, and because it was a good staging platform from which to head west after the hurricane season was over.

There was also a certain momentum involved. We had planned to spend the previous summer in Fiji, but had been thwarted by weather considerations into going to the Gilberts instead. And one of the motives that powered our plan change was the promise to ourselves that if we didn't go to Fiji this year, we'd go next. So there was that.

And then there were all the peripherals, the kinds of reasons that tip the scales when major considerations leave the decision still in balance. Friends we hadn't seen in years would be there. There were lots of places to gunkhole that were close to Suva Harbor. There was the Lau group, which someone had described to me as "the most beautiful cruising grounds in the world!" There were boatyards, some marine supplies, and food was plentiful, varied, and cheap. American Express had an office in Suva, making the transfer of money to us from the U.S. both easy and quick.

Given the same set of circumstances, I would not now make the same decision. I would not spend the hurricane season in Suva Harbor.

The fly in the ointment was overcrowding. That year there were 30 foreign yachts whose skippers elected to hole up for the summer in Suva. Thirty yachts added to all the resident yachts and local fishing and small boat fleets were enough to cause a traffic jam when hurricane warnings sent everyone running for shelter and a fouled-up mess when strong, shifting winds repositioned too many boats anchored in too small an area. During our worst storm, when Hurricane Meli passed close to Suva but fortunately didn't score a bull's eye, all the damage to boats was a direct result of overcrowding. If Meli, whose maximum winds reached over 120 knots, had hit us full force, you probably could have put the remains of 30 yachts into one garbage bag.

In the beginning we had no notion of the dimensions of the threat. We concerned ourselves with seeing to our ground tackle, picking our anchoring spot, and planning where and how to store all our deck gear below. Game plan outfitted and outlined, we had done all we could except keep an eye and ear on the weather. Forewarned is forearmed, and we absolutely depended on being warned.

Impending dangers are the jumper cables that quickstart my motivation. When we were preparing to go to sea, I read all the info I could find about hurricanes. 'Hurricane' is a title of degree, bestowed on tropical storms that are having tantrums. 'Fury' describes a hurricane's most prominent quality. Blind fury is frightening, and I prefer not to be in its way.

The North Pacific High is my mnemonic guide to the wind's patterns. Sailing from Hawaii to California in the summer, you're advised to go north over the high for favorable winds. That helps me remember that in the Northern Hemisphere the winds revolve clockwise around a high. A hurricane begins as a tropical depression (low), and its winds circle the low in a contrary direction to that of winds circling a high. Just to complete this theme of opposites, in the Southern Hemisphere everything is reversed. With Fiji being in the southern latitudes, we knew that the winds of any hurricane we encountered would form a pattern like this:

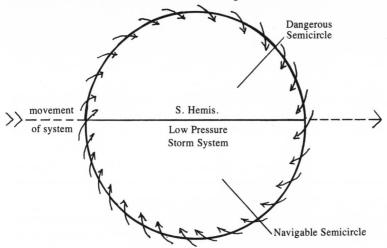

We also had to take into account the fact that the whole wind system travels, and as it matures it can move at speeds of 20 knots. The arrow through the figure divides the storm into two semicircles, and indicates the direction it is traveling. In one semicircle the movement of the storm adds to the speed of wind (with regard to a stationary point), and in the other subtracts. Sum and difference. The sum half is called the dangerous semicircle, the difference half the navigable semicircle.

One more point, just to keep things in perspective: the force of the wind (on a stationary object) increases as the square of its speed. I have spent a few miserable nights at anchor in 30-knot winds, knowing that the force exerted by 120-knot winds would be 16 times as great. When a hurricane threatened, this fact alone made me consider trading *Sea Foam* in on a cave.

Before satellites, radio, and record keeping, sailors were dependent entirely on watching the barometer, and on "reading" the ocean's waves and swells. A skipper might get a few hours warning from this, but no more. Suppose he got six hours warning while at sea, and in six hours his boat can travel 40 miles. Forty miles *might* make a difference to him. But the difference between sailing 40 miles in the right direction and 40 miles in the wrong direction is 80 miles, a more significant distance, particularly in the case of the tight-assed, tornadoish, small-diameter storms that are characteristic in the South Seas. So in the old days you kept an eagle eye on the barometer, kept a record of wind shifts, watched for widely spaced swells, and hoped to God you guessed right. Experience helped; but even so, many more boats got caught in hurricanes then than do now.

Today, using information from satellites, weather bureaus can normally give us several days' notice. (Exception: when the hurricane forms right over you.) The weather will broadcast that a low is developing, and where. At any stage of development a hurricane can dissipate, but if it matures, it goes from tropical disturbance or depression (low) to tropical storm to hurricane.

Statistics reveal that hurricanes have occurred in certain areas according to a seasonal pattern. Historically, the months of greatest threat in Fiji have been January, February, and March. The 'season' starts in September and goes through April. On an average, six or seven hurricanes will occur somewhere in the Southwestern Pacific during the season, and some part of Fiji will be hit by two or three of them. But a particular place in Fiji, such as Suva, Nandi, or Levuka, can go for decades without seeing hurricane-force (64 knots or more) winds. So if you hole up somewhere, the odds are excellent that you won't be hit. After much agonizing, Nancy, Craig, and I decided to take the chance. Nevertheless, it was a crapshoot with our boat and, as experience would prove, with our lives. Fortunately we rolled our point, but I'd think twice before risking another pass.

It's breakfast time. I've managed to come up with tea and coffee, and have retired to let one of the real chefs take over. This morning it is Craig, making pancakes, cooking bacon, filling the cabin with good-to-be-alive smells. Sipping reassures me that my smoker's/drinker's mouth is merely encrusted with the detritus of pleasure, and that flushing it repeatedly will revive moribund taste buds. Thus comforted, I turn on the radio to WWV. The two tones that beep out the seconds form a minor third, and their insistent repetitions give me a sense of permanence.

"They're playing our song," I say. The humor is jaded—I've made the same remark some dozens of times—but it serves to notify whoever cares that I'm alive and willing to speak. An answering silence tells me that everyone is still groping through pre-conscious fog.

"Tropical cyclone Fay is near 10 south, 175 east, moving south 5. Winds at center, 40 knots. Radius gale, 50 miles."

It's an effective reveille. The sleep curtains of privacy are raised. Glances zap from Connie to Craig to Nancy to me. Is this going to be the one?

I turn off the short wave and turn on a local station. Fiji weather broadcasts roughly the same information. A tropical cyclone alert is in effect for northwestern Fiji. And though Fay is moving slowly, my speedy calcs conclude that if it grows and continues to move in its present direction, it will wipe us out four days from now. And there's no reason to believe that it won't do so even sooner.

WWV broadcasts are the definition of promptness, and mental alarms cue us to tune in to the weather just a minute or two beforehand. Radio Fiji, however, is not nearly so hung up on time. The schedule, published in the local almanac, is ignored, and we find to our frustration that we are always tuning in late. I hate to have the radio playing constantly, but eventually I quell my quirk and let it play, adding fuel to my distaste for all things that threaten me, and Fay in particular. Fay continues to move in our direction, biding her time and intensifying.

By next morning Fay has grown in strength (to 50-knot winds) and girth (to a gale radius of 120 miles). Still over 300 miles north of us, the storm continues to move toward us. Now a few boats make their move, reanchoring in the places they've selected to ride out the weather. We remain behind Mosquito Island, waiting and seeing.

The reasons for waiting are at least two. For one, we still have plenty of time. Fay can turn and go in another direction. The second and most important reason is that there is no sense making haste to stake out 'the best place,' even if we knew what the best place is (we don't). But what might be the best place from a technical point of view—i.e., most protection, best holding ground—will not be the best place if everyone in the harbor decides to anchor there. In my nightmares I see a bay of bouncing, bumping boats. Brr.

The following morning—it is now 48 hours since we first heard of Fay—she boasts winds of 60 knots, with gale force winds 150 miles from the center. The first gusts will hit us in 10 hours. Many boats that have been tied stern- or bow-to the Tradewinds' quay cast off and reanchor in the bay, making that particular small area even more crowded. We are undecided whether to move over by the river mouth or stay where we are.

Suddenly I have an anxiety compulsion I can't resist. Although our ¾-inch nylon rode is still serviceable, it's by no means new. Over the years it has chafed through and broken, and subsequently been spliced. After months of lying-to an anchor in coral sand, the line has probably picked up a beach full of abrasive, enough to cause God knows how much internal fraying between the fibers. Cancer of the rope. Time to replace.

"Do we really need it?" asks Nancy, her eye on the balance sheet.

"My stomach acids say we do," I say.

"Can we afford it?"

"What's afford? It's insurance, actually. I can't face a hurricane with iffy rope." (We had a working rode of 300 feet of $^5/_{16}$-inch chain—the rope rode was extra.)

"And how come you didn't think of this before?" she asks.

"Because," I say, "hurricanes are suddenly real, scary, not just a number in a book." No matter how much you read, until you've stared down the barrel of a killer's gun, you have no idea of what it was really like at the OK Corral.

There's no nylon line in Suva's marine supply stores, but I do find 250 feet of 1-inch polypropylene and 72 feet of ⅜-inch short-link chain. I buy it, and arriving back at the Tradewinds I discover a group of yachties surrounding a dense cluster of dead Bloody Marys under which, somewhere, I assume is a table.

"Happy Hurricane!" The speaker is the owner of a 26-foot, shoal draft sloop who has managed to get his vessel up the river and snugged down in a forest of mangroves. His self-satisfaction would have irritated me if I didn't remind myself that during thousands of miles of blue water sailing we were undoubtedly far more comfortable than he.

"You all set up the river?" I ask.

"Be'r b'lieve it," he says. Suddenly I wish our draft was five feet or less so that we could get up the river too. And I would love to have the Bloody Mary that is offered, but I refuse. I say good-bye to the group and row moodily out toward *Sea Foam,* up-the-creekers' parting toasts echoing in my ears. Nancy greets me as I arrive.

"Suva weather says Fay's going to pass north of Viti Levu," she says. "They predict we'll get winds no stronger than 30 knots max."

"Fantastic," I say. "It's a reprieve." A great weight falls from my shoulders. Somewhat sobering is the possibility that Fay will turn around and hit us from the other direction, so I'm glad to see that Craig has already done some preparing: jib stowed, awning down, sailcovers lashed with extra line, and everything movable put below. We ready extra anchors, but because Suva weather continues to reassure us that the storm is passing, we don't put one down. After a good supper we go to bed, my usual forebodings uncharacteristically dormant.

Something wakes me a little after 1 A.M., and I go on deck for a look. The wind has changed directions 180 degrees—indicating that the storm center has passed us—and is blowing 25, gusting 30. We are so well protected from chop that *Sea Foam* is virtually motionless. The only indication of anything unusual is the whine of wind in the rigging.

I sit in the companionway, lip-chewing. Should I wake the crew and put out another anchor? The wind seems to be steady, our present anchor is holding. Wouldn't I be being overcautious? Then, while I am still debating, *Sea Foam* swings broadside to the wind, drags 150 feet with startling speed, and goes hard aground on the mud.

I start the engine, thinking that if the mud is soft, *Sea Foam* can bull her way into deeper water. No way. However, the roaring engine does succeed in getting everybody topside.

The first thing we need is an anchor set offshore to keep us from going further up as the tide rises. I row out with the anchor, while Craig pays out 300 feet of rode. When I toss the anchor over, one of my oars goes with it. I drift back downwind to *Sea Foam*, steering with my one oar, and finally retrieve the other, which Connie had spotted drifting by. But my temper, fueled with embarrassment, has taken creative flight, and the air in my vicinity is filled with the ozonic smoke of electric invective. My attitude is hardly improved by the simultaneous appearance of a rain squall and a drunk Fijian in an outboard who, when he isn't actually hindering us by trying to help, is threatening to cut our lines accidentally with his propeller.

To set an anchor, you pull on the line till the anchor bites into the bottom. Craig and I heave together. Unbelievable! By hand, using no windlass or winch, we haul the 40-pound Danforth, 72 feet of chain, and 250 feet of line all back to the boat. I am now convinced that while we were asleep the bottom where we are has turned to grease.

Craig rows the anchor out this time, and we are only able to pull back 20 to 30 feet of line. Now one anchor, at least, is set.

Our next job is to retrieve our truant plow anchor—the one that betrayed us into our present dilemma—and reset it. With such treacherous holding ground we are not about to trust only one. Once again Craig and I, without the use of the windlass, hand over hand in all 200 feet. I row it out again in a slightly different direction, and once more it appears it will slide all the way back to the boat. Suddenly it catches with a definiteness that indicates it has hooked on a rock.

With both anchors set, there is nothing to do but wait for the tide to come up. By first light we're afloat, and it's a simple and uneventful task to reanchor in deeper water. We have endured an uncomfortable and worrisome night, but the only damage has been to our sleep and self-esteem.

(Fay, having missed Suva, attacks Fiji's eastern islands. Sustained windspeeds of 60 knots are recorded by weather stations. Several villages are destroyed, and one is inundated by a tidal wave. One life is reported lost.)

Fay was a fire drill. There was a great shift of boats from where they were to where they went. Some problems to which we'd given a low priority were upgraded. We had a chance to talk tactics with other skippers. But we still didn't have a gut understanding of what it would be like if a hurricane nailed us with a Sunday punch. Meli would teach us more, but even now, with my increased respect for the wind's force, I don't believe I can fully comprehend a hurricane's raging capacity to deal out terror, destruction, and death.

On February 15, *Sea Foam* and several other boats set sail for the Astrolabe Reef, 40 miles south of Suva Harbor. A flotilla cruise, it was just the opposite of a reach for seclusion. In the middle of the hurricane season, eight boats were cruising the Astrolabe. The Astrolabe would be a terrible place to be caught by a hurricane, as it provided no place to hide. The island of Kandavu, close by and to the south, offered a good bay for one or two boats, but certainly not for all of us. The bay was on Kandavu's north shore and about an hour away, but I don't believe any of us had ever been down there to have a look. *Sea Foam*ers certainly hadn't. In an emergency, with no buoys or beacons, piloting into an unfamiliar bay would require clear visibility for spotting underwater hazards. The hours preceding a hurricane would most certainly be overcast, making the water opaque.

So what in the hell were we all thinking of?

I know what *I* was thinking. I was thinking that we'd have plenty of time to make it back to Suva. If not, I might head for the bay I mentioned, or maybe for one farther away on the south side of Kandavu (which I'd never been to, either). But those plans were necessarily vague, because if I'd clarified them I'd have had to face the reality that poor visibility would make them unworkable. Going to sea wasn't a very good option, in my opinion. Nearby there were too many islands and reefs to be blown onto. To get far enough away to have what I'd consider ample sea room for a hurricane would require leaving port long before most of us would be convinced that the hurricane was going to move on us.

So we just assumed that our number one plan—going back to Suva Harbor—would work. A fool's paradise can be as reassuring as any other kind.

By the time the end of March rolled around, the fear that we might be hit by a hurricane had weakened. The worst months were over. In our Sailing Directions, whose incomplete statistics covered the years 1904–23, a little box showed that the South Pacific would see 2.1 hurricanes in March, 0.3 in April. Only half of these would hit some part of Fiji, favorable odds indeed. Complacency had moved aboard and was unpacking her things . . .

The low that hangs over the ocean in the space between eastern Fiji, Samoa, and northern Tonga fails to excite anyone. Even when it's upgraded by Fiji weather to a cyclone with winds of 40 knots, no one pays much attention. After all, it's 400 miles away and forecast to move southeast. Poor Tonga, we think, compassionately. How unlucky to be hit, even by such a dinky storm, with the season so close to being over. It's March 26, after all—practically April. Bummer.

March 27 is a morning like many others. Coffee and tea lift our eyelids to half mast. A knock on the hull brings me topside. It's Peter.

"Hurricane Meli is headed this way," he says, sitting in his dinghy and holding on to *Sea Foam*'s bulwarks. "It's supposed to be here this evening sometime. Right now they're talking about max winds of 50 knots."

"Shit, I thought we were out of it. Want to come aboard?"

"No thanks. I think I'll row around to the other boats. People aren't monitoring the weather that closely any more."

"OK. Thanks a lot. I sure wasn't listening, either."

I go below and turn on the radio. Eventually we hear the hurricane alert, broadcast every hour on the half-hour (give or take 10 minutes). Meli's approaching, all right.

Of the skippers who are tied up to the Tradewinds' quay, one or two will stay put, but most are going to anchor out, adding to the congestion. Some will move over to the river mouth. *Sea Foam*ers talk it over, and we decide to reanchor, farther from the channel, but still in the Tradewinds Bay. We have no appetite to go back where we were during Fay, even though where we've chosen to anchor doesn't offer much room.

After lunch we make our move. The winds will likely come up out of the southeast and swing clockwise 180 degrees. We lay out two anchors, one to the southeast, the other to the west. Now we can control our swinging if the wind does as it should. This is important in a small area where boats on moorings will swing in a small circle, while boats on anchors will swing in much larger circles. I don't like the situation, and once again consider our decision to stay in a harbor where there are so many boats. But there's no time for that now.

We've miscalculated and placed our anchor so that we lie too close to another boat that's on a mooring. We could solve the problem by taking in some of our scope, but we decide we'd rather move the anchor. By now the winds are blowing 30 knots and gusty, but this doesn't bother us. We are completely protected from seas, from fetch. We move our poorly placed anchor about 150 feet, but before it sets we've dragged it back to within 20 feet of where it was when we started. We decide to leave it, as the wind is already shifting, and soon we'll be lying off our second anchor, too, and the problem will be solved. The hour's worth of hard work wasn't necessary, but who's to know?

Supper is a dish of nerves (I'll have seconds, please) with paranoia for dessert. The radio now ups its forecast to maximum winds of 60 knots, but our bed is made. There is little left to do but worry, so I go topside to watch the fury build.

The wind has already backed around from south-southeast through south and is now south-southwest. This clockwise shift tells me that unless the storm changes its path (which is possible) it will move in a westerly direction and pass us to the south. We'll be dealing with the navigable (less violent) semicircle, something to be grateful for. I'm also grateful for the hotel. Its blazing lights give solace in the rainy blackness, beacons of a battle shared.

The boat that earlier lay dangerously close to us now lies a comfortable distance away, and with the wind change all the other boats have repositioned as well. One by one I pick them out and identify them. On the far side of the bay, a ketch is slowly dragging its anchor. There are people on deck taking care of the matter, and people on the decks of other nearby boats prepare to cope, to defend themselves by fending off. Everyone I know who has sailed for any length of time has dragged anchor, but I find it unnerving to see someone having so much difficulty so early in the storm. Better now, though, I think, than later, when the full strength of the wind will make remedies difficult, or impossible.

I go below. It's my turn for the dishes, but Nancy has done them, freeing me for captainly concerns. I'm only half grateful, as there's a part of me at the moment that would rather be a dishwasher than a captain. I turn on the radio, and we hear that the hurricane winds have begun to blow.

"Tell us about it," snaps Nancy. The weather isn't the announcer's fault, but anger helps, and he's convenient. The worst of the storm should be over by morning, we learn. It's always nice to know the tunnel does have an end, even if you can't see the light yet.

"We'll stand watches, naturally," I say. "The usual rotation: Nancy nine to twelve, me till three, Craig three to six. OK?" It's OK. "Check topside every ten minutes at least." Everything is a compromise. In Fay, we broke loose our anchor and went aground in under three minutes. But most emergencies will be caught with checks made every ten minutes, and to have someone sitting in the driving rain for three hours would increase our safety factor very little. At least that's the way we all feel about it, and such feelings have a truth of their own.

Sea Foam, lovely old wooden boat, is a marvelous womb. Below, with the hatches closed, the sounds of the storm are far away. Sometimes I can't sleep under stress, but other times I can drop off like a cat. This night I drop off, and am surprised that Nancy should awaken me so soon.

"It's not soon," she says, handing me a hot cup of coffee. "It's midnight. We've swung around some more. Otherwise, everything's about the same."

I go topside. The air is warm and moist, but it's not raining. The gusts are stronger, and the whine in the rigging is awesome, but with no seas and no rain much of the terror factor is missing. I orient myself to our new position. Across the bay the same ketch is dragging, whether again or still I can't tell, and two other boats are having trouble, as people are on foredecks doing anchor drills. I get the feeling that ketch has been the cause of misery to more than her own crew, but she is also comic relief, and for this I love her. We swung a full 180 degrees, and I figure we'll lie in this position for the rest of the storm. Good, because our anchor is holding, and no other boat is too close to us.

Below I make another cup of coffee and check the time till the next weather report. There's 20 minutes to wait. I'm looking forward to hearing about Meli on the radio. Usually it happens that the weather misery we're having never makes the airwaves, leaving us feeling like unsung gladiators battling phantom enemies. This time I'm sure our battle will be recognized, and the news will validate the seriousness of our struggle.

It starts to rain again, and a terrific gust catches us off the bow and heels us over. I rush topside and am dumbfounded at what is going on. In 10 minutes we have swung another 50 degrees and fetched up in a nasty position. In front of us by no more than twenty feet is *Kenosha,* a ferrocement ketch. Behind us, her bowsprit no more than five feet from our mizzen boom, is *Sea Witch,* our sister ship, with all hands on deck. Behind *Sea Witch* is an island, so close that there's no way she can drop back. What was a well-disposed defense has realigned into a nightmare.

The noise of the engine starting brings Craig and Nancy rushing on deck. *Kenosha* takes in about ten feet of scope, we take in five feet, and *Sea Witch* drops back five feet. By 1 A.M. we've done what we can. The wind is now gusting 60 or better, and the rain is like grapeshot. I can barely see what only a few minutes ago were the brilliant lights of the hotel patio. Craig and Nancy go back to their bunks, and I sit in the companionway. The hatch is open, but the wind is blowing so hard not a drop of water comes in. The air is warm, the only good thing about tropical hurricanes, but I'm cold from tension and fatigue.

Because we are helpless. The boat in front of us has no engine, and there is only a couple on board. No way can her skipper reanchor, even if he wants to, which he probably doesn't. After all, he's been moored there for months. *Sea Witch* and *Sea Foam* have intruded on his territory. But we can't possibly reanchor. Our chain goes directly under *Kenosha,* and since we've shifted, our second anchor is almost directly in line with our first. *Sea Witch,* last in line, has the same problems we do. If *Kenosha* or *Sea Foam* should drag even a few feet, we'll all be in trouble.

Sea Witch and we run our engines much of the night, jockeying the boats for just a few feet more clearance and easing the strain on the anchors. Daylight finally comes to rout Darkness Fears. The weather remains nasty, but the gusts gradually grow less strong. By noon we've retrieved our ground tackle and have reanchored in our old spot. Meli has passed, leaving us shaken and tired, but otherwise intact.

We go ashore and give thanks at the Ritual of the Grateful Bloody, and learn what happened to others. Who acted cool, who panicked. One 50-foot fiberglass ketch had its anchor line fouled by a commercial fishing boat, and had to spend the storm tied up alongside the fishing boat's steel hull, receiving considerable damage from the bashings. Ashore, trees were downed, cane fields flattened, streets flooded, and two people lost their lives. A bad enough storm, but the weather warnings worked, our defenses held (barely), and our decision to risk laying over in Fiji is vindicated.

Or is it?

Forty miles to the south, a 40-foot trimaran and a 30-foot sloop were cruising together at the Astrolabe Reef, where *Sea Foam* and others had been cruising only six weeks before. The sloop's skipper had a ham radio aboard and was in the habit of talking daily to other hams in the Fiji area. He didn't come up on the air Wednesday morning (the day after Meli), nor on Thursday morning. His friends were worried.

Thursday the *Fiji Times* was full of pictures of Meli's mayhem. But 24 hours after the storm, the report was still that only three people had been killed. A plane hired by the *Times* flew over some of the outer islands and reported whole villages wiped out, the houses and grass huts flattened or completely blown away. The plane couldn't land, however, and with communications out, there was no way to know about injuries and deaths.

Ngau, just north of the storm's path, reported winds of 110 knots. People survived by sheltering in a government-built, cement-block building. With many communications facilities knocked out, and especially those in villages hardest hit, circumstantial evidence cried out that there must be pockets of tragedy, places in desperate need of help with no way to call for it.

On Thursday evening, 36 hours after the storm had passed, a radio operator (with no training in electronics) at the station in

Nakasaleka finally hooked up the antenna wires properly, and the story of what happened to the village of Ono finally got through to the authorities in Suva.

The small island of Ono was located in the lagoon formed by the Astrolabe Reef. The night of the hurricane, most of the villagers took shelter in the stone church. The church collapsed, killing 21 and injuring others. Not a house was left standing. There were dozens of injured. Aid was desperately needed.

The next day, sea planes flew down to bring the most serious cases to the hospital in Suva. On one of the first flights was Eric, skipper of the trimaran, frantically seeking searchers to help him look for his father and fiancée, both of whom were missing. Eric's story, as I remember it, was as follows:

The morning of the storm, Vern, his wife, and a friend set sail for Suva to pick up mail. When Vern heard on the radio that Meli was heading west, he feared that Eric might not get the news, and came back to warn him.

The two friends discussed the options: (1) run for Suva Harbor; (2) try to get into the little bay on the north shore of Kandavu; (3) stay put. They decided to stay put because the forecast predicted winds of only 50 knots; because they were worried about whether they could make it back to Suva and get secured before the storm arrived; and because if they stayed where they were, they had a whole day to rig ground tackle.

The two skippers dove down and secured their anchors, in some cases wrapping the chain around a coral head. They cleared the decks and stowed everything below. Then they waited.

The last forecast they heard upgraded the expected windspeed to 60 knots. Frightening forces—history recorded at least one reaction of "oh, shit!"—but one could still reasonably hope to deal with them. Nevertheless, as darkness fell and the winds began to blow, each skipper had a hunch that it was going to be a far worse storm than they had suspected.

Before long their worst fears were realized. The wind blew so hard it was sometimes impossible to take a breath while sitting in the cockpit. Spume blown off the surface of the ocean combined with rain to make an opaque wall of water. Dressed in wetsuits to protect themselves from the stinging rain, Eric and his fiancée went up in the cockpit. Eric ran the engine to take some of the strain off the ground tackle.

In the sloop, Vern and his crew prepared for the worst by donning wetsuits, and getting fins and snorkels ready. They also put their passports and money into plastic, ziplock bags. The force of the storm was terrifying, the noise unbelievable. The wind actually dismasted the little sloop, and the fact went unnoticed by the crew sitting in the cockpit. It was only later in the lull of the 'eye' that they saw what had happened.

Suddenly the winds flipped the 40-foot trimaran upside down, throwing Eric and his fiancée out of the cockpit into the water, and trapping Eric's father inside. Eric swam around calling his fiancée's name, but it's doubtful he could have heard her or she him, even if they'd been screaming in each other's ears.

The eye of the storm brought respite from the wind, the spume, and the noise. Eric could see the flashlight carried by Vern's group as they swam ashore. He knocked on the trimaran's hull and begged his father to dive down through the hatch and swim out, but the father, a poor swimmer, said he couldn't adding that he'd had a full life and that Eric, whom he loved very much, should save himself. Eric, frantic, and with some unformed notion of getting help from the others, swam ashore. Before the four could take any action, the eye passed over and the storm was on them again. They could no longer stand up. It was all they could do to crawl on their bellies to the high ground at the center of the island, where they found some shelter under an overhanging rock. When morning came and they could see, there was no trace of either yacht.

Searchers later found some wreckage of Eric's trimaran, and the body of his father. His fiancée was never found. Vern's sloop sank where it was anchored, and was not found until several weeks after the storm, long after Vern had gone back to the States.

Hindsight makes brilliant tacticians of us all, but the fact is that the outcome of any of Eric or Vern's options depended on Meli's caprice as well as on other unknowns. Even if the two skippers had chosen to do something different, Meli could have acted differently too. If those of us who 'prudently' took refuge in Suva Harbor had been hit with the killer force winds that struck the Astrolabe, we too would have lost our boats and perhaps our lives.

The change in my attitude brought about by Meli is more one of degree than of substance. In making a future decision to remain in Fiji during hurricane season, the possibility of being hit by a killer must be given more weight. An ounce of prevention—staying out of the area—is by far the safest choice. Failing that, I would gear my defenses vis-à-vis ground tackle and a sheltered anchorage to a superstorm and little warning time, rather than to a storm of 60 to 70 knots and three days advance notice. In other words, I would plan for the longshot worst, and be grateful if the extra work and expense was unnecessary.

Misguided by the weather information on the radio, Eric and Vern greatly underestimated Meli's potential and had the bad luck to be hit squarely by the dangerous semicircle of a superstorm. But the rest of us in Suva Harbor were also remiss, and must share some of the responsibility. It was only the spin of the wheel that made them and not us the victims.

XVI / UP YOUR MAST

W ooden masts are dying out. Today's new generation of sailors will, in the twilight of their lives, remember the slapslap of Dacron on aluminum with the same degree of nostalgia my generation holds for tar and oakum, canvas and manila. The Moderns are multiplying, overwhelming the Traditionalists by sheer numbers, and although there are still a few Trad cells dedicated to the cult of wood, their role is more Curator-of-the-Heritage than State-of-the-Art Sailor.

And if wooden masts are dying out, so, certainly, are the deadeyes and lanyards of yesterday's shrouds. No longer is it even necessary to know how to do a wire splice, as shrouds are made to order at the factory. They may even be rods instead of wires, and be swaged to their end fittings by machine. Mods point out that the technology is superb, and that the new rigging supports the mast better and fails less often than ever before.

But even though there is far less likelihood of a shroud or stay (and therefore a mast) breaking under load, the possibility does exist. When it happens, today's boatman is not expected to fix his own gear himself, but to pull in to a shipyard which, if it can't fix or replace the broken item, will have a new one flown in. I'll concede that there's nothing wrong with this way of living if you have plenty of money and are always within reach of a shipyard and competent service. I'll also concede that it would be nice (for a change) to have frustration stem not from a rebellious splice or an obdurate nut and bolt, but rather from the failure of minions to do my work as well or as fast as I would like. However, the farther we sailed from urban shores, the less likely we were to find minions capable of doing a decent job, and even less likely to find the needed parts.

A Trad can almost always find something to work with, however. Rope and chain, nuts and bolts, wood and fasteners are all available in almost any port. When all is said and done, the best way to go is still the old style, where you carry your independence with you in the form of tools, parts, and the knowledge acquired from books, manuals, magazines, other cruising sailors, or best of all, from experience.

The best experience is to build your own boat, and those who did so were unquestionably the most able and helpful of cruising skippers. Second were those who had rebuilt or restored one that was run down. Third were those who'd had years of experience maintaining boats—either theirs or other people's. Finally there were those who, like myself, were learning through trial and error what it took to maintain their own particular boat.

Whatever his experience, each skipper felt as though he was an expert on the care and feeding of his own craft, and any inference to the contrary would draw angry and sometimes everlasting reactions. I always rejected anyone's suggestion that we *Sea Foam*-ers either had become or were becoming expert sailors. First of all, it wasn't true. Second of all, the responsibility scared me—I didn't want to be a nautical authority. Leave that to the real sailors. However, I did feel that we were becoming expert *Sea Foam*ers, which is quite a different story: expert in making our boat go where we wanted to go, in keeping her together, in making a life aboard her that was fun and rewarding. Any threat to this cherished self-image I greeted with the extreme reactions of the insecure.

One such threat was to have a guest whose seamanship was unquestioned go forward and look up *Sea Foam*'s mast while we were under sail. Upmast-looking is something a one-upper should be trained to do from birth. Coupled with lip-pursing and head-shaking, it is the single most intimidating act that you, as a guest, can do to an inexperienced skipper. Fredrika Long, solitary round-the-world voyager and author of *Singlehanded Sex,* pointed out that *mastus erectus* is a male potency symbol equalled only by the Washington Monument, and any threat to its adequacy strikes archetypical discords of unbearable stridence.

We sailed *Sea Foam* for almost two years before I ever sighted up her mast under sail. Furthermore, I had sailed on very few other boats, and had never looked up their masts, either. I was like an adolescent who'd never been in a locker room shower. When I finally did look up *Sea Foam*'s mast, I had nothing to compare with what I saw—no 'norm'. To be candid, I never did develop a feeling for what the ideal working *Sea Foam* mast should look like. And it follows as the day the night, if you don't know where you're going, you can't get there from here.

The first person I remember looking up my mast was a guest who was daysailing with us in the Bay of Islands, New Zealand.

DB was a pleasant young man in his thirties who had sailed around the world several times and logged roughly 10 times more sea miles than I. If I had listened or asked questions I could have learned volumes. As it was, I devoted my psychic energies to defending my skipper's self-image. A budding circumsailor, I'd gotten this far without his help, right? What could a young upstart possibly tell me about my own boat? Defenses of this kind are the most important qualifications for membership in the AA (Assholes Anonymous).

Sea Foam's mainmast was thick up to the spreaders, four-fifths of the way to the top, at which point it continued upward at a smaller diameter, giving the visual effect of a clippership's topmast. When we were flying the jib in stiff breezes, tension of the jibstay would pull the tip of the mainmast forward, bending the mast at the spreaders. This is what DB pointed out to me, beginning what was to be my four-year battle to tune the standing rigging so that this bend would not occur. I was never totally successful. Constant fiddling with the stays and shrouds helped, but success was in percentages (less than 100).

One obstacle to a satisfactory solution was the designed-to-be-sloppy, deadeye-and-lanyard rig. The stretch inherent in the lanyards made some movement of the mast inevitable. There were no permanent backstays, so the fore- and headstays had no counterpart aft. Aft support came from the rake of the mast, the shrouds, and from the springstay and running backstays. The design had serious weaknesses, I now realize, but at the time I hadn't enough experience to know that the oddball rig we'd bought was not sacrosanct, and that I could have made some changes for the better. As it was, I merely tried to deal with what I had, and ended up feeling frustrated.

The main reason for worrying about a mast bend is the fear that it will be followed by a mast break. I gradually became convinced that some bend in our mast at the spreaders was not threatening; because it was supported there by shrouds, forestay and running backstays, the out-of-column aspect wasn't important as long as it didn't exceed a certain point. But what was that point? One afternoon in Majuro on a daysail in a brisk breeze, Don Coleman sighted up *Sea Foam*'s mast, and signaled me to come take a look. I'd never seen such a bend, and though I later lessened it by adjusting the standing rigging, I wondered what the limits of the mast's flexibility would be, and hoped I would never discover the answer.

Following this, we sailed from Majuro to Tarawa and then Fiji, most of which was hard on the wind, and some of which was in stiff (20–30 knot) trades. On two occasions the mizzen running backstay (which supports, through the springstay, the tip of the main) let go because of a hardware failure. Thank God I wasn't sighting up the mainmast at that point—the sudden strain must have bent it like a longbow. In spite of the backstay failure, the mast didn't break. However, we may have cracked it, as later events would prove.

Two friends, Ian and Claire, flying back to New Zealand after having delivered a boat to the U.S., broke their flight in Suva in order to spend a few days with us. Ian had built his own 40-foot, ferrocement sloop, built his own ham radio at age 14, and was for a time one of BMC's top motor mechanics. His competence aboard a boat was exceptional. The five of us took *Sea Foam* to the nearby island of Benga, powering all the way (there was no wind, a matter, perhaps, of good karma) and ended up anchored in a little cove on the west side of the island. It was early March, still in the middle of the hurricane season, and the weather was heavily humid with a sultriness that was unrelieved by the frequent thunderstorms. The water in our cove was murky from fresh water running off the hills that both protected us and made us the focus of venturi-amplified winds.

The side of the cove where we first anchored was less sheltered from the gusty squalls than the other side, so we decided to move. The decision was poor. We got to the other side without incident, only to discover that the holding ground was bad, and that there were too many coral heads and no swinging room. Then, in coming back to our first spot, we ran aground on a coral patch. Craig, in the crosstrees, saw the patch only as a shadow and could not judge its depth. Fortunately we were going slowly, there were no squalls for the moment, and we were able to back *Sea Foam* off the coral with no trouble. Afterwards we put out two anchors against the blasts of wind that assaulted us, and because we were on a lee shore where a dragging anchor would have seen us on the beach in less than a minute, we stood watches. Soon, however the weather improved, and we were able to relax for dinner and a good night's sleep.

I don't know what got into Ian. He was not by nature a one-upper (though he would be superb at it if he chose), and when he sighted up my mast I knew it was because he wanted to find out what was going on and not because he wanted me to feel badly. But for some reason, having sighted up it, he decided he wanted to *go* up it. And he wasn't aloft three minutes before he made me feel very badly indeed.

"You've got big trouble here," he hollered down from the cross-trees. "There's a crack in the mast, and there's rot inside."

The sinking feeling in my stomach was intense. Ian descended, and I went up in the bosun's chair to have a look. There was no question about it. Right at the spreaders where the diameter of the mast decreased was a flat shoulder of wood on which sat a bronze collar. Around the collar were tangs to which were fastened the shrouds, forestay, main throat halyard, and staysail halyard. Just above the collar was a crack in the wood, across the grain, and when I put the blade of the knife into the crack, there was no doubt that I'd struck rot.

My first question then was and still is, why hadn't it broken? Why hadn't it snapped in any one of a dozen situations during which we'd been sailing hard with the jib up? When the running backstay failed? And had it cracked under stress and the rot gotten in afterward, or had rot started first, weakening the mast and causing the break?

The next day as we powered back to Suva violent thundersqualls and lightning underscored my gloom. Ian and Claire had to return to New Zealand to ready *Nunki*, Ian's sloop, for a trip east around South America and up into the Med, but they offered to interrupt their plans so that Ian could help me solve our mast problems. Much as I would have appreciated his expertise, I refused the offer. He and Claire had seasonal weather to contend with for their own trip, and I would have felt guilty delaying them.

I felt guilty enough as it was. It's a skipper's job to know what's going on everywhere on his boat. The way our mast maintenance had worked out, I had taken the job of varnishing the mizzen and Craig the main. But the responsibility to check for trouble is solely the skipper's. It had taken a guest to discover trouble that I should have been aware of.

Once, in the office of a movie producer, I saw a beautifully calligraphed sign on the receptionist's bulletin board: ASSUMP-

TIONS ARE THE MOTHERS OF FUCKUPS. Assuming that something is OK without checking is asking for trouble. But this is only one of the roads to oversight. Another is just plain losing track of when you last checked something. When was the last time I'd gone aloft for a look? I couldn't remember.

One way to avoid Mother Assumptions is to use inspection schedules. The list we used on *Sea Foam* for maintenance, Nancy called our 'born again' list. As fast as chores were crossed off the top, new ones would be born again at the bottom. But we never applied time factors that would have made our list a schedule. We decided to varnish the spars when they looked like they needed it, and we figured that in the process of sanding and varnishing we'd notice anything wrong with the mast or rigging. But without specifically deciding to *look* for trouble, often you don't see it.

I associate trouble shooting with diagnosis of an ailing system. But a check-up means you go *looking* for trouble, ailing system or no, and this takes courage. Trouble can be expensive, time consuming, and often frustrating and baffling. Sometimes I was courageous, and sometimes I wasn't. And sometimes I was so reluctant to confront the possiblity of certain kinds of trouble (like rot in unreachable places), I would avoid thinking of it, and eventually block it from my mind.

I never could learn to welcome trouble, which is silly. Trouble faced at a time and place of your own choosing is far better than a surprise attack at sea during a storm. But why should I get into the grimy bilge to inspect the electric bilge pump? Turn it on, and if it works, leave well enough alone. Never mind that the bilge pump hose might have worn through (a rat once ate a hole in ours), the wires frayed, or that the bilge might have accumulated a kind of debris that made clogging the pump a foregone conclusion. Twice our pump clogged up at sea in rough weather. Once a matchbox had worked its way down from a locker. Another time, sawdust from a project in the forepeak made its way aft. Both times, while being tossed about by seas and working up to my armpits in sloshing bilge water, I had the chance to reflect on how much easier it would have been to take care of the problem in the sunny sanctuary of our last anchorage.

Strongest of all motives for an if-it-works-don't-fix-it approach is the Can Of Worms syndrome. COWs are inevitable, particularly on an old wooden boat. Something that looks like a snap to fix turns out to be but one link in a chain of problems which, once discovered, leave you no option other than to fix them all. One day, on a daysail in Suva Harbor, a friend pointed out that a cheek-block for one of the running backstays was starting to come loose from the deck. Back at anchor I tightened down on the lag screws. They seemed to bite, but on a hunch I removed one. It looked perfect, bright, fine. I tapped it with a hammer and half of it fell away in the sickening manner that crystalized bronze has of destroying your confidence. Of the four lags, three were crystalized. "Why wasn't the block through-bolted in the first place?" I demanded huffily. By the time I'd drilled all the way through the deck, the deck beam, and the sheerclamp, and removed much of the galley to gain access to attach the nuts, I realized why. A day and a half later, having repaired only the port side, I logged the end of my bout with another COW.

So, as we powered back to Suva and watched the lightning lance the hills and trees of Viti Levu a couple of miles away, I thought about aluminum masts, and how they don't ever rot. I thought about our coming battle with the trade winds as we tried to make our way home to California. I thought about the time it would take to have a boatyard fix the mast, and the money it would cost. I visualized *Sea Foam*, dismasted and helpless in midocean, and knew we were lucky to discover the trouble while we were in a good position to deal with it.

So why was I finding it so hard to feel properly grateful?

As soon as Ian and Claire left, I made the rounds of Suva's shipyards. There were three possibilities. The government shipyard couldn't squeeze us into their schedule for six months, Carpenter's yard for four months. The third yard, and my last hope, agreed to send a man out to inspect the mast and give me an estimate. One week later I got a message that they, too, were too busy and unable to help me. The whole process—many trips to town on the bus, hunting down the right person to talk to and having to return for an appointment because he was busy now—took three weeks. March became April, time grew short, and we began to get desperate.

The three weeks were not a total loss, however, as during my quest I had been able to research available types of wood. Our masts were made of straight-grained, Sitka spruce, the best, but of course there was no Sitka available in Fiji. My next choice would have been Douglas fir, and Fiji used to import tons of it. Recently, however, they had planted their own stands of fir, and to protect their fledgling industry they'd banned Douglas fir's importation. In true bureaucratic fashion, imports were banned before their own stands of timber had reached harvest size. The result: fir was unavailable.

I made two bus trips way out into the boonies to the government forest products labs to see what local woods might be suitable. The buildings were modern, the personnel courteous and helpful. Each type of wood was displayed in a kind of museum of woods, with descriptions of each one's characteristics and uses. One of the commonest, a wood called Dakua Macadre, seemed to be best suited for masts, and after I'd determined this on my own, I checked out my decision with the head of the lab. He confirmed my choice.

The next step was to find a carpenter who could take on the job of scarfing a new section into the old mast. Leroy, a man who had built his own boat, figured that together we could do the repair in the Tradewinds parking lot, behind the dive shop. I had a tarp, and we borrowed some others to make a shelter to keep the mast dry. Using a block and tackle from the yardarm of a friend's schooner, we plucked the mast and laid it on *Sea Foam*'s deck. Three of the hotel maintenance crew helped us carry it ashore. A trauma for me was to saw our mast in two. Psychologically it felt like circumcision without benefit of gas.

Leroy and I went to three lumber yards before finding a pile of select Dakua to choose from. We bought six two-by-tens, twelve feet long, and glued them together with resorcinol to make a solid, twelve-foot ten-by-ten. The hotel loaned us their pickup to haul our juggernautical creation off to another friend of mine at Fiji Woods, a woodworking shop with a bandsaw big enough to shape logs. We cut long, male V's on each end of our timber, then carted it back to the Tradewinds and inserted the male V's into the female V's we'd made in the lower and upper sections. At first they didn't fit well, but a half-day's work with a handsaw made them fit closely enough for a strong glue joint. Using 18 borrowed clamps, we put together a whole mast with a square timber for a midsection. It took a couple of days for me to scrounge up an electric plane to shape the timber, and another week for Craig and me to strip off all the old varnish and apply five new coats. The end result was a mast that was *nearly* straight, and I was pleased. I thought I knew its strength, and I was sure I knew its cost—about one-quarter the cost of having it done in a yard. When another friend offered the use of his mainsail gaff to step our new stick, *Sea Foam* was back in business. From unstep to step, the project had taken three weeks.

But peace of mind was not as healthy. I was sitting at the Tradewinds pool one afternoon after the mainmast was repaired and restepped.

"What kind of wood did you use?" asked a New Zealand expatriate, a seaman. I told him. "That's terrible wood for spars," he assured me. "Jim Speir used it for his spars on his outrigger canoe voyage from the Gilberts to New Zealand. Every one of them broke. It's real brittle—you'd better watch it."

So in spite of the fact that I sat there with a handful of literature from the Fiji Forestry Department—test results that showed Dakua Macadre to be both stronger and more limber than Douglas fir—I was suddenly insecure. No matter that another friend later told me, "There's always some asshole who's got to say something like that after the fact," I couldn't forget what the New Zealander had said. Every chance I got, I inspected our repair for signs of weakness, and though it survived every blow, I was always worried that it would fail during the next one. The bottom line is that if you really want to shake a skipper's confidence, go for his mast. It'll get him every time.

XVII / SUVA - SUVAROV

When we first decided to sail back to California instead of sailing on around the world, we planned to sail south from Suva toward New Zealand until, as we neared New Zealand and the winds became favorable for sailing east, we would curve around in a great swoop and end up in Tahiti. From Tahiti to Hawaii is a 2,300-mile piece of cake; and the 3,000-mile sail over the Pacific High to San Diego is, in the right season, a milk run.

"But we've been to New Zealand," said Nancy.

"Are you ready for the alternative?" I asked. "Beating against the trades for 2,000 miles? In *Sea Foam*?"

The enormity of the prospect silenced us all as we considered our fat, comfy home, whose reluctance to go to weather was only exceeded by our reluctance to try to coax her to do so. There's a saying among cruising folk that gentlemen don't sail upwind. But the fact is, you don't even have to *be* a sailor to go downwind. For example, you could go from the Galapagos to the Marquesas, 3,000 miles of favorable trade winds and current, without ever raising a sail. If you did decide to put up any sail, the idea would be to get it up, make it fast, then kick back and enjoy the scene, man.

On the other hand, we had to take into account our previous trip from New Zealand to Tubuai (one of Polynesia's Austral Islands), an off-the-wind but stormy and soggy saga that soon exhausted our reserves of humor and dry clothes. The thought of climbing out of a warm bunk and into clammy clothes several times a day made me shiver, and my admiration for intrepid, weather-defying skippers was qualified by the thought that I'd rather see than be one.

"Why don't you talk to George?" asked Nancy.

Nancy's suggestion that I consult someone else never fails to infuriate me. The implications are clear. (A) I don't know what I'm doing. (B) So-and-so *does* know what he's doing. (C) If I weren't so stubborn, maybe I could learn something. Having sailed X number of miles and finding most of the places I aimed us at while avoiding the obstacles in our path, I considered myself experienced.

"Of course you are, darling," was Nancy's answer, "but George has delivered three boats from Samoa to Hawaii, and he *knows.*"

Grumpily, I consulted.

"I just tack along a corridor between 10 degrees south and 14 degrees south," said George, knowingly. "The east-west current isn't as strong there as it is nearer the equator, and the trade winds are lighter than they are farther south. I try to make all my easting before I head north."

"Sounds easy," said Nancy, nodding with the reverent attention she reserved for consulting experts.

"At least it'll be warm," said Craig.

"We can stop in Tonga and trade all our old clothes for baskets," Nancy added. Baskets, high on Nancy's passion list, were somewhat farther down on mine.

"You know, if you're patient, you can wait for the right winds." George was confiding now, equal to equal, sharing skipperdom's secrets. "The trades blow like hell for 10 days to two weeks, but then they drop off. Sometimes after that you get some really weird wind directions. Usually you can count on a slant." A slant in this case meant wind from anywhere other than due east, thus making one tack more favorable than the other.

Even talking to George we weren't completely convinced, but at least we felt it wasn't *totally* crazy to adopt a plan that would allow us to stay warm.

We motored nearly all of the 450-mile passage from Suva, Fiji, to Vava'u, Tonga, so that by the time we reached Vava'u, we had no more idea of the strength of our mast than we did when we left Suva. But more than a month of gunkholing in northern Tonga's protected anchorages and dramatic scenery convinced us the mast was strong. We left. Nancy was happy because *Sea Foam* was loaded with baskets and no longer encumbered with our old clothes. Craig was happy because the ocean was calm, and there was a good chance that this time he wouldn't get seasick. I was happy because the trades, which for two weeks had blown their brains out, had finally died.

Our destination was sort of Suvarov, 850 miles to the east-north-east. I say sort of, because one of the ways to defeat a wind god determined to slam you with headwinds is to have multiple objectives. (Another way is to leave port with a bunch of boats that are heading in another direction, the idea being that even if you're a wind god, you can't screw all of the sailors all of the time.) Thus Nancy, Craig, and I loudly asserted that Niue Island or Palmerston Island would be lovely (due east); Aitutaki would be delightful (southeast); and Pago Pago, though north and not very far east, offered the enticements of cheap diesel, cheap liquor, American groceries, and old friends, not necessarily in that order. Sort of Suvarov, however, was where we wanted to go.

Nancy and Craig really enjoyed our good weather, but I could not, knowing that the only thing it could do was get worse. Our second day out we found ourselves in a trough of variable winds, squalls, calms, and sloppy seas. During the night the wind rose to 30 knots, and we labored along under reefed main and staysail. Then, early in the morning, an uncommonly strong gust teamed up with a bellicose wave and knocked us down. Among the sounds of chaos—the clatter of the cutlery drawer as it popped out and strewed its contents all over the galley, the crash of the kettle as it leaped out of the sink and flew two feet to slam into the stove— was a sickening thud, and I looked behind the companionway to find that the box containing our three batteries had torn loose from its moorings. Bad luck: I'd planned other diversions than disconnecting wiring, removing heavy batteries, and rebuilding a battery box in the confines of a boat made punchy by slugging seas. On the other hand you could call it good luck, too, in that if a small tool box hadn't gotten in the way, the battery box would have slid a couple of feet further and taken out all the wiring, the diesel fuel line, and lodged in a virtually inaccessible hole.

Normally I saw nothing wrong in relaxing with a book while Nancy and Craig were topside doing sanding, painting, or varnish work. After all, we each worked at our own pace. However, I was absolutely incapable of doing a messy, dirty repair job without involving everyone. The sight of someone lying on his bunk in cool, clean detachment while I sweated, dripped and performed unappreciated miracles of improvisation infuriated me. Craig must fetch and carry, Nancy must hold the light, and both must keep up a continual chatter of encouragement and praise. Without this support I was reduced to fuming, swearing impotence. With it, usually only achieved by coercion, my amiability grew in inverse proportion to theirs. The battery box job took four hours, and whereas

I ended up with a cheerful feeling of satisfaction, the crew finished by acting petulant and put upon.

The weather worsened. By nightfall, we'd double-reefed the main and were being forced northward by an unsympathetic, 30-knot wind. My first celestial fix in three days showed that my DR was 60 miles too optimistic. A note in the log (entered long after the fact) pointed out that if you divide 60 miles by three days of current and leeway, the loss per day is not all that great. But taken in a lump it was hard to swallow. Going to weather was turning out to be work, and not the easygoing pleasure of lazing downwind.

Nine days after leaving Tonga, we were 90 miles west-south-west of Suvarov and happily able to lay a course only 20 miles north of it. During the past seven days we had been hard on the wind on the starboard tack, and all the standing rigging had loosened. Even the stretch inherent in our sloppy, deadeye-and-lanyard rig couldn't account for that much slack. Because of this, we were forever tuning the running backstay to keep the mainmast as straight as possible in the strong winds. The scarfed-in piece of Fijian Dakua was proving itself, flexing nicely, but it was nerve-wracking, knowing that the only way we'd discover the mast's limits would be to break it.

At midnight we turned south on the port tack. I was worried, because it was impossible to see how the mast was doing in the darkness, and thus impossible to properly tune the port running backstay. Just before dawn, a violent squall hit us and tore the mizzen running back turning block right out of the deck, taking three planks with it. We tacked immediately, amazed that the mainmast had survived. It had all happened before on our Tarawa-to-Fiji passage, and we knew what to do. We quickly took the strain off the masthead by lowering the jib (the main had been double reefed for days). This done, we put *Sea Foam* back on the port tack and power-sailed, hoping the engine's help would add enough speed to get us into Suvarov before dark. I managed to grab a few sun lines between squalls, and my estimated position gave us hope. At 1500 we sighted High Island, westernmost *motu* (islet) on Suvarov, and by 1700 we realized there was no way we could make it through the pass before dark. We decided to heave to for the night.

Like everything else to do with boat handling, heaving to is something that needs practice. On several occasions I've risked my reputation for sanity by spending half an afternoon backing and filling to see how *Sea Foam* reacted under various conditions of speed and rudder, how much way she carried, how windage affected her, how tightly she turned, and at what point she began to lose steerageway. A do-it-yourself, know-your-boat project. But I had never analyzed how much *Sea Foam* sideslipped and forereached when hove-to, and now I could only guess how she would behave.

We were five miles north of Suvarov. I began with the premise that the southeast wind would push us to leeward at one knot. From the pilot chart I figured the current to flow southwest at one-half knot. Fore-reaching (forward drift, as opposed to leeway) would be desirable in our case, working us slowly to windward and making our next day's sail a little freer. Hove-to on the starboard tack with double-reefed main and staysail flat amidships (not backed) and with the helm lashed hard to windward, I estimated we would fore-reach at one-half knot. Solving the vectors, I concluded that by dawn the next day we'd be 16 to 20 miles north-northwest of the pass. This conclusion had all the validity of any conclusion that's based on three premises, one of which is wrong.

Gray, grim dawn revealed that we'd get no celestial fix unless the weather improved, and that heavy and nearly continuous rain squalls made visibility as poor as you could get. (Fog, in this part of the world, is unknown.) The wind blew 30 knots—even harder in the squalls. With double-reefed main and staysail, and with a few hundred revs from the engine to help us point, we careened across the faces of 20-foot waves like a skier on a breakneck traverse.

By the time we'd covered 30 miles we knew we were lost. The main had a three-foot tear, acquired when the reef tiedown at the leech cringle had chafed through, putting a sudden increased strain on the next reef point. The three torn-up deckplanks left a gaping hole, and water that we took on deck was going directly into the bilges. If we couldn't find Suvarov, what should we do? Continue on to Hawaii in our nearly-disabled vessel? Put back 450 hard-won miles to Samoa where there was a shipyard? Angry and frustrated, we decided that no matter how long it took we would heave to till we could get a fix, by which time, we all gloomily agreed, the current probably would have pushed us halfway back to Tonga.

There was something about rough windward passages that made everything seem worse than it was. It came from the constant heeling, from pounding into the waves, from the wind wailing relentlessly in the rigging, from water finding its way everywhere. Tension had built up in each of us. The repair list had increased as the square of the number of days spent beating into strong winds and big seas. We were depressed by the knowledge that we'd thousands of miles left to go before reaching Hawaii, and instead of a delightful interlude of rest and relaxation, our visit to Suvarov was looking like a sentence of two weeks at hard labor. Nancy seemed more down than any of us, probably because she knew we'd have to take everything washable off the boat, rinse or wash it to get rid of the salt, hang it up to dry, and then stow it all again. The repair of the mainsail would probably fall to her, also.

(Subsequently, when we were sailing reefed for long periods, we'd add a second tiedown at the leech cringle, loosely tied. Then, if the working tiedown let go, the sudden strain would be taken by the backup tiedown, and not by the sailcloth at the first reefpoint.)

The wind dropped, the seas leveled, but the skies remained leaden (300 percent cloud cover, if you counted all the layers). We bathed and shampooed in the nearly constant rain, but even this failed to have its almost sure-fire cheering effect. I decided to encourage the crew by starting on the chores, and fetched my rigging knife topsides. Within 30 seconds I had cut the fleshly part of my forefinger to the bone, and the dramatic spurting of blood made Nancy cry.

We were all agreed that wind and current had doubtless forced us to the west of Suvarov. Still, there was always the outside chance we were east of it. Suvarov was a symmetrical, diamond-shaped atoll with seven-mile sides and with points at the cardinal points of the compass. Almost all of its *motus* were in the northern half of the lagoon. The southern half was mostly reef awash and was extremely dangerous to approach. Two years earlier, in clear weather, we'd found ourselves approaching from the southeast, but that time visibility was perfect. This time we'd tried to do it right, making our approach from the north, hoping by so doing not to become another statistic in Suvarov's alarming total of wrecks. Now we were hove-to with no idea where we were. If west, we would drift away from it. If east, we would drift toward it. Feeling foolishly overcautious, when night came we decided to stand watches.

Nancy woke me at 2330 and tumbled into bed, exhausted. I fixed a cup of coffee and went topside. The wind had shifted. Now a mere zephyr teasing the sea's surface to tiny feathers, it was blowing gently out of the west. The overcast remained total. Our world had shrunk to cocoon dimensions. All would have been serene but for a sonorous underlayment of sound, like a squadron of jets taking off in the distance. Like tympani. Like *surf!*

Napehairs at attention, I summoned Craig on deck.

"How far away?" I asked him. He would have no more idea than I, but his opinion would help me think.

"Three miles," he said, cocking a knowing ear.

"We're *east* of it."

"Right on, Sherlock," he agreed.

My nerves insisted we were really much closer than three miles, but no matter. I started the engine and powered for one hour due east. I was sure we wouldn't drift back to the breakers in the five hours of darkness that remained. By dawn we had drifted back just far enough to pick up the sound of the breakers again. Daylight proved that the reef was still a full, unbelievable *eight* miles distant.

My inner critic later reminded me that for the second time we'd approached Suvarov from the dangerous sector; that I should have had a better idea of how fast *Sea Foam* would fore-reach when hove-to; and that if the wind had continued to blow hard from the east, shrieking in the rigging and drowning out all other noise, we'd have been pushed up onto the reef before we ever heard the breakers, whether we were standing deckwatches or not. As it was, luck was with us, the wind shift made the acoustical conditions perfect, and we were able to locate the reef from what must be the maximum distance for hearing surf.

Three hours later we were at anchor in Suvarov's familiar and favorite lagoon. A 25-pound yellow-fin tuna, caught as we came in the pass, lay on the floor of the cockpit. Thirteen people from six other boats shared our barbecued fish on the beach that evening. Squiggling our toes in the cool, coral sand and watching a flamboyant sunset, Nancy and I looked out at *Sea Foam*'s regal silhouette. The sharp edges of the memory of our passage had already started to blur. Much of our easting had been won. Our doctored mainmast had passed a tough test. One way or another we'd make the repairs *Sea Foam* needed. I looked at Nancy, and our smiles reflected the fact that we'd been right to choose the warm way. If we'd had to face our new set of problems in cold, rainy weather, I knew for sure we'd have turned back. As it was, the pure pleasure of life in this idyllic setting had already pumped up our flaccid resolve.

XVIII / COMMIES / AMERICANS

W hat are we going to do?" demanded Nancy, plaintively.
Usually she was the positive one, while I tended to be negative. Being out of phase—at opposite ends of the attitudinal scale—was not necessarily being at loggerheads. Rather, it brought balance by keeping the tenor of our ways more even. When we were *in* phase, elated or depressed together, the graph of our moods showed spikes or peaks, too many of which left us giddy. (Example: out of a clear blue sky on a Sunday in 1971 I suggested we give up our lucrative jobs, sell everything, buy a boat, and set sail for the South Seas. Because we happened to be in phase at the time, our setting sail two years later was inevitable.)

Now, however, Nancy's pessimism was being offset by my determined optimism. I knew that in her present state of mind she'd jump at any suggestion to sail back downwind the 450 miles to American Samoa, sell the boat for whatever price we could get, and hop a plane for home. Determined not to let this notion take root, I was bustling around busily making notes, humming, chewing the end of my pencil, assembling tools and materials, and acting as if everything was under control. No one was fooled.

Our problem was that we had to deal with a mind-numbing list of repairs. The most serious item (we thought) were the three deck planks that had been torn up by the mizzen backstay. We had to refasten and recaulk them, and then secure the ripped-out turning block in such a way that the same thing couldn't happen again. Other repairs on our list were less dramatic, but the length of the list was boggling. With thousands of miles left to sail, the crew's morale was registering 'discharge'.

"Furthermore," I said to Craig, "we've got to find out why the hell the rigging loosened so much. Someone will have to go up the mast to see what's wrong." Craig, who in conversations of this sort is used to responding to the name of 'someone,' had started to move even before I'd finished speaking.

"You should see it," said Craig, after inspecting the mizzen-masthead. "You know the tang, the way it sits on a flat shoulder of wood? Well, it's sunk down into the wood, peeling back the outer layer like a banana skin. It must have gone down an inch or more." His description ordained that I go up and have a look for myself.

The tang, a bronze collar, had been forced two inches down into the endgrain of the shoulder on which it rested. I assumed that this was just wear and tear from our punishing windward passage from Tonga, and at first I thought I could repair it from the bosun's chair. Twenty minutes of trying to use a hammer and chisel among all the shrouds and lines that collect at the masthead convinced me I couldn't.

"No way," I said, on regaining the deck. "We'll have to unstep the mast and lay it down where I can work on it."

Had we not had the recent experience of removing our mainmast for repairs, the thought of unstepping our 40-foot mizzen (which stood almost as tall as the main) while anchored at an uninhabited island might not have occurred to me. But quite frankly, if I couldn't fix it, I was prepared to sail the rest of the way to Hawaii as a cutter. Fortunately, I didn't have to put this resolve to the test. Three skippers from other boats in the lagoon spent an hour assisting us, and by using the main gaff and a block and tackle, removing the mizzenmast went smoothly. It was one of the few times I've been grateful that we had a gaff-rigged main.

When I removed the tang and inspected the area underneath, my heart sank. The reason the wood had peeled back was rot. After I'd chiseled away the peels, we all stood and stared. The sight was as attractive as gangrene, and just as insidious.

A little digging with a knife disclosed the cause of the rot. Someone had routed out a channel in the otherwise solid mast, and had laid in a coaxial cable for a radiotelephone antenna. A subsequent owner had run a wire up the outside of the mast for an anemometer, and had secured the wire to the mast with bronze boatnails. Not knowing the location of the cable (whose channel did *not* run down the central axis, but was close to the surface), he had, unwittingly, driven one of the nails right through the cable, short-circuiting it. The sudden malfunctioning of his radio must have mystified him for a time, but once he'd diagnosed that the coax was useless, he'd cut off the ends and sealed up the holes. Although even now the seal looked OK, it had leaked, water had gotten in, and rot had started. It was our karma to discover this when we were about as far as we could get from shipyards, carpenters, lumber mills, and hardware stores.

One good thing about a rig that uses deadeyes and lanyards: a person has flexibility if he feels like shortening his mast. Luckily we'd ordered our new mizzen sail cut shorter so that we could raise the boom to clear the windvane.

"We can always lower the boom again if we have to," I said, to which Nancy grumbled that, in her opinion, Fate had already done so.

Bravely I dug out the rusty crosscut and bravely sawed. Eleven cuts and 11 inches later I stopped to assess. Any further mastshortening would make it necessary to resplice all four of the shrouds; and although I had done some wire splicing in New Zealand, I figured now that if I didn't absolutely have to, I didn't want to. Besides, the rot had already decreased from 60 percent of the cross-sectional area to about 10 percent, and I chose to believe that it would, if I persisted with the saw, shrink to nothing in the next cut or two. I decided to stop where I was, arrest the malignancy with an epoxy rot-killer, and trust to luck that there wasn't another pocket of rot further down the inside of the mast. (The only way to find out for sure, Craig pointed out, would leave us with an impressive pile of one-inch spruce discs, and no mast.) Within three days of unstepping it, the mast was back in place. The deadeyes looked a little silly, being only seven inches apart instead of matching the main's eighteen inches. The two-foot, decorative mast tip was missing. And the mizzen shroud pinrails were at leprechaun level, forcing us to get down on our knees when making fast the halyard (a not-unreasonable position, given our present circumstances). Nevertheless, I felt confident that we had strengthened the mast enough that it would get us home to California.

One week later we had completed nearly everything on our list, including replacing the torn-up deck planks; refastening the backstay cheekblock to a new timber that spanned two deck beams; and Nancy had washed the salt and dirt out of all the cushion covers, pillow covers, pillow slips, sheets, towels (bath and dish), and all our clothing, and had repaired the three-foot tear in the mainsail. It was then that she made a declaration of independence.

"To hell with this working dawn to dusk. I think we should start quitting early enough to have some fun, like walking on the reef, or visiting one of the other boats, or snorkeling."

"How about a picnic?" I suggested, sneaking a glance at the list of things left to be done. "Over by the wreck. We can pick up some diesel while we're there."

"Hardly what I had in mind," said Nancy. However, she and Craig both brightened at the prospect of an adventure and a change of scene.

The wreck still lay there washed up on the southern reef, the only object higher than sea level for five miles. Two years before, when we had syphoned off 90 gallons of diesel fuel, we had made only microscopic inroads into the tons of fuel that remained. Now we hoped to tank up for the next leg of our homeward voyage. There was a nasty rumor that a large motoryacht had been through Suvarov and had tapped the hold, taking what fuel they needed, and then letting all the rest drain into the sea. We couldn't believe that someone could be that selfish, and fully expected to find that there was still plenty of fuel left for the taking.

We anchored on a sandy patch and, armed with syphoning hose and jerry cans, rowed one-third of a mile across the reef to its outer edge, where the wreck lay stranded. A quick inspection proved that people could be that selfish after all. We rigged a syphon, but in short order discovered that the liquid that was left in the tank was mostly water. Sobered by the knowledge that we'd have to make our last, long leg to Hawaii with a minimum amount of fuel, we rowed back to *Sea Foam* and sailed back across the lagoon to our anchorage.

That evening, everyone got together on the beach to fry fish, boil coconut crabs, and overeat. I was still fussing with the idea of getting diesel from the wreck, and wondered aloud if I could count on diesel and water not mixing. By airing my problem I learned that one young skipper had served some time on a tanker.

"You're right," he told me. "Motor oil will homogenize with water to a certain extent, but diesel fuel won't. The whole operation of a tanker is geared to this. They fill empty tanks with water for ballast, clean them with water, and they couldn't do this, of course, if there was any danger of the water and oil mixing.

"Funny thing, they use a special paste called 'thieving paste,' stuff that turns purple in water. Tanker captains used to steal a little bit of fuel from each bunker and sell it on the side, making up the difference by adding water. Now they've got this paste that they can smear on a dipstick so they can tell how deep the layer of

water on the bottom really is, which keeps the captain from thieving." Then, with the panache of a magician pulling a rabbit from
a hat, he added, "I just happen to have some thieving paste on
board. You're welcome to use it."

Armed with the magic paste and a dipstick, we attacked the
wreck a second time. The dipstick showed a total of 18 inches of
liquid in the hold, but only the bottom 13 inches turned purple,
indicating water. Carefully fixing our hose to draw only from the
top five inches, we were able to syphon off the 70 gallons we
needed. Later we used the paste to check all our fuel containers,
and were comforted to learn there wasn't a trace of water in any
of them.

One by one, all the other yachts departed. No feeling can equal
having a whole, South Sea island to yourself. With our boat repairs
finished, we now had the time to enjoy it. Small chores remained,
but mostly we spent our days walking the reef, exploring the island, or snorkeling.

One evening I caught a shark on a hand line, and having noted
a little smoke oven erected by an earlier visitor, I decided to smoke
some shark meat. For two days we tended the fire, periodically
checking our progresss, and because the idea (and most of the
vigil) was mine, I had a heavy investment in the outcome. For
days I chewed on the charred, desiccated disasters in defiance of
the crew's obvious distaste. It was two weeks before I finally admitted the truth and tossed the whole lot overboard.

We moved to the Seven Sisters, a cluster of *motus* on the eastern
reef. The largest Sister was a rookery for thousands of terns, frig-
ate birds, and boobies, and as we walked around the island I was
reminded of the Hitchcock movie, *The Birds*. We were the nervous
targets of numberless powerdives, with the boobies, by far the
most aggressive, bottoming out a scant three feet above our heads.

At night we went walking on the reef looking for lobster. We
found them, green-shelled and red-eyed, usually tucked up under
the ledges of the ubiquitous tidepools. Having spotted one, we
would transfix it with a flashlight, reach down and pick it up. "But
you've got to be quick," said Craig, as a big one flipped out of my
gloved hand and darted off into the safety of coral catacombs. In
30 minutes we found six, each weighing over two pounds, and
stored them overnight in a burlap sack that we hung over the side
of the boat. In the morning, perfect weather made us suddenly

decide to leave, and because none of us can face lobster our first day at sea, Nancy decided to can them. Our canned lobster turned greyish yellow, and though the one time we tried it the taste was OK, the color turned off our enthusiasm for a second try.

We motored out the pass a little after noon and pointed our bowsprit east. The wind was smack on the nose, but very light. We were powering. The weather had mentioned a ridge of high pressure, and that we'd have light airs for a couple of days. Good weather to make easting in. As Suvarov dropped astern, I felt that we were leaving the kind of perfection that people think of when they dream of sailing off to the South Seas and finding their own place in the sun. The last time we left I'd felt that we'd never be back, and that if we did come back it wouldn't be nearly as perfect as my cherished memory of it. I was wrong. Now we had been there twice, and our second visit had been an affirmation of the first. Would we be back yet again? I doubted it. We were leaving Suvarov for good, letting go, giving it up for the next person to discover, and I couldn't help wondering if it would mean as much to him or her as it had to us.

"Next stop, Hawaii!" I said as Suvarov sank into the quicksand of our past. Then Nancy dropped a bomb.

"Let's stop at Penrhyn."

Penrhyn, northernmost of the Cook Islands, was only 450 miles from Suvarov. True, we had heard that the islanders were extremely hospitable, and that visiting yachts were a celebrated rarity. But we were on our way and I wanted to keep going. Momentum is a quantity to be reckoned with, and my courage for seeing a project through often depends on it. But I knew with Nancy, direct confrontation wouldn't succeed. For one thing, it always spoiled my love life, at least for a few days; and for another, the more emphatically I denied her her wishes, the more difficult it was when I finally had to back down.

The trick was to say 'yes' but mean 'no,' the islanders' way of *not* granting a request. I was reminded of the day I finally understood how it worked. We were in the post office in Tarawa.

"Can I buy 10 aerograms, please?"

"Tomorrow," was the reply. He didn't really mean tomorrow, he just meant 'no, not today.'

"Don't you *have* any aerograms?" I demanded, my incredulity showing.

"Yes," was the response, accompanied by a lifting of eyebrows. Fortunately I'd been warned, so I understood him correctly to mean, 'yes, that's right, we *don't.*' Now, when Nancy said "Let's stop at Penrhyn," my answer was a calculated "Tomorrow."

"Don't you want to stop at Penrhyn?" she demanded.

"Yes," I said, knowing she wouldn't know if I meant 'yes, I do,' or 'yes, I don't.'

"You don't really want to stop, do you Mom?" asked Craig.

"It'll break up the trip," she said, "and I think we should."

Debates with Nancy are hopeless. I continued heading east for 48 hours, proving that I was indeed a decisive skipper, at which point we swung north and set a course for Penrhyn. Another low-lying atoll, we apprehended it trying to hide in a parade of squalls that marched through the leaden-skied morning. By noon we were outside the pass.

"I'm not going in till visibility improves," I said. We had no chart, and the Sailing Directions warned that the lagoon was riddled with coral heads.

"This *is* good visibility," said Craig. He should know, as he always cons us from the spreaders. But he has, on occasion, let his desire to get the anchor down pollute his judgement. We hove-to outside the pass while we ate brunch, during which he and I continued to explore the subject of visibility on a dialectic level of 'it is not'—'it is too.'

"All right," I finally agreed. "We'll approach the pass slowly. If you can't see coral heads plainly enough to keep us from running up on one, we turn around, OK?"

"OK," said Craig. The only thing wrong with my plan was that the tide was streaming in through the narrow pass, and by the time we were close enough to judge the visibility, we were committed. As if *Sea Foam* were a slippery pumpkin seed being squeezed by the giant fingers of the reef, we popped through the pass at eight knots and, once in the lagoon, threaded our way toward the village through a minefield of coral heads. But they were just as Craig had claimed they would be: eminently visible.

Many books describe the ideal conditions for piloting in coral: sunlight overhead or slightly astern, clear skies, and a faint ripple on the surface. But nowhere have I seen the conditions we found at Penrhyn described. The overcast must be complete, heavy and dark, and ideally there should be a ripple. In these conditions, coral heads stand out plainly. You will not have the shades of color for judging depth, however. Also, there is danger in the sunlight's breaking through the clouds. If even a trace of direct sunlight strikes the water, reflection of the cloud cover will make the surface of the water opaque and blind you to underwater hazards.

The Penrhyn officials greeted us with a cool politeness that I attributed to our having arrived on the Sabbath, a holy day that Penrhynites kept with uncompromising strictness. Nope. They were reticent because Penrhyn was not a port of entry for the Cook Islands, and I hadn't yet come up with a reason for our unauthorized presence.

"Is there something wrong with your boat?" prompted the chief administrator.

Mental gears ground, then meshed, as I remembered the rules of the game.

"Uh, yes, there's, er, a part of our steering gear that needs fixing." This was true, although we could have repaired it at sea. Our excuse, however, brought smiles to official faces, and we were welcomed ashore to the village of Omoka. Our karma being what it was, the following day a local came to visit, and tied his 20-foot, wooden skiff astern on a short painter. The skiff fetched up against our stern, demolished the windvane linkage, and legitimized our presence.

The next morning I cornered Walter the chief administrator.

"What do you do at night?" I asked him. I already knew what he did on Sunday nights, which was (when opportunity presented itself) to entertain unexpected guests with drinks, dinner, and more drinks, and then watch them with amused concern as they weaved dinghyward, littering the landscape with giggles.

"We have the dancing," said Walter. "Drop by the house this evening and I'll take you."

At 8 P.M. we gathered on his veranda. A frenzy of distant drumming underscored the deepening darkness.

"That's the band," said Walter. "They're warming up. The dancers will be there in an hour or so."

"We're preparing two teams," he said later. "They're both planning to take the next boat to Rarotonga (the capital of the Cook Islands) to dance in our Independence Day competition. Tonight I'll take you to see the Communists. They're about to have their dress rehearsal. The other team is called the Americans."

In answer to our unbelieving questions, Walter elaborated. "For years this place has been divided into two teams, or factions. No one really knows how or when it started, but we think that it started in church. Now the schism infects every aspect of village life, from volleyball games to dance competitions. As for the names, 'Communist' and 'American,' they have no political significance. But they do indicate the pitch of rivalry we sometimes reach."

When we arrived at the Communists' rehearsal place, nothing was happening, so after 30 minutes of standing around unnoticed in the background, Walter suggested we go watch the Americans. We homed in on the beating of drums, and found the hall where rehearsal was already in progress. Americans promptly welcomed us and gave us ringside seats. These were the slender threads on which our affiliations hung.

During the following days, Nancy got involved with the Americans helping to make the grass skirts that were intricately decorated with seashells and coconut shells. I went to every rehearsal and exposed profligate amounts of film. Craig made friends with one of the drummers and hung around the bandstand, watching the girl dancers out of the corner of his eye. We made one more attempt to catch the Communists' act, supposedly dress rehearsal night, but it was another no-show, and back to the Americans we went. In the minds of the locals, this constituted a commitment.

The day came for the arrival of the island steamer that was to take the dancers, bands, retinue, and fellow travelers to Rarotonga. Greeting a ship is an art form, and the Penrhynites had it down pat. The little packet motored up the lagoon heralding its own coming with the raucous music of the Rakahanga (a neighboring Cook Island) dance team's band, players perched precariously on cargo hatches. The boat docked, but no gangplank was lowered until the Rakahangans, Americans, and Communists had all sung songs to each other. Blossoms were hurled. Walter made a welcoming speech to the passengers who were patiently pressed to the rail. Finally the gangplank was lowered, and people streamed ashore to start planning the night's festivities. The Rakahangan dancers had intended to give a special performance for the whole village, but the Americans cornered them first and the Communists were excluded.

Big party. Dress rehearsal, three costume changes. Nancy and the other wardrobe ladies beamed proudly as young men sweated into their grass lava-lavas, and young girls ran relieving fingers around the hard edges of their coconut shell bra cups. Strobe lights flashed, shutters clicked. Generators coughed and died, but pressure lamps didn't. Speeches were made, hats were passed and money was collected. Tea and cookies were served. Finally, at 3 A.M. people dissolved into the darkness and sought sleep, perchance to scheme.

Because throughout the evening, Bare Fact and Naked Truth sang a sobering song: there ain't enough room on that small, rusty, interisland bucket for everybody who wants to go.

"What will you do?" I asked an American friend.

"Aw, we'll get on somehow, and when they ask us to leave, we'll just sit. (All were going as deck passengers.) They ain't gonna make *me* get off."

The captain stood at the head of the gangway with a list. As he called the names, the designates filed past him. For each legal boarder there were four who swam, climbed hand over hand up the docklines, or slipped past the captain when a friend distracted him. Finally the list of 40 names had been called, some 200 people had gotten aboard, and the captain gave the order to drop the gangplank. The obedient first mate promptly did so, thereby dumping a late-returning, first class passenger into the water.

The chief administrator offered a prayer for a successful voyage. 'Amens' were fervent. Interisland ships are almost always overloaded, but this was ridiculous. The little ship moved away from the dock in a cloak of silence, as 80 percent of the passengers tried to pretend they weren't there.

"Well, they're gone," said Nancy, much later and for the umpteenth time. We were suffering from the deflated balloon feeling that always follows the closing of a successful show.

"I never thought they'd make it," I said.

"They didn't," said Craig from the companionway. "Here they come back."

The ship docked. No singing, no bands. Sheepish faces as everyone debarked with belongings.

"I stopped outside the pass and tried to get them to work it out democratically," said the disgusted captain, an ex-Penrhynite himself, "but they're all too damn stubborn. I'm not going to take *any* of them."

The chief administrator, the captain, the radio officer, the heads of the Island Council, and a select multitude of Communist and American VIP's crammed themselves into the radio room and spent the whole afternoon trying to get a ruling from the authorities in Rarotonga. The windows were open, and outside, a couple of hundred Omokans waited patiently. By nightfall no decision had been reached.

Conferences. Smoke filled rooms. Whips and wheels moved that months and months of rehearsal and costuming shouldn't be wasted. The ship should not sail away half-empty. Penrhyn must be represented on Independence Day. The Communists had the smallest team and were the logical choice. Cell heads were contacted and the outlines of a plan were drawn.

American Intelligence, never slackers, had long ago installed agents-in-place. Couriers, racing along crushed coral paths in the dead of night, carried news of the plot. Forewarned of a secret early departure, the Americans planned to be there to board the ship, by force if necessary. The captain, whose multitentacled information network was better than anybody's, advanced the time of his departure another hour and only notified the Commies at the last minute.

The Americans found out, but too late. The gangplank was already ashore, and a mere dozen or so of the more athletic were able to leap the gap at the last minute. As the ship pulled away, scores of fulminating, frustrated partisans milled about on the quay. One Communist sympathizer uttered something inflammatory (later quoted as *nya, nya*) and the bruhaha was on. The most severe injury was suffered by Walter who, in trying to stop a Communist grandma from braining her American niece with a six-foot two-by-four, took the brunt of the blow on his upper arm.

The ship, even now, had 40 more passengers than life jackets. The captain, however, was under tremendous pressure from local kin, and opted to proceed with the 750 mile voyage. Rumor had it that if the authorities in Rarotonga counted the number of passengers that arrived, the captain would lose his ticket; and that if there was an accident en route resulting in loss of life, he'd go to jail— dire predictions that never came to pass. Nor did either the Rakahangans or the Communists win the competition. The Americans, however, who were determined not to waste all the time and effort they'd spent in preparation, soon lined up a (paid) New Zealand tour for later in the year . . .

It was our last Sunday. The week before, we'd gone across the lagoon to Penrhyn's other village and attended church to hear some excellent singing. Having been to one church, not to attend the Omoka church would have been rude. We were late, our usual style, and discovered to our horror that we couldn't slip quietly into a back pew—the only entrance was in front. Blinded by embarrassment, we marched down the aisle, and slipped into the first available seats. Later, at a friend's house for coffee, I was taken discreetly aside.

"Why did you sit with the Communists?" demanded our hostess.

The expression of horror on my face must have reassured her, as she smiled immediately and continued. "That's OK. But you will not make that mistake again, yes?" And having definitely cast our lot with the Americans in Penrhyn's microcosmic cold war, I repledged our loyalty by affirming, island fashion, that yes, we would not.

XIX / PEARLS

We left Penrhyn on August 6, the day the Cook Islanders celebrate their independence. Friends stood on the shore by the village of Omoka and waved to us as we eased *Sea Foam* out into the lagoon, around the point, and headed for the pass that led through the reef into open ocean. We had intended to stay in Penrhyn two days and had been there two weeks, partly because I had gotten an infection in my foot that was now healing, and partly because Penrhyn was a difficult place to tear ourselves away from. The northernmost Cook Island and hundreds of miles from its nearest neighbor, Penrhyn is inhabited by people who combine the warm hospitality of the lonely wilderness dweller with the acidulous independence of the recluse. Both sweet and vinegary they are, and you don't forget them easily. We might have stayed longer if we hadn't been so late, late, late in the execution of our master plan.

We ourselves had never made the trip north to Hawaii, but talks on the radio with skippers who had sailed up from Tahiti or Samoa convinced us that we should try to get as far east as possible before getting into the North Pacific trade winds. The magic words were: "cross latitude 10 degrees north at longitude 150 degrees west, and your last leg will be an off-the-wind piece of cake." I chuckled knowingly as I listened to the radio. Boat after boat was sailing a more direct course from Samoa to Hawaii via Christmas Island. Their last leg, I informed the crew, would be a battering battle to windward, and while their boats might be up to it, *Sea Foam* was not. We would take the long way, the smart way around. We would make our easting against the reputedly lighter trades in the South Pacific rather than against the stronger northern trades. To sailors used to loafing lazily along a westerly, downwind course, making 'easting' connotes an awesome task. Having plenty of easting is like being at the top of a ski slope instead of at the bottom. The reverence given the concept 'easting' was once more proven when we announced over the radio that we'd left Penrhyn (9 degrees south, 158 degrees west) bound for Hawaii (roughly 1800 miles due north) on a course of east-southeast, and not one of our otherwise sensible sailing friends questioned our sanity.

By the end of the tenth day we were up to our ears in easting. We'd used up two-thirds of our diesel, and now we were just sitting, saving the rest of our fuel for the doldrums. All over the South Pacific, sails were flapping helplessly as the trades, or any other winds, refused to blow. Records for long passages were being set for Samoa to Tahiti, Rarotonga to Tonga, Bora Bora to Suvarov, Taiohae to Ahe, and, most unfortunately, Penrhyn to Hawaii. Two days ago, we'd made 24 miles in 24 hours. Yesterday gained us 48 miles, an improvement that failed to have us dancing and shouting. On the other hand, the surface currents that normally would have been stealing away our easting at a rate of 20 to 30 miles per day had, without the wind's impetus, wound down to zero. Someone had cried "stop the world" and the Lord had complied. The ocean was dotted with sailors sitting, and for me, hand in hand with universal calm came the nervous urgents.

I have a vivid memory of going topside at sunset and being impressed by the stillness. There were no swells. The water was glassy smooth. For 360 degrees the horizon traced an uninterrupted straight line. With no clouds, haze, or pollution to diffuse the colors, the sky was like the pictures taken from space vehicles: above the blood red wound of sunset was a lavender band of twilight and then, overhead and to the east, the black-purple of night. I could feel in my bones that the world was really round and that we were a mere pinpoint on its surface. The feelings of loneliness and isolation were total.

Calms bring boredom, which we combated with varying success by reading, and by waging war on the playing fields of Backgammon, Othello, Four Score, or Mastermind. Then, when Nancy or I got tired of having Craig wipe the deck with us, we'd get out the pearls. We kept the pearls in a 35 mm film container, but when we wanted to look at them we'd pour them into a large salad bowl. Sometimes we'd think of the future, of coming wealth. Other times my mood was reflective, and my mind would drift back to when we got them. Most of the pearls, particularly the smaller ones, were anonymous. But some, like the biggest one, or the large black one, or the three perfectly matched gold ones, recalled individuals . . .

"You may think," said our friend, Dago, "that the days of pearl trading in the South Pacific went out after Conrad and the advent of culture, but you'd be wrong. They're still finding natural pearls in Penrhyn. Nice ones. And they trade 'em cheap. I got me 10 grand worth."

I was impressed. Throughout our travels in the Pacific we'd run into sailors who claimed to have traded for rubies in Sri Lanka, diamonds in South Africa, and opals in Australia. The stories always sounded inviting, but one had to accept a certain amount on faith. Without exception, each hero had a scruffy boat that suffered from a lack of maintenance money—hardly evidence of bottom-line, fortune-hunting success. Dago, on the other hand, had a luxe boat that burgeoned with expensive gear and lent credibility to his claims.

"I'll get 'em to Europe—I have ways—and turn a thousand percent profit on them. You guys should go to Penrhyn—they'll trade for anything. They're dying to trade. Opportunity of the century."

"Not me," I said. "I don't know a damn thing about pearls." After a lifetime of coming out on the short end of schemes, I *thought* I'd learned not to don the wheeler-dealer's hat. It never fit, and always ended up giving me a headache. But this was not the case with Nancy, and I knew that all her receptors were bleeping. What I didn't know, as I put pearls out of my mind, was that a fire had been lit on her hearth of hearths, a fire that wouldn't die until she'd seen for herself what pearl trading was all about.

On Sunday afternoon when we arrived and dropped anchor in front of Omoka, the village was devoid of lifesigns.

"Except for church, people don't go out on the Sabbath," Walter told us, "but it's all right to entertain in your own home." I never did figure out how the guests were supposed to get there. That evening as we sat on the porch of Walter's waterfront home, looking out over the lagoon, we asked about Cook Island politics (the Cook Islands are self-governing, but New Zealand still sends them money—a type of independence I'd tried, long ago and without success, to establish with my parents) and told about our cruising experiences. Conversation never flagged. But pearls were never mentioned.

"How are we going to let them know we'd like to trade for pearls?" Nancy asked later as we lay in our bunk. "I don't want to appear eager."

"Maybe we should dress up," I suggested sleepily. "What's the pearl trader's uniform?"

"I get the feeling you're not taking this seriously. If you don't help, I get all the pearls."

"I'll help," I mumbled. "Just tell me what to wear."

Nancy needn't have worried. The next morning we had hardly ingested our first sips of coffee and tea when we were startled by loud thumps on the hull. We groped topside to find two of the long, narrow outboard-powered skiffs that are the Penrhynites transport. Men and women greeted us with anticipatory smiles. Two more skiffs stood off, waiting their turn.

"Trade for pearls?" we were asked, and at our 'yes,' a dozen people trooped aboard and started fingering our intimate possessions like bargain hunters at a flea market. Things that they couldn't see, they asked for, and soon the contents of every locker and storage area were spread all over the boat. "Kinda rusty" was the standard comment about my tools; "kinda mildewy" about my clothes; "kinda stiff" about my paintbrushes. Their lack of enthusiasm was not reflected in the tempo of trading, however. They came to trade, and trade we did. There was a certain competitiveness among them that went beyond need, and led to their determination that first-comers should leave no good deal undealt.

When we had passed through Tonga, we had unburdened ourselves of much of our excess junk in exchange for Tongan baskets and woodcarvings. We thought at the time that we'd pretty well cleared the boat of nonessentials. But in Penrhyn we unearthed boxfuls of dispensables, and to keep the gears of commerce turning we eagerly reclassified many of our erstwhile essentials 'non'.

But in all fairness, we had not yet fallen prey to pearl fever. We were still sticking to restrained parameters. We only traded things that we could afford to throw away, or whose value in a dock sale was negligible. We weren't greedy. And we were oh so careful not to misrepresent our gear, not to cheat our naive, native friends who were so obviously babes in the Caveat Emptor Woods.

"No, I'm not trading that," I told one young man who was sniffing around our portable Honda generator. "It's not working right." (We had hung on to it, even though it wasn't putting out full power.) At this point, I learned the power of reverse psychology. If I'd claimed that the generator was perfect, his reaction would have been just as skeptical as it was now, for opposite reasons. But because *I* was reluctant and not he, he thought I was holding out on him.

That night we sifted through our tiny trove. Some of the pearls were blemished or oddly shaped, acquired before we realized that if we complained of the quality of the pearls they showed us, they'd dig deeper and pull out a cache of nicer ones. But many of the pearls were truly beautiful, and we couldn't help playing 'what if'. What if they were really worth a lot of money? What if they brought the cash we needed to restore *Sea Foam* to Bristol condition before selling her? What if they made us rich enough to *keep* her?

"Pipe dreams," I said to Nancy. "Unrealistic."

"Yes, but isn't it fun?" So saying, she slid off into smiling sleep, anticipating tomorrow.

The next couple of days were repeats of the first, except that we became more businesslike. We found a piece of black velvet on which to examine proffered pearls. We developed a routine of remarking on their roundness, size, color, blemishes. I appropriated a green visor from Nancy and a jeweler's loupe from Craig, and thereafter felt so professional that I fooled myself into thinking I knew what I was doing. Fate, the king conner of Condom, was setting us up for the kill.

A radio conversation finally did it. We were talking to Clark, a friend whose every utterance had always rung with the clear tone of truth. His wife had been a cottage jeweler for years.

"You say they still find natural pearls, not cultured pearls, in the lagoon? Have you any idea what they're worth?" By the time he'd finished giving us examples of pearl sizes and their value, our eyes were like a squid's eyes, grotesquely bulging. Quick calculations made us prospective millionaires, and Sanity jumped ship.

The man who had wanted my generator returned, but now my reluctance to deal was an act, feigned to fan his flame of desire. When I finally gave in, a profligate number of pearls changed hands.

The same thing happened with our all-band radio receiver. I'd bought it, used and unkempt, and it had become less kempt with the years. I kept it in an out-of-the-way place, usually throwing a pillow over it when we had guests. On our *Lissa* trip to the States I had brought it along, and had given it to a repairman for an overhaul. The following day the lady from the shop phoned me.

"You've got to come back," she said firmly.

"Why?" I demanded, somewhat peevishly. It was a 30-mile

drive, round trip.

"He won't open it," she said.

Grumpily, I retraced my tracks. The back of the radio was closed with duct tape. I removed the tape, applied some penetrating oil to reluctant hinges, tried to open it, and the back fell off in my hand.

"See?" said the repairman self-righteously.

"No problem," I said huffily. "Just tape it back on when you're done."

When I picked up the set from the repair shop, its back was taped on neatly. The bill was explicit: "removed two spiders and blew out their webs. Regarded circuitry with wonder. Replaced back, and recommend that no further action be taken—after all, it does still work ($15.00).

I kept the radio as much because of inverted snobbery as because of a financial inability to replace it. But in Penrhyn, it went on the block for pearls.

"One of the bands doesn't play," I said, "and sometimes you have to shake it to get it to work at all." This to a coveter who eventually built up his pearly offer to irresistible heights.

Random scenes that stuck in the mind:

—Watching Nancy whose unwillingness to trade her sewing machine was only exceeded by her eagerness to trade all my shoes and clothing, as her objections dissolved in a beaker of pearls . . .

—Encouraging Craig, who spent one afternoon diving with the locals and another diving with Nancy; remembering the three of us sitting up in the cockpit half the night, shucking oysters by the light of our kero pressure lamp; and seeing myself eat more raw oysters than I had appetite for, just so I wouldn't feel quite so greedily murderous . . .

—Trading the kero pressure lamp . . .

—Saitu Joe . . .

Saitu Joe deserves more than cursory mention. He arrived at *Sea Foam* at suppertime from Penrhyn's other village, seven miles across the lagoon; invited himself, his wife, and three noisy children for dinner; and mystified me with repeated demands for "blushes and rine." He was immensely proud of his English, and totally unaware that he reversed all his 'l's and 'r's. I finally understood him when he shouted "*Paint*blushes! *Anchor* rine!" We learned to accept his peremptory manner, and never could find the heart to correct his English. One day I had to laugh, however. Joe had reluctantly given us our largest and most beautiful black pearl for $60 and our plywood dinghy. He then cast off with too much family and too little freeboard, and, having gotten no more than 100 feet from *Sea Foam,* he, his wife, and two children silently and stoically sank.

One Sunday Saitu Joe invited us for lunch. We admired and discussed his collection of bibles, some of which were written in Cook Island language, and some in English. Soon, however, conversation ground to a halt. Saitu was Sunday somber, and during our previous chats I had just about exhausted my small talk. Suddenly, apparently on a signal from the kitchen, Saitu Joe broke the silence by standing up and roaring "R – r – *runch!*"

I laughed, helplessly, till the tears came. Saitu Joe looked both puzzled and offended.

"Joe," I said, when I could speak, "I never in my life heard anyone sound as hungry as that." With this he laughed too, and we were still friends. Since then, however, it's a *Sea Foam*ism to say, at appropriate times, "What some people won't do for a flee runch."

We finally found wind in the doldrums—a westerly—which, with the Equatorial Countercurrent, pushed us all the way to 146 degrees west, giving us an extra hundred miles of easting. This was 200 miles further east than we'd planned, a good thing overdone. It's true that we then had fair winds all the way to Hilo, and that we never again had to sail closer-hauled than a beam reach. But instead of sailing the 1800-mile rhumb line, we covered 2800 miles and took 30 days to do it. Those who had taken the direct route arrived in half the time. In my next life I too would try the direct route, and would no doubt be clobbered by headwinds. One never knows.

What we do know is that we traded the following items for pearls: five sheets; four blankets; one new flag halyard; two old jib sheeets; one 440-pound test trolling line; one electric drill and bits; one saber saw and blades; one extension cord; one tap and die set; one socket wrench set; old clothes; newer clothes; all our old paintbrushes; all our fishing lines, leaders, hooks, and lures; one Honda generator; one pair of binoculars; one Zenith all-band receiver; five bolts of material; one sewing machine; two bottles of perfume; one gaff (for landing fish); ten shackles; one electronic calculator with spare batteries; three-quarters of all my small tools; Nancy's and my diving gear; all but two of our towels; all our footgear (except for one pair of zories each, at which point mine broke and were useless); one of our three anchors with 40 feet of ⅜-inch chain and 60 feet of ¾-inch nylon line; two old sails; all our plastic containers; two 50-foot lengths of garden hose; one .22 rifle and ammo (with tacit official approval, although I still look nervously over my shoulder at the words 'gun runner'); one big black tarp (leaky); patches for tarp; one dinghy with oars; paint; two wrist watches; one travel alarm clock; one magnifying glass with built-in light; one handbearing compass; four pairs of scissors; one basketful of assorted sewing stuff; two cooking pans; one pound of real coffee; three yards of acrylan awning material; and $65 cash. At conservative second-hand prices, we figured we might have netted $1,000 for all this at a garage sale. But our pearls . . .

On reaching Lahaina we took our pearls to an appraiser. His opinion was that we might be able to realize $500 for all of them. For a while, Nancy was depressed. But she couldn't remain so for long, and soon she was punctuating her pearl stories with bursts of laughter. Craig, with his pearls as a built-in inventory, took a course in jewelry making. As for myself, I was delighted when Philip (son) wanted a pearl for his fiancée's engagement ring, and pleased to be able to give Sarah (daughter) a pair of matched pearls for a graduation present.

But the law of conservation of experience is still valid. Nothing is wasted. When later we were desperate to sell *Sea Foam* in a market whose high interest rates had brought boat buying to a halt, we were able to walk away from an apparently generous offer of glittering opals, and to wait, patiently, for something more liquid. Not only do we have our Penrhyn pals to thank for a crash course in the art of barter, but I'm positive that what finally closed the sale of *Sea Foam* was our promise to the new owner of the warm welcome he'll be given when he sails into the Penrhyn lagoon and offers to trade for pearls.

XX / PAINTING *SEA FOAM*

Y ou would think that by the time we'd owned an old wooden
boat for eight years we would have learned how to paint it.
Unfortunately, this was not the case. Long before peer group pressure had forced us to adopt yachtsmen's attitudes toward painting
and varnishing—attitudes that required unreachable standards of
perfection—we had quit the marina life and headed for the South
Pacific. From then on, most of our time at anchor was spent in
ports where, if there were any marine stores at all, they served a
workboat clientele.

Throughout our cruising years, Nancy and I did what we could
with what we had, but soon I succumbed, willingly, to the goal of
the workboaters: protection, as opposed to beautification. Yachtsmen are never satisfied unless their topsides are a paradigm of
smoothness and gloss. But workboaters are ecstatic if the usual
array of chips, scratches, peels and rust streaks are temporarily
covered with paint. Thus the beauty in my paint jobs resided in a
pleasing pattern of visible brush strokes punctuated with a random
distribution of drips and sags. I called this individualism, but my
yachtie friends had other, less complimentary descriptions. Nancy,
although painfully slow, was a meticulous painter. Even she admitted that if she had to paint the topsides by herself, by the time
she got all the way around the boat, the place where she'd started
would be cracking and peeling.

There are two schools of thought regarding boat maintenance.
The first is the school of Diligence. Dils, or Dillies as they are
sometimes known, make a constant effort to keep their boats in
perfect condition. A Dil's boat is never unkempt, but unfortunately
its appearance is so cherished that the boat is never used.

Initially we were Dillies. The biggest risk in going sailing was
not that we might hit another boat, or blow out a sail, or risk the
rig with an unexpected jibe. The biggest risk was that we'd scuff
the brightwork. A scratch on the varnish, a smudge on the top-

sides, a tiny streak of rust—any or all would send us into fits. Soon, instead of sailing, we were spending most of our free time in self-improvement, trying to patch up our personalities, to save each other from falling into depraved nitpickery. And failing.

The second school is the Prodigal School. Prods stray from the paths of the righteous by letting appearances go. Prods are loose, and allow their boats' looks to reach rock bottom before lifting a finger. Outcasts, they are not welcomed back into the Dilly fold until they see the light and complete the penance of rejuvenation. The greatest thing about the Prods approach is that between marathon efforts there is always plenty of time for sin (sin being a Dilly's term for 'having fun'), and the change from grungy to gleaming is always so dramatic that it cheers the most jaded soul, and can even masquerade as progress.

As we cruised farther from the various influences of advertising, marine stores and other yachties, we gradually moved into the Prod camp. Our carefree periods were filled with sailing, swimming, diving, shelling, surfing, reading, studying, photographing and writing—the core of our cruising lives. Then, two weeks before haulout, we would become 70-hour-a-week moles, sanding, preparing, varnishing, painting, and, on relaunching, *Sea Foam* would be cosmetic perfection. "Beautiful," our friends would say. "She really looks good!" Greedily we Prods would drink up the praise while the glasses of the Dillies went unfilled. It's always the return to grace that draws acclaim.

But I must admit that the last time we went too far. We put off till tomorrow what we should have done yesterday "because we'll be in California soon, and we'll want her pretty for her new owner, and if we do it now we'll just have to do it again when we get there." The only problem was that it took us eight months to sail home instead of an expected three, and long before we reached San Diego, the attrition of thousands of miles of mostly on-the-wind sailing had eroded *Sea Foam's* appearance more than ever before.

"Oh, Herb," moaned Nancy. We were standing on the dock, staring at *Sea Foam's* sad-sack mien.

"Just remember *Lissa*," I reminded her. *Lissa's* arduous passage had left her looking disreputable. The first broker that saw her said we'd be lucky to get X thousand dollars for her. With a little time, and some paint and varnish, we'd sold her for three times that amount.

"But I don't want to make a career out of fixing up *Sea Foam,*" said Nancy. "We've got things to do, places we have to be."

"We have to do *some*thing," I said. "Nobody'd give us anything for her the way she looks now."

We talked with a friend, a perfectionist who makes his living buying, refurbishing, and selling sailing yachts.

"Topsides are most important," he insisted. "Go for that real, yachtie gloss, a smooth, fair job. That's the first impression a buyer has, the most lasting. Take the hull right down to bare wood. You won't regret it."

My thoughts would have been to bring everything up to a passable level—topsides, decks, spars, interior. His idea was to take one area at a time in order of importance and make it as nearly perfect as possible. Our friend is expert at what he does, and he failed to reckon with my ineptitude, with Nancy's snaillike pace. Somehow, spurred on by his advice and encouragement, we managed to achieve what a generous critic might grade as a fair topsides job. But even after two weeks of hard work in the yard, we still hadn't painted the red stripe.

If it had been up to me, years ago the red stripe would have been painted white like the rest of the topsides. But Nancy maintained that this was a prominent feature of *Sea Foam*'s image, and that especially now, when we intended to sell her, we shouldn't give it up. Because we didn't want to stay in the yard any longer, we decided to finish doing the topsides by painting the red stripe while tied up in the slip.

"I'll paint it," offered Nancy. "It's fussy, cutting it in and all. My kind of job."

With her usual care, she went about preparing to paint. Our slip was right by the gangway in a large marina, and everyone who entered or left had to pass us. From my various projects on deck I could follow Nancy's progress just by listening to people's comments.

"Still working on the red stripe?"

"You still sanding? Jesus, you're slow."

. . . a few days later:

"Sure is going to look good when you get her all painted up."

"You do good work. When you get done with *your* boat you can come by and paint mine, haw haw."

. . . next day:

"Looks like it flatted out on you."

"Kinda lost its gloss in spots, didn't it? Must've been the fog."

. . . a couple of days later:

"You sanding that red stripe *again*?"

"Don't you ever quit?"

. . . a few days later:

"Painting her again, eh?"

"Gonna get it right, this time?"

. . . next day:

"You know, I painted my cabin sides last month, and my paint blistered just the way yours did."

By now Nancy was functioning at 'slow burn'. After six weeks (to be fair, there were some rainy days), she had carefully sanded and painted the port side stripe four times, and the fourth time it had flatted out along its whole length. So far, sidetie authorities had tipped us to the fact that we'd made the following mistakes:

1) Painting too late in the day. Paint still wet when the dew falls loses its gloss ('flats out').

2) Painting too early. Tiny beads of moisture are still on area to be painted. Paint blisters.

3) Painting early enough, but thin paint too much with a drying retardant that insures better flow ('flow' being a paint's ability to merge and obliterate brush strokes to form a mirror surface), to the extent that the paint dries *too* slowly and flats out in the evening dew.

4) Painting when your karma's bad. Fog comes in, flats paint.

Nancy was, for one of the few times that I've known her, truly depressed. In spite of the fact that she'd made a huge number of new friends, she knew that at her present rate of progress it would take her the rest of her life to get the red stripe painted.

"Let me try," I suggested, and the Bottle Imp was passed. I sanded and painted—most carefully for me, because if there's anything I hate more than painstaking work it's doing the same job twice. The result was perfect. I phoned Nancy, pleased with myself, boasting a little. (She had not only quit the job; she'd left the county to visit her mother.)

"Terrific," was her generous reply. "Maybe I'll come back to the boat again now."

I didn't call her back the next day when the red paint shriveled—

literally shriveled—and dried in wrinkly patches. I needed her back too desperately to let a little thing like honesty stand in my way. What I did do was stand and stare mournfully at the damn stripe, trying to psych its malevolence. Why was it doing this to us, now, when time was so important? My emanations were puzzlement, which-way-do-I-turnville, why me-dom.

This was all that passers-by needed. Their hearts came forth disguised as gifts of advice.

"Paint's not thin enough," said one expert. I had thinned it till it had turned more orange than red.

"Must be bad paint," said another expert. It was the most expensive paint that I could find.

"You put it on too thick," said the third expert.

I decided to ignore the wrinkles temporarily, and turn the boat around. It was time to do the long-neglected starboard stripe. I sanded, filled dings, sanded again, and dusted. I assembled paint, thinner, rags, a new brush. I wiped down the stripe, checking for unseen moisture. Then I opened the paint can.

The paint, where it had dried on the inside of the lid, was beautifully wrinkled. The sides of the half-empty can were coated with wrinkled paint. Even the skin which had formed on the paint's surface had a permanent ripple, as if windblown. Suddenly I was struck with the realization that the paint had come with the wrinkles included.

The next day I arrived on the dock with a new can of red, purchased from a retail chain that specialized in inexpensive paint. My confidence was magnified by the blue-skied, optimistic weather. Friends, fellow marinians, psychological partners in the outcome, offered warm smiles, good wishes. With all systems go, I finished painting the stripe in two hours. It dried perfectly. The color was slightly different from the port side, but I couldn't care less. I knew now that I could finish off the other side with just one try, given the right attitude. At last the red stripe problem was over, and we had solved it in a brisk two months.

My success gave me courage, whistling and humming, I tackled other areas of the boat. Paint ceased to sag and drip, partly because I'd bought stronger glasses, and partly because I'd learned that paint is basically deceitful: just because it fails to sag or drip when you brush it on doesn't mean that it won't do so the minute you're out of eyeshot. I learned to go back over my work, a refinement that my previous method had disdained, to catch the drips and sags unawares. And my varnishing—it was superb. If only I could have varnished in seclusion and merely presented the results to a critical world.

"D'you mean to tell me you varnish with a *sponge*?" Mere underscoring can't begin to communicate the scathing scorn of my friend, George. George was a craftsman, had built his own boat, and approached varnishing with the same reverence that Japanese approach teadrinking. His varnishing brush, which he kept enshrined in a hermetically sealed glass case in his yacht's salon, was made from the finest badger hair. I never could find the slightest imperfection in any of George's varnish work; but *he* could, and when I would praise his work he would point out my crippled critical faculty by showing me where and how he'd screwed up. The fact that I applied varnish with one of those inexpensive sponge-brushes strained our friendship to its limits. The fact that I was content with the results cost me George's respect.

Little by little I noticed some cooling in George's—as a matter of fact, in all my friends'—attitudes. No longer were their smiles spontaneous and friendly, but instead were forced and half-hearted. As project after project went forward without a hitch, those that would speak as they passed numbered fewer and fewer. Finally, more often than not I wouldn't even get a flicker of recognition when they walked by, silent and tight-lipped. Progress on *Sea Foam* was moving along at an exceptional rate, but I was living a lonely life, locked away from the world in my cell of self-satisfaction.

When the loneliness became unbearable, I knew what I had to do. One weekend, when foot traffic was heavy, I got out an apple box, sat on the dock, and stared moodily at the red stripe. At first, people continued to ignore me as before. George ignored me also, but I noticed that he made several unnecessary trips past me. Finally, he stopped and spoke.

"What's happening?"

"Oh, I'm thinking of redoing the red stripe."

"How come?"

"Well," I said, shaking my head, "if you look closely, you can see brush strokes where it's lapped in a couple of places. Looks pretty bad, actually. I'm surprised you didn't notice it."

"I noticed," said George, the flicker of a smile belying his apparent implacability, "but I thought you were satisfied with it. Thought maybe you'd painted it enough times and decided to call it quits."

"I can't understand what happened," I said.

"Aw, the paint was probably drying too fast. Don't know if I'd do it over if I were you, but I'm sure glad you're unhappy with it." At this thought he brightened visibly before striding purposefully away.

The word was passed. One by one, people resumed speaking to me as they walked by. Occasionally I had to stop what I was doing to point out the places on the red stripe where you could see the overlaps of the brush strokes. I was invited here for coffee, there for a beer. Progress slowed a bit, but the climate of camaraderie went from winter to spring. I knew I was really back in the fold when I overheard through a porthole the remarks of passers-by:

"Poor bastard hasn't got that red stripe right yet. But he's OK— he hates the way it looks."

"Yeah. I hear he's upset about his varnish work, too. Going to strip it all off and redo it using a proper brush."

This last was pure rumor and totally unfounded, but I like to think that George had a hand in starting it, and that he did so because he felt I was worth redeeming.

XXI / HAWAII - CALIFORNIA

B ecause of our habit of spending extra time wherever we stopped, we arrived in Hawaii months later than intended, and then spent several weeks enjoying our first taste of America in years. Craig finally had to leave, and Nancy and I were facing the voyage to California alone.

Though by now we'd been cruising for over six years, only once had we ever taken *Sea Foam* out sailing by ourselves. We were in Papeete. Somehow we'd managed to get rid of all our crewmembers at the same time and decided to celebrate by sailing to Moorea for the night. A sort of second honeymoon, we said. Moorea was 12 miles from Papeete, not an excessively challenging passage for experienced cruising folk, but the idea that we would have only ourselves to depend on worried Nancy and brought out the bravado in me.

"Of course we can," I reassured her. "Besides, half the reason I wanted to go cruising was to sail, you and me, hand in hand, into the sunset. And it's ridiculous—we've owned *Sea Foam* for two years and we've never sailed her anywhere by ourselves."

"What if something happens?" she asked, lip-chewing. Her faith in herself as a sailor was minimal, and in me was based more on her loyalty than recognition of my talent.

Our trip to Moorea was slow, as out of deference to Nancy I put up only about 50 percent of the appropriate amount of sail. We finally made it, entered Cook's Bay, and dropped the hook in front of the Ai Maio Hotel. It was the cocktail hour, and I had my eye on the busy, open-air bar.

Cook's Bay was a fully protected but comparatively deep anchorage, and I had dropped our anchor and 200 feet of chain into 60 feet of water. It was a place where the bottom dropped off quickly. More scope and we'd have swung too close to shore. Further from shore and we'd have had to anchor in 100 feet.

"Reverse!" I yelled from the foredeck, and watched *Sea Foam*'s 55 horsepower diesel resolutely drag our anchor across the bay. Too little scope. Try again.

Bringing the anchor back aboard should have been a snap. Our electric windlass functioned; but the gypsy was worn, and the chain had a habit of disengaging itself, whereupon we would lose more scope than we'd recovered. The solution we'd adopted was to press a piece of wood down on the chain as it came over the gypsy. I was impatient, and decided instead to help the windlass by hand-over-handing the chain. Almost immediately I caught my hand between the chain and the gypsy, much like running it through a washing machine ringer, and the weight of 200 feet of suspended steel rode made the mistake unforgettable. As I am totally without stoicism when it comes to pain (mine), my shouted swearings offended the sensibilities of all English-speaking people within hearing, and from the murmur of appreciation that came from the Ai Maio bar, those who had understood me lost no time in translating for those who hadn't. Even though our second try at anchoring was successful, Nancy refused to go ashore to the Ai Maio with me, and for the next month the thought of going anywhere hand in hand was enough to make me cringe.

So the prospect of sailing 3000 miles, just the two of us, was awesome. In fact, it was driving us to drink.

"Isn't it a little late?"

"How come you're sailing to California at *this* time of year? You must be nuts!"

"Man, when the isobars get this close together, you'd never catch *me* out there."

These and other encouraging bits came *gratis* from the Old Salts at the Hawaii Yacht Club. "There's nothing like a dose of Old Salts to give you courage" whispered Nancy as we exchanged grim glances, swallowed hard, and ordered another round from the bar. We had committed ourselves, and were therefore pressed for time. None of our alternatives—remaining in Hawaii for another six months; leaving *Sea Foam* and returning for her later; having her delivered—seemed to make sense. Even the thought of taking a crewmember was discarded, for the same sorts of reasons that will make one hesitate to pick up a hitchhiker at night. We knew of no one who wanted to go, and the one stranger who approached us appeared to be so spacey that thoughts of being cooped up with him (not to mention worrying about how he might react in emergencies) were vivid enough to make us decide that no matter how scary it was, we'd rather go it alone.

On a glorious October afternoon we powered out the Molokai Channel in the company of a huge container ship which, I observed, kept disappearing in the troughs of gigantic swells. Nancy pointed out that my observation was somewhat subjective, as more likely *Sea Foam* was doing the disappearing. But whatever meteorological violence was causing the swells must have been far away, as the wind in the dangerous Molokai was gusting an anaemic four knots.

For three days the wind remained light, coming up only in the afternoon to a maximum of 12 knots. But the huge swells continued, and though they merely lifted us gently up and down, the valleys produced a strange backwind that required tying lines (preventers) to all three booms—mizzen, main and staysail—to prevent them from jibing. I hated preventing everything, as it was one more task to remember if we had to come about or make sail changes. But time isn't critical in good weather in mid-ocean, and prevention was certainly preferable to jibing every 15 seconds.

Our anxiety that we would have more wind than we could handle soon gave way to irritability caused by too little wind. Windvanes need wind to function, so we were forced to steer whenever we were under power. Instead of being thrown together constantly, our interpersonal life consisted in sleepy grunts as we passed each other at the change of watch. This put one of my worries—too much togetherness—at least temporarily on hold.

The weatherman reported a continual series of gales and storms in our path, and my confidence, which had been convalescing in the sunshine, had a relapse. So, on the fourth day, when the headstay broke at the masthead in a light breeze, my first reaction was "Hot damn, we get to go back." To me, a stay of execution was a stay of execution, but Nancy saw the bleaker side.

"Sure, we get to go back, spend money, repair the stay, and start out again even later."

"When we leave, we'll go by way of Maui and spend a few more days with Chris," I said. At the thought of another visit with her older son, Nancy smiled, and I consoled myself with the thought that after all, if you're going to be late, you might as well be *really* late.

Our second departure was no more auspicious, and demonstrated how often our concepts are trapped by language. When you're sailing along and the wind suddenly comes from another direction, you say "the wind has changed." To me this means that the wind, tiring of blowing from one direction, has decided to blow from another. The change would occur even if the boat were standing still. The idea that the wind where you were has *not* changed, but that the boat has crossed a border between Eastwindland and Northwindland, for example, had never occurred to me— after all, in most cases the distinction is academic. In our case it was not. *Sea Foam* sailed well, full and bye, about 65 to 70 degrees off the wind. We set out sailing north. A hundred miles from Hawaii the wind changed, heading us west of north, so we tacked and sailed on a course a little south of east. After a few hours the wind changed again, heading us much too far south, so back we went on the starboard tack and headed north. Three days of these gyrations won us less than 100 miles of real progress, and convinced me that there was a definite line, north of which the wind was blowing from the northeast, and south of which it was blowing from the east. Finally, however, the wind god released us from our endless task and allowed us to sail north-northeast to a rendezvous with our very own gale.

During spring and summer in the North Pacific, a semipermanent high sits between Hawaii and California. The high is a great blob of calm which sailboats, unless they carry enough diesel fuel to power through it, must sail around. Winds revolve clockwise around northern hemisphere highs, so the summer sailing route is to go over the top of the high, which usually requires going to 40 degrees north, or farther. Nancy and I agreed that fireplaces, slippers, armchairs, and electric blankets are for cold weather. Sailing is for warm weather, and the idea of sailing so far north in what was now November elicited a unanimous "no way." As opposed to a quick trip in clammy misery, we chose to beat against headwinds in warmer latitudes for however long it might take—weeks, if necessary. Besides, we learned the hard way that the high was in its 'semi' state. The weatherman would report it in a particular place. We'd make our plans. Then, within a couple of days, the high would move off, or a low would swallow it up. Next thing we knew it would reappear 2,000 miles to the west, moving toward us at 600 to 700 miles per day. Against such an agile adversary, evasive action applied from a pokey sailboat was futile. But we had heard that sometimes you can pick up fair winds as far south as 29 degrees north, so we decided to sail up to an absolute limit of 33 degrees north, the latitude of San Diego, just to see what was happening. The worst we figured could happen was we'd have to come back south again. We've been getting daily weather reports via direct contact through a ham with the National Weather Service. Nothing grim threatens. Satellites inform us of the locations of highs, lows, gales and storms, and how fast and in what direction they are moving. What they can't predict is where a gale is forming. But as we approach 29 degrees north and the wind swings to the south, the falling barometer fails to dampen our spirits. It is, after all, our first fair wind. The weatherman says there are no storms or gales for hundreds of miles. We don't know it, but we are about to assist in a birth.

The low that develops is just to the north of us, which is lucky, as its winds, revolving counterclockwise, send us scudding toward San Diego. But when the windspeed reaches 30 knots, bouncing us along at 7½ knots under only a double reefed main and staysail, we begin mumbling things like "enough is enough." *Sea Foam*, however, is handling the seas easily, and there seems to be no need to reduce sail further.

It rains, off and on, and the wind is chilly, so most of our time is spent below, letting the vane steer. One of us comes topside every few minutes to have a look around. At mid-afternoon I see, approaching from the west, a line of evil, black clouds.

Almost all fronts are presaged by an increase in the size of the waves, often leading the wind by as much as several hours. Our front, being brand-new, gives us no warning. We are suddenly hit with the strongest winds we've ever encountered. Even with the small amount of sail area we have up, we're slammed all the way over onto our beam ends. Time and experience have taught Nancy and me how to gauge the speed of the wind, but beyond a certain point it's hard to be objective. Nancy presses me for a number, and I say "In excess of 65 knots." A nasty bastard.

I tell Nancy to stay aft in the cockpit and handle the sheet and the gaff preventer while I go forward to try to pull the mainsail down. Fortunately at this stage the wind is still gusting, as it's only between the gusts that I can make any progress. It takes me 20 minutes to haul the sail down, sort of furl it, and tie two ties to hold it. The wind blows more steadily, but with even more force, until moving about on deck becomes impossible. Getting the staysail down is, I decide, too dangerous. I retreat to the cockpit.

Nancy goes below. A wave breaks over the boat and tries to snatch away one of our lazarette hatch covers. I catch the cover just before it goes overboard, and nearly go with it. New game, catch the hatch.

Even with only the tiny staysail up, the strongest gusts are laying us over at a frightening angle. I figure that if *Sea Foam* should founder, our chances of taking to the life raft are zero. I go below to find Nancy sitting on the cabin sole—It's too rough, even to stay on a bunk," she tells me. Her face is ashen, reflecting my own fear. I climb back up to the cockpit, but there's nothing more to do. The ocean has gone crazy. I can't see the surface for the sheet of blown spume that covers it. The screaming of the wind is painful. I fish two lifejackets out of the lazarette and stagger with them down below. Together we sit and wait, holding hands through our 90-minute nightmare.

When the front has passed, the 30 knot winds that remain seem like gentle breezes. I sit on the bunk, wrapped in blankets, shivering, heavy-headed, nauseous, my heart beating rapidly, my breathing short. Nancy, to a milder degree, has similar symptoms. We both have a craving for tea, and I swill down two scalding cups of it, laced with sugar. I have no idea whether I am suffering a heart attack or the effects of adrenalin shock, but for the next 24 hours, the slightest exertion brings back the symptoms. Both of us are awed by what might have happened, what might yet happen, and we spend some time going over what Nancy can do if she has to make it into port with no help from me. But I recover, and two days later I write in the log: "My health must be better, as getting the main down this afternoon was a struggle, but I felt OK afterward. It would be convenient if I could refrain from getting sick or dying while at sea. Nancy agrees."

We continue to sail east. The gale moves east with us, matching our speed, maintaining our relative positions. We become almost fond of it, our very own gale, and we are pleased by our daily progress. The variable winds—from 15 to 40 knots—are hard to use efficiently. The days are gray and the nights are black, but otherwise time stops in a world that's nothing but wind, rain, sog, cold, and worry. Our gale finally weakens and moves off to the northeast.

Now the weather grows colder. We have left the tropics for the first time in 2½ years, and our clothes and attitudes are both inadequate. When I go topside, I wear a shirt, sweater, and foul weather jacket. My lower body is clothed in salt-encrusted shorts, and no shoes or socks. I have only one pair of shoes and one warm pair of long pants. Nancy has only one pair of knitted longjohns. They have horizontal black and yellow stripes, making her look like a redheaded bumblebee. It would be disastrous to get these things wet. Consequently, each time we go topside we strip off our warm things, and get dressed on coming below. This routine has two effects: (1) it makes us reluctant to go on deck for anything less than a survival move and (2) having put it off too long before deciding we *must*, we then go through a Laurel and Hardy, quick-change routine. The continuing squall-calm weather cycle makes the salon a locker-room madhouse. Watchkeeping consists in peeks; faces stick out of the companionway hatch for a quick look every 15 minutes, much like a gopher surveying a hostile world from the mouth of his burrow.

We've been pumping the bilge when the water gets to a certain level—about every twelve hours. Now suddenly the interval has decreased to 90 minutes. A wooden boat works in rough weather, and it's not unusual for her leaks to increase. Rarely so dramatically, however. I check all the through-hull fittings, the stuffing box, and the hose connections, particularly those connecting the head. Nothing. I finally find the leak where two planks meet behind a butt block, way back under the water tank and absolutely inaccessible.

We're hove-to, and have been all night, as the wind has decided to blow out of San Diego at about 30 knots. We have 600 miles left to go. Even though the waves are 15 to 20 feet, we'll be comfortable and safe—as long as the leak doesn't increase or the weather worsen. Nevertheless, I suddenly want someone on shore to know of our potential danger. I mention our leak to a ham with whom I have a daily conversation, just so that if we fail to come up on the air one day he'll know that it might be because we're in trouble. He prefers not to be solely responsible, and suggests that I check in to the maritime mobile net, a network of amateur radio operators who meet daily for the sole purpose of keeping track of and giving aid and comfort to yachts at sea. With some misgivings, I do, and our situation, for the moment only a threat, balloons into a great, emergency radio network that includes the Coast Guard, the National Weather Service, and over a dozen hams, all of which makes me feel foolish and premature. On the other hand, it's comforting to know that the Coast Guard can air drop us a pump if the situation gets beyond our own pumps; that there's a cutter to the south that could steam to our aid if we start to sink; that the Coast Guard wants our position daily so they can track us all the way into port; and that hams will keep communications open 24 hours a day if necessary.

That same afternoon, the bobstay breaks.

We are below. The wind is still blowing 25, too much to use our jib to windward, so we're just marking time under stays'l and reefed main, waiting for a change of weather, making maybe two knots to the north and sliding off to the west at about the same speed. We are below, reading, getting through the day, when the sudden 'thunk' of something breaking rouses us, and we rush topside to see what is the matter.

Sea Foam's bowsprit is waving up and down like a giant pumphandle, the headstay sagging and tautening. The bobstay, which runs from the midpoint of the bowsprit down to the stem at the waterline, has broken. As both fore- and headstays terminate on the bowsprit, the masts have no forward support whatsoever.

We douse the sails. I loosen the fore- and headstays, and then run the jib and staysail halyards forward to the anchor winch. With no sail up the masts are OK, but the 12-foot bowsprit is still waving around from the motion of the boat. As it is fastened *under* the foredeck instead of outside on deck, (the more usual arrangement), there's danger of worse damage to come. My private nightmare— trying to finish the passage with a gaping hole in the foredeck— forces me to a quick decision.

The bobstay, a seven-by-seven stainless steel wire, having chafed through the thimble and subsequently the strands of the wire itself, has broken at the cutwater. I detach it from the bowsprit and make a new bobstay out of two parallel lengths of ⅜-inch chain, and only then confront the fact that making a new bobstay is one thing, but putting it on is something else.

"Can you hang by your heels?" asks Nancy. We are standing together on the foredeck, peering over the side at the fitting, at the waterline. *Sea Foam*, lying a-hull, sits quietly in the troughs for maybe 30 seconds. Then, responding to the rhythms of the waves, she pitches violently for 30 seconds, sometimes even burying her foredeck. This, with small variations, is the cycle, a cycle I am reluctant to experience upside down.

"Where's Craig?" I demand, momentarily slipping a mental cog.

"It's just you and me, Babe, remember?" says Nancy.

Painfully, I drag myself back to the here-and-now. "I'll try it from the bosun's chair," I say.

We hang the chair over the side, and I climb down into it. The tasks I have to do are: remove a cotterpin from a stainless steel clevis pin; remove the pin; insert the shackle that's on the end of the new bobstay; replace the clevis pin; and insert and bend a new cotterpin. All this I must do underwater, and I don't dare drop *any*thing. My personal problems are: I'm being continually plunged into and snatched out of the water; even clinging with both legs and both hands, I need all my strength to keep the pitching hull from bashing me; without my glasses (which I can't keep on and couldn't see through dripping wet anyway) I can't see; and try as I will, I can't stop comparing my up and down dunking to the tantalizing things I do with fishbait. I'm hardly encouraged when Nancy tells me she's going to go sit in the cockpit because she can't bear to watch. Finally, after 30 minutes of non-success, I climb back on deck, discouraged, dripping, and shaking with cold.

"Let's wait," Nancy pleads. "The weather's bound to get better someday."

But we have had similar or worse weather for the whole trip. I watch the bowsprit waving around, and imagine the damage that worse weather could do. In situations like this, one merely thinks of the alternatives and chooses that with the least frightening consequences. The possibility of my fixing the bobstay from the bosun's chair is certainly in question, but the possibility of our making it to San Diego swimming is not. I climb back into the chair.

This time it takes me only two minutes to learn how to wrap one leg around the stem and push against the hull with the other, steadying me enough to free both hands. Still, my usual style would be to drop things and be clumsy—I've often in the past spent ten minutes or more under perfect conditions trying to get a cotterpin straight enough to remove it from its hole. Be that as it may, I now proceed to finish the job without a mismove in a record three minutes. I'm convinced that my blind fingers were inspired, perhaps by the blood that flowed from my scraped legs; perhaps by untapped skills in the cobwebbed attic of my brain; or perhaps even by the same guardian spirit that stopped the tradewinds, enabling us to hear the surf on the reef at Suvarov. Suffused with grateful thoughts, I climb aboard and swap hugs with Nancy.

The bobstay crisis is a turning point. From then on the weather is sunny, the winds fair, and *Sea Foam* races like a horse to the stable. Our last night at sea is windless, however, and dawn finds us under power with me at the wheel. As the sun rises, the sight of Point Loma warms my heart. Five miles to the south, a large navy ship idles slowly along toward the coast. Perhaps it too is coming home after weeks at sea. Another ship, a destroyer, catches up with us, then slows to match our speed and becomes our personal escort for our triumphant return. A third ship, laden with antennae, a freeform electronic sculpture, steams out of the channel and heads for us. Warm bubbles of pride and patriotism jacuzzi my soul. To record this extravagant welcome for all posterity, I bring my camera topside and snap with reckless abandon.

At the appearance of the camera, the mood changes dramatically. Outrage electrifies the air. Our destroyer escort puts on a burst of speed and effectively surrounds us by running circles around *Sea Foam*. Strings of choleric flags are raised, and the commanding officer wears out a whole sailor sending me semaphore—to no avail, as I don't understand it. What I do understand is that Big Brother is huffy, and that we might well end our 6½ year cruise by being shot out of the water. Suddenly inspired, I wave the U.S. ensign, and the destroyer steams off in a flurry of fume and a flounce of foam. Relieved as I am, I am even more puzzled. Would a spy really use a camera in full view of God and the U.S. Navy? And wouldn't even a *dumb* terrorist equip himself with an American flag?

Never mind. It's a crisis passed. Nancy gropes topside, fisting her eyes and stifling yawns, bringing coffee. She won't believe me about the destroyer. She gushes over passing pelicans. I remark on an unusual bird, and she giggles out of control. "That's a *sea* gull, dummy." It seems like I haven't seen one in years. The pall of smog that hangs over San Diego sobers her. A pack of sunbathing seals, piled up on an overpopulated channel buoy, brightens her again. Ever in character, I point out the bad news: a fabulous chapter of our lives is about to end. Ever irrepressible, Nancy points out the good news: an exciting, new chapter of our lives is about to begin.

EPILOGUE

At the several dozen slide lectures we've given since our return, there were always some people who were considering such a cruise of their own. Three questions kept recurring. The first is: "How could you bear to sell *Sea Foam,* give up cruising and move back onto land?"

To be sure, selling *Sea Foam* was a difficult decision. My whole identity was vested in the role of skipper of *Sea Foam*, cruising sailor, writer of cruising adventures. If not he, who was I? The very nature of that question would have goaded me into testing it—when something becomes that important it's time for a change. Of course we loved her, and giving her up was wrenching emotionally—but no more so than moving out of the house in which one grew up.

On the other hand, my sense of proportion was satisfied. To have continued to cruise as we were doing on a day-to-day, catch-as-catch-can basis would have struck me as running a good thing into the ground—the red stripe would have become a pair of red shoes, dancing its unwilling wearers into eternity.

"She did what we bought her for and did it well, and I know I'm going to miss her a lot later on," said Nancy. "But it came time to sell her. It was just time, that's all."

The second question always asked is, "Did you change?" Yes, we changed a lot: older, fatter, poorer, but richer in experience. I now work days instead of nights, as a writer, not as a musician. We live in the rural Northeast instead of the urban Southwest. And we live a simple life more or less contentedly on one-quarter of our former income. If you wish to attribute any of these changes to cruising's influence, so be it. But as far as I'm concerned, the only change that surely resulted from cruising is that today I write about sailing subjects, whereas if we'd done something else I'd be writing about other things.

To the last question—"Was it worth it?"—the answer, for Nancy and me, is also yes. However, Nancy can get mightly wistful pointing out that the house we sold for $40,000 in 1973 brought $120,000 in 1976. And I have to point out that during our 6½ years of cruising we made 26 passages requiring our spending three or more nights at sea. Of those, only seven went smoothly enough to be called benign. Three out of four times we could expect one crisis or more—could expect to be scared, pummeled, lost, sick, challenged, or in jeopardy. Seventy-three percent of the time, some form of unpleasantness obstructed the smooth flow of enjoyment.

Recently I was at a slide presentation given by a couple who had sailed around the world. At the end, a person from the audience asked them why they did it. "It was a challenge," said the husband. The wife remained eloquently silent.

I can just see it, a precruising scene, Nancy and I and our six offspring sitting around the breakfast table in Newport Beach, California.

ME: I want to buy a boat and sail around the world.

CHORUS: Why?

ME: It's a challenge. Pass the marmalade?

CHORUS: You want us to go along? Help you play hero?

ME: Naturally.

CHORUS: Up yours.

Challenges, they say, make a man come face to face with his alter ego, sometimes to the discouragement of both. It's true that the worst moments make the best stories, and that I've often sat at my typewriter wishing, for inspiration's sake, that worse things had happened on our most recent passage. But to go to sea to meet challenges? No way. If we were to sail oceans, we had to accept the fact that a certain number of challenges went with the territory. But I didn't have to like it.

Nancy says, "It was worth it because of the friends we made, and because we saw places we wouldn't otherwise have gotten to." For me there was that, but there was more. I've always loved boats. Any kind. I wasn't a bit surprised that my son Philip's first word was 'boat'. Some of the best moments of my life have been on boats.

Take, for example, the sailing high. The sailing high comes from a harmony of all the rhythms of sea, wind, sky, boat, and me. Usually it follows bad times, thus erasing the blackboard and flushing the spirit's toilet. Gone are the nightmares and fears. Who can be afraid on a beautiful day or night with a good breeze and the wake hissing and bubbling? Who can feel poor when the sails are full and the spirit is full? I can't remember ever feeling more in tune, more alive. It's a time for thanks.

We had been in Maine for a month when I got a call from our boat broker that he had a buyer. I flew to San Diego alone for the sea trials, which was a very strange sensation—up till then, Nancy and I had shared every aspect of owning and operating *Sea Foam*.

All went as planned. In the late afternoon of the day that we hauled out for survey, I suddenly found myself alone on board. The broker, the surveyor, and the new owner had left. At that moment the familiar saloon seemed totally foreign to me. Stripped of our personal gear and no longer the vehicle of our dreams and adventures, *Sea Foam* was a strange empty shell. Today is the first day of the rest of her life, I thought, filling in for an absent Nancy in the summing-up department.

I climbed down the ladder from *Sea Foam*'s deck to the ground and noticed that the sounds of the boatyard had stopped. The workers had gone home. Next to *Sea Foam* was a sleek, pert, 28-foot wooden sloop. A couple in their early sixties were sitting underneath her on the cradle sipping gin and tonics. Their hospitable smiles shone from pink faces ringed with bright blue dust, residue of a day's sanding.

"Like a drink?" They spoke in unison. I would have been happy to stop to reminisce over a cool one, but already I felt as though I'd left the fraternity. I hadn't done much that day except be present during the survey, and for a moment I envied this pleasant couple for their involvement, and their shared feelings of hard-earned reward.

"Pretty boat," I said. The compliment won me two broad smiles. I left them to their contentment and headed for the gate that led from the yard. There I turned for a final look. The first time Nancy and I ever saw *Sea Foam*, she was hauled out of the water in Long Beach, California. Since then we had sailed her to fifteen countries, raised one son aboard, and had given a taste of traveling by sea to all five of our other offspring. Now I was seeing her for maybe the last time hauled out of the water in San Diego. I allowed myself a moment of melancholy, the melancholy I always feel for endings, happy or sad, just because they're endings. Suddenly the old couple caught sight of me standing there and waved goodbye. I waved back. Then, the mood broken, I walked away, thinking now only of the flight I had to catch, and Nancy awaiting me at the other end.